D1067738

INVESTIGATIVE SOCIAL RESEARCH

Volume 29, Sage Library of Social Research

FRONTISPIECE

"In this history I have made use of set speeches some of which were delivered just before and others during the war. I have found it difficult to remember the precise words used in the speeches which I listened to myself and my various informants have experienced the same difficulty; so my method has been, while keeping as closely as possible to the general sense of the words that were actually used to make the speakers say what, in my opinion, was called for by each situation.

And with regard to my factual reporting of the events of the war I have made it a principle not to write down the first story that came my way, and not even to be guided by my own general impressions; either I was present myself at the events which I have described or else I heard of them from eye witnesses whose reports I have checked with as much thoroughness as possible. Not that even so the truth was easy to discover: different eye witnesses give different accounts of the same events, speaking out of partiality for one side or the other or else from imperfect memories. And it may well be that my history will seem less easy to read because of the absence in it of a romantic element. It will be enough for me, however, if these words of mine are judged useful by those who want to understand clearly the events which happened in the past and which (human nature being what it is) will, at some time or other and in much the same ways, be repeated in the future. My work is not a piece of writing designed to meet the taste of an immediate public; but was done to last forever."

Thucydides, *The Peloponnesian War.*

Investigative Social Research

Individual and Team Field Research

JACK D. DOUGLAS

Volume 29
SAGE LIBRARY OF
SOCIAL RESEARCH

 SAGE PUBLICATIONS   Beverly Hills   London

For information address:

SAGE PUBLICATIONS, INC.
275 South Beverly Drive
Beverly Hills, California 90212

SAGE PUBLICATIONS LTD
St George's House / 44 Hatton Garden
London EC1N 8ER

Printed in the United States of America

Library of Congress Cataloging in Publication Data

Douglas, Jack D
 Investigative social research.

 (Sage library of social research; v. 29)
 Bibliography: p. 227
 1. Social science research. 2. Social sciences
—Field work. I. Title.
H62.D69   300′.7′2   76-21663
ISBN 0-8039-0675-7
ISBN 0-8039-0676-5 pbk.

FIRST PRINTING

CONTENTS

ACKNOWLEDGMENTS

The work and ideas this book reports on have been team efforts in the complete sense. I have tried to indicate ideas that have been contributed by specific people, but this is necessarily only a partial acknowledgment. My closest co-workers bear equal responsibility for the glories and ignominies of this work.

I owe special thanks to those who have done so much work with me over the years at such great cost to themselves. In most instances they have had to literally pay their own money to do their research work, for our work has almost never been financially supported by anyone. Again and again, to the point of hilarious absurdity, we have been confronted by government and private agencies with ludicrous questions like, "Well, yes, the field research might be interesting, but how will you know if it's true when you have no official statistics of survey information?" We made our way as best we could. This was easy for me, but hard for them. Their dedication is deeply gratifying. It does not make me optimistic about the future of our society or our discipline, but it does help prevent me from despairing totally.

Undoubtedly I owe most to the intrepid and inimitable John Johnson, whose own work on field research, *Doing Field Research,* has set a high standard of creativity, meticulous empiricism and courage for us all. Without that work, and his general stimulation, I probably would not have done this one. I also owe a great deal to all the other brave field workers with whom I have worked—David Altheide, Paul Rasmussen, Carol Ann Flanagan, Carol Warren, Robert Gilmore, Steven Phillips, Phillip and Sharon Davis, Dennis Stouffer, Steven Siegel, Andrea Fontana, Kerry Teeple, Kenneth Lieberman, Lauren Kuhn, Peter and Patti Adler, and many others, especially the people who helped us so much but must remain unnamed—like John, Jason and Denise. Then there are many more with whom I have worked intermittently' and less intensely, both graduates and undergraduates. In addition, there are the people whose creative and critical thoughts have helped greatly in general—people like Bennet Berger, Fred Davis, Joseph Kotarba, Joseph Gusfield,

Stanford Lyman, Howard Becker, Peter Manning, Richard Brown, John Anderson, Charles Freeman, Scott Fuller and many more.

I hope this work will stimulate them to further critical and creative thoughts and that those will in turn stimulate me to. . . .

PREFACE

When I look back over the work of my first twenty years as a sociologist (which began with my voluntary commitment to sociology at the age of nineteen) I find it hard to believe I have written this book. The ideas on research methods and the view of American society presented in it are startlingly different from those I had then. It is not that I was naive about American society at that sophomoric age. My vastly varied childhood and adolescence, which ranged geographically and socially across the spectrum of American society, from the slums of Baltimore to the richer suburbs of Cleveland and the North Shore of Chicago, from the barrooms and trailer camps of Miami to the barrooms and middle-class suburbs of the San Fernando Valley in Los Angeles, had given me the inside experience of much of this society and made me all too aware of the evils of it.

Rather, that very detailed knowledge of the pervasive cacophony of conflict, "immorality" and "deceit" in American society had caused me to seek the peacefulness and silence, the blissful serenity, of the library. This had led, more or less accidentally, to my being a scholarship student at Harvard. There I found my booky and abstract interest in society prized and rewarded, which was exciting for someone who had been chased and beaten by toughs in schools across the country for his childhood bookiness. I became a de facto monk and buried myself in the catacombs of the library. On three occasions I did venture to use my experience of American society to write papers in graduate seminars: One for Robert Bales on the complex and conflictful nature of class consciousness in American society; one for David McClelland on a phenomenology of anxiety; and one for Cora DuBois on the youth rebellion that was growing in the late 1950s. Bales told me I should seek psychiatric counselling for megalomaniacal tendencies; McClelland reminded me he was not William James and agreed to just forget the paper, rather than flunk me; and DuBois, more sympathetic, thought my work involved "purple prose" (which it still does).

Except for some of the anthropologists I knew, the atmosphere was permeated with abstract functionalism and experimentalism. It complemented my monkish tendencies beautifully and by the time I got to the graduate program in sociology at Princeton, which was also very functional but had more roots in social reality, I was committed to making sociology really scientific. I had continued studying mathematics since my work in calculus as a freshman and even added some biochemistry and neurophysiology. Like many young social scientists, I was hoping to be the Newton of social theory, creating the classical synthesis of the "social physics" of American society. And I was planning to integrate it with our hard scientific knowledge of the structure and chemistry of the brain.

By the time I left Princeton I was ready for a year of mathematical models at Johns Hopkins.

But by then my doubts were growing. I was deeply involved in work on suicide rates that would out-Durkheim Durkheim. But throughout all of this abstractness, I had never lost my commitment to understanding the basic facts of everyday life. I had developed an abstract model of suicide hinging on the crucial variable of "felt control." (The term "felt" presaged terrible troubles, but I never thought of that.) Like mathematical ("hard data") types generally, I had worked backward from the statistical data. But unlike mathematical types I did not stop in midstream and work back to other mathematical abstractions. I kept moving toward the real individuals who committed real suicides. And I was finding I couldn't make any real connections between their internal experiences, as revealed in personal documents and case studies, and the abstract variables.

Worst of all, I was discovering that the statistics were coming unhinged. It was a terrible shock to discover that all available evidence indicated those statistics were not in any reliable and valid way connected to the individual realities. (I suffered a minor anxiety neurosis for months over this—nightmares, cold sweats, and so on. A couple of bright and friendly sociological wags have suggested that I and others went through "conversion" experiences, but actually I was not being converted to anything—I was being diverted, rejecting something that simply wasn't working, that couldn't be honestly clamped down on the brutal realities of human beings.) About a year later my frantic casting around for some way to make the concrete realities fit my theory combined with some crucial hints from sources such as Schutz, thereby leading to the adoption of an upgoing case study approach and, thus, to The Social Meanings of Suicide (1967).

My first research experiences outside of books and the library happened inadvertently. While I was studying suicide, real people insisted on imposing their concrete realities on me—a friend attempted suicide; a student's mother successfully used the student's attempted suicide to get her grade raised by threatening me in frightening detail with the responsibility for her life; a distraught mother wanted my help in getting the officials to recategorize her son's death as homicidal rather than suicidal.

After that work I did an in-depth interview study of coroners, comparing one county with another, to see how the coroners categorized suicides. I learned a lot, but was continually plagued by the knowledge that they could be lying about the crucial matters to make themselves look more scientific. I was particularly suspicious because most of them made it look more scientific than did one candid coroner who had worked in a big city and insisted that the whole thing was "no better than if you threw the death certificates up and counted as suicide those that stick to the ceiling." From then on I moved toward more in-depth field research, but only by slow steps. Anyone who compares this work with my more abstract statement of field methods in *Research on Deviance* (1972b) will see that the progressively in-depth studies done by me and my many co-workers, especially John Johnson, have led to varying methods. (For a good critique of the earlier view see Warren, 1977.)

These ideas or methods have developed out of the research. Most of the crucial ideas of this work have come from looking back at how we did it. That is, in our many different studies our continual focus is on reaching the truth, getting at what goes on naturally, as experienced by people in natural settings. We simply devise ways of doing this, certainly by drawing upon past experience and ideas, but always necessarily dealing with the concrete setting that we face. Things such as the phased-assertion tactics (discussed in Chapter 8) for penetrating fronts were simply tried and found to work. So we began to realize how we were doing each technique, thought about it more abstractly, developed a descriptive name for it, tried it more consciously, modified it, and used it again.

This approach assumes there are some underlying, common-sensical means of recognizing the truth *before* we have any scientific methods. Otherwise, how would we know when any particular methods used had achieved truth? This is obvious about all scientific methods now, yet it was resisted for centuries, largely because of the desire of scientists to use the powerful rhetoric of absolutist truth inherited from medieval theology. (They were fighting fire with fire.) We have explicitly committed ourselves to this approach. Animal thought and the human mind, both its symbolic components and its subsymbolic components, have evolved over a few billion years in intimate interaction with the way the world is made up. Our basic feelings and ideas about truth seem to work, more or less. My purpose is not to pretend to revolutionize the primordial modes of thought, to supplant them with some shining new model of truth; rather, one of the overall purposes of this work and ones related to it (especially *Existential Sociology,* 1976a) is to examine more closely how we know what is true and what false in our everyday, common-sensical ways of thought and action. But I do not pretend we are doing the same form of thinking here that a carpenter does. There is a basic similarity, but what we are presenting here goes beyond that. We try to show what the basic structure is in order to better use it, and certainly we use many specific devices that are only dimly recognized in most common-sense activity.

This basic approach assumes there is a necessary interdependency between the nature of the social world we wish to study and the specific methods we should use to study that social world. (One would say in philosophical terms that ontology and epistemology are necessarily interdependent.) Our basic, largely common-sensical view of what the social world is like is of basic importance in deciding to get more truth about that world, and what methods to use in getting it. This means that we must deal continually with what the social world is really like and show how the methods are related to that social world. It means as well that when we have different goals of truth, different kinds of data we want to achieve, we want to use different methods to get there.

In Chapters 1 and 2 we shall draw out this argument further and try to show that we use different methods to get different types of information in different kinds of social groups. This leads us to conclude that most, but certainly not all, of the types of information sociologists want to get in American society can be gotten *only* by the use of natural involvement and field research methods, at least as the primary source of understanding. The rest of the book is concerned with showing how we use the major forms of natural involvement and field research methods to achieve these goals. In doing so, we necessarily deal at great length with what our society is like today. This book, then, is necessarily as much about the nature of everyday American life as it is about the methods used in studying that life.

Of course, the focus is on the *problems* our kind of society poses for field researchers trying to study it, on the evasiveness, secrecy, deceits, frontwork, and basic conflicts and problems of our society, rather than on its openness and truthfulness. This must be kept firmly in mind in reading the book. American society is generally more open, friendly and truthful than other societies, but that has nothing to do with the work here. When people are open and honest they don't pose much of a problem, though it may be problematic to know reliably that they are being open and honest. As an example of extremes, if a field researcher wants to study the architecture of office buildings, he doesn't have any problems of honesty; he just looks at them. They aren't hidden or hard to get at. But it's different if his interest is in what goes on in the board of directors' meeting or in the private dens of the president and executive vice president. This is very hard to do and, indeed, to the best of my knowledge, only Melville Dalton (1958) has succeeded in doing any of it.

I have drawn upon the gamut of field research works, but the focus is upon the field research studies I myself have been directly or indirectly involved in. The reason for this is the same as the focus on field research in the first place. These are the studies I know in full context, studies which I know when to trust and when not to trust. They are the ones I can best evaluate. One of the sad facts of sociological life is that almost all research reports (probably all) are laundered, as Paul Rasmussen has called it. This does not mean they lie or that they are aimed at some secret political goal—few are. It means that the authors choose to leave certain important parts of the context out, certain details about what really happened, how they really got the data or failed to do so. I know of any number of studies in which the author's fundamental way of knowing the things he reports was through direct personal involvement, a fact that has been carefully hidden from the readers because revealing it would stigmatize him as a creep, a weirdo, maybe even a criminal. In all instances I know of, these sociologists have been unhappy that they felt it necessary to do this and in each case with which I am familiar they have not lied. They have merely evaded the issues. (See Chapter 4 for an extensive treatment of evasions.) This is all right for people who are primarily interested only in the substantive issues of the work, but not for those who want to know how the work was actually done. To do that one needs to know the context in detail and with maximum trust.

This does not mean that all will be revealed. On the contrary, this book contains explicit instances in which I have shown how and why I have laundered the data. In some cases the demands of intimacy are the reason. In others it is simply that I have to protect my subjects and co-workers or I won't have any subjects or co-workers. (Some readers may think this is overly dramatic, but it is supported by some famous recent examples, such as the case of a young sociologist who did a fine thesis and almost lost his degree when his actual methods were revealed.)

Some of my co-workers and I have gone far beyond other sociologists in trying to start a whole new mode of honest reporting of methods. This will be apparent in this work, since many things are revealed here which will seem weird and even shocking to some people. I personally am willing to accept the costs, but I cannot ask others to do so. (Some, like the intrepid John Johnson [1976] have done so and have set an example for us all.) Even the tone of many of the accounts, which sometimes approaches a rollicking tone, closely represents the way the research was actually done. Anyone who ever listened to our research tapes would find they range all the way from deadly serious to uproariously bawdy. That's the way people are, that's the way we are, and that's the way it has to be done, whether one is studying nude beaches, drug dealers, businessmen or politicians. Anyone who conducts such studies with puffed-up professorial methods is usually put off, shut out and put on. (There are times to be professorially formalistic, but it should be put on and off like the pose it is.)

The revelations of these real methods, especially when combined with the proposal that the investigative paradigm is essential to exposing the truth about our society, is likely to inflame the moralistic fervor of many sociologists and government bureaucrats. There is, after all, a considerable body of literature in sociology denouncing some of the more genteel and laundered methods of the traditional Chicago field researchers. And government bureaucrats have been trying to regulate and strangulate such free speech for some time.

In view of this, one might expect that I would deal at length with the tortured moral arguments posed by the revelations in this book. I considered doing so, but the thought made me chuckle. In the end, my mirth became uncontrollable and drowned out the considerations. Upon reflection, the reason is almost obvious. Anyone who knows what really goes on in American society, and who has any sense of fairness and practicality, will immediately recognize that all of our methods are by comparison still genteel and certainly harmless. Every person in our studies, and most of the scenes, are carefully protected by the cloak of anonymity—except to ourselves. Consider this in relation to the standardized practices of the massive news agencies in our society, which every day purposefully set out to expose and destroy the projects and careers of thousands of individuals and groups—and not infrequently do their exposés with full knowledge of suicide threats. (See my study, *Newspower*, 1977a.)

Or consider our methods in relation to standardized police, prosecutorial and judicial practices which use threats of years in prison to extort information about other people, and lies and mental cruelty to elicit confessions which may result in lifetime imprisonments. Or our methods in relation to standardized industrial, governmental and private espionage which not only may destroy nations but may certainly destroy countless lives and investments. Or our methods in relation to standardized political attacks on persons and groups; or in relation to the pervasive practices of falsehood and betrayal aimed at gaining advantages over other people in everyday life—in seductions, adultery, betrayals, business deals, radical attacks on the fabric of society, the milking of welfare programs, and many more. There is no comparison except in the minds of the ignorant and the absolutist moralists who can see only black and white. We know of no single instance in which our research has injured anyone, but we know of scores of individuals we have helped to keep out of jail, to stay alive (by getting medical help), to try to understand their problems better, or simply to find a little more joy in their everyday lives.

Our studies reveal that in fact there are few people in our society who are so ignorant or so truly moralistic. Rather, we find that prudery and priggishness are normally assumed for rhetorical reasons or because of secret emotional conflicts that produce self-deceptions. Everyone in our society is already attacked from various angles for precisely those "reasons." I feel a bit more in a good cause, that of trying to reveal truths about us all which may in the long run be of vital help to us all, is not too much to bear. Let them launch their fiery brands; and let government bureaucrats hatch their secret plots to gain greater power by brandishing moral rhetoric. We are equal to the challenge.

This work should be viewed as a field research report on the forms of field research that seem necessary in getting at the truth about our complex, conflictful and problematic society. It is irremediably open-ended and tentative. I hope it will stimulate efforts to devise even more effective investigative methods and that the truths our methods expose will be used to better the lives of us all, rather than to fuel self-serving and futile moralizing about the phenomena exposed.

April 21, 1976   *Jack D. Douglas*
                                                                    La Jolla

Chapter 1

Introduction:

TRUTH IN SOCIAL RESEARCH

The goal of all social research is to discover, understand and communicate truth about human beings in society. Sociologists, anthropologists, political scientists, economists, journalists and others involved in doing social research may differ over whether these truths should be about matters of immediate practical concern to society or whether they should be more abstract truths that can become useful only over the long run. But there has never been much argument over whether our goal was truth about humans in society. There has, however, been considerable and growing argument over the nature of truth and how we know what is true.

Most people agree that the medieval theories of truth were *absolutist*. They were matters of faith and were not to be questioned, under pain of excommunication and possibly death. But few people are yet used to seeing the basic theories of truth held by scientists as being just as absolute. Indeed, most people still think of science as having been born in revolt against the ideas of absolutist truth. But the history of philosophy and science have made it progressively clear that lying behind scientists' willingness to argue about facts and about the truth of specific theories has always been a metaphysical foundation of absolute truth, an unchallengeable scientific epistemology.

The crux of this scientific epistemology has been the theory of absolute objectivity (see Douglas, 1970c). There are two basic ideas in this theory. First, the internal, subjective experience of human beings is seen as being the realm of the shadows of the cave, of uncertainty and untruth, while the external realities of objects, of the realm of nature, is seen as being the realm of certain, objective truth. Second, the rationally devised methods of scientific experiments and verification procedures control or eliminate the subjective realm from science and leave us with absolutely objective knowledge. This is, of course, the classical epistemology of classical science, which reached its unchallenged zenith in the 19th century. It has since been challenged and overthrown philosophically in the natural sciences by the revolutions of relativity and uncertainty. But much of the everyday workings of the natural sciences still operate under these assumptions, and this epistemology is still dominant in the general public view of science.

Von Hayek has argued in his brilliant historical work on the origins of the social sciences, *The Counterrevolution in Science,* that by the early 19th century, when the social sciences were being founded, these absolutist ideas about scientific methods were simply taken for granted—they were considered absolute. Those who created the social science disciplines had one basic goal: They wanted to build absolutely objective sciences of the social world. They unquestioningly applied the natural science epistemology of absolute objectivity to the social world. If anything, the social science literature of the 19th century is more insistent upon the ideas of absolute objectivity, especially about eliminating the subjective element from their work, than that of the natural scientists, presumably because the social scientists felt they faced a greater problem in eliminating the subjective element from a study of humans and because they were so anxious to prove to a scoffing world how truly scientific they were. Their works bear all the marks of defensive rhetoric.

This epistemology is the cornerstone of such classic works as Durkheim's famous and still widely studied *The Rules of Sociological Method* and continues to dominate much social research in all disciplines. The only significant change took place in the 1940s and 1950s when the earlier palace coup in the natural sciences and philosophy of logical positivism became widely accepted as a modification of the theory of absolute objectivity. As in the natural sciences, the social scientists had slowly become aware that not all was well with the epistemology of absolute objectivity. Above all, the ideas of relativity and uncertainty had made it doubtful that absolute knowledge was possible, even of the physical world.

Given this challenge, logical positivists in the social sciences decided to cut loose their absolute methods from the idea of absolute knowledge. They now insisted that all knowledge of the world is relative to the basic assumptions and methods one uses in doing the science. There are, then, competing models of truth, which must be accepted or rejected on terms other than those of truth. For example, there are aesthetic ideas or pragmatic ideas of what is useful. The effect of this, as with any palace coup, was to allow social scientists to continue using their classical absolutist ideas of absolutist methods of control and verification independently of whether those methods produced more truth than some alternative methods. Questions of truth were now mute—no need to bother worrying about it because it all depended on one's assumptions and we happen to choose these classical methods of quantitative analysis, experimental controls, etc. Methods thereby became divorced from questions of truth.

In recent years this approach has been carried to its extreme by those ethnomethodologists who define *all* questions of truth as being irrelevant. To them sociology views all accounts of truth and falsehood as being merely more accounts to be studied by methods which are simply assumed to be the correct methods for doing such analyses. Truth is now eliminated both for the social phenomena and for methods. In its most solipsistic form, ethno-methodology equates science with superstition—or anything else. (See Mehan and Wood, 1976.)

The two major streams of social research are those of controlled, experimental, quantitative procedures, and of field research.[1] Each has been dominated, though to varying degrees, by the same classical epistemology of absolute objectivity. Each in recent decades has largely separated research methods from the basic questions of epistemology, of truth. Moreover, each has separated research methods largely from the general nature of the social world, from the concrete subjects of study, and from the personal research experience of the persons writing about research methods. Research methods have been presented in separate courses and the textbooky approach to learning methods has presented them as iron laws of procedures for approaching any kind of research subject, for any and all purposes of research. These works on research methods are now commonly called "research cookbooks" by students and professionals.

This work takes a basically different approach to social research. It begins in this chapter with a general, but necessarily brief, discussion of the most basic questions of truth, of how we arrive at truths about the social world. It then tries to show that, using basic ideas of truth, we find that the social world in which we live, especially American society, is a complex, conflictful, and problematic world in which people, both unintentionally and purposefully, often (but not always) construct complex ways of hiding important parts of their lives from the outside public, especially researchers. Social research methods must always be constructed in accord with the basic ideas of truth and the basic goal of achieving truth in this kind of social world. Our analysis of the basic ideas of truth and of the problems of achieving truth in this society lead us to see truth about the social world as being highly problematic and partially dependent upon the goals and methods of research. We eliminate the idea of absolute truth and substitute a more problematic, multiperspectival conception of truth; we eliminate the idea of absolute methods, substituting a multiperspectival conception of methods which argues that our choice of methods must always be made in the light of the degree of reliable truth we are seeking and the problems we face in the concrete settings we are studying. We shall see that this method makes the researcher, the live and socially situated individual, the ultimate "measure of all things." For this reason, and because our argument leads us to see direct experience of the social world as the most important basis of all truth about that social world, this work is based largely on the direct experience of myself and my many fellow workers. The research is permeated by our concrete experience; most of this experience is research experience, but many instances are taken from everyday life in which we were simply living, not doing sociology.[2]

The Kinds of Truth and the Common-Sense Tests of Truth

The traditional absolutist approaches to truth assert that there are certain absolute methods of knowing the truth and that these methods have produced certain absolute facts. The logical positivist approach allows one to choose his own epistemological assumptions and model of truth. I propose a different approach here. Instead of asserting that this epistemology or that one is correct, let us look at how human beings in fact do their truth-seeking and truth-knowing. What do people mean when they talk about the truth and how do they arrive at or test their truths?

The rationale for this approach is relatively simple. The human mind has evolved over the eons in direct relation to the natural world in which we live. The ideas of truth that we have about that world have grown out of all this concrete experience. These ideas of truth work for people most of the time. Let us begin with these common-sense forms of truth and truth-seeking and try to improve them, to build upon them, rather than sweeping them aside and imposing some bright new asserted model.[3]

When we do this we find that there are certain basic forms of truth or natural types of truth that overlap but are quite different from each other.

First, there is transcendental or religious truth, which is not tied down to concrete observations of the real world. Transcendental truth is most distinct from the other three types. It may well be the most important form of truth to most people or everyone, but it is not what we are dealing with here.

Second is aesthetic truth, or truth of internal feelings about symbolic forms. It is more directly related to the world of concrete social experience that concerns us, but it is too removed to have much interest for us.

Third, there is philosophical or abstract truth. Philosophical truths are usually derived ultimately from the realm of everyday practical affairs, but are largely independent of immediate experience. (What is often called philosophical is really transcendental. Those theological forms of thought do not concern us.)

Fourth is the massive realm of everyday-life truth. In our concrete experience of everyday life we continually make complex decisions about truth and falsehood by using complex feelings and ideas. It is this realm that most concerns us and from which we derive our ideas about truth in social research, though complemented with the abstract ideas that philosophers and scientists have derived from practical forms of everyday life activity. (While it is obvious that any systematic analysis of everyday life epistemologies would be an immense work in itself, we shall examine them only briefly here so that we can put our more concrete work into this general context.)

In everyday life we tend to use roughly four tests of truth in deciding what is true and what false, though we are rarely conscious of them in this explicit form.

First, we use direct experience of things. "Seeing is believing." "Experience is the best teacher." People sum it up in many ways even in everyday abstractions. Most importantly, they use it all the time, commonly without saying anything about it. Direct experience seems to be the most pervasive, fundamental test of truth. All four of the everyday tests are used in conjunction and they are chosen partly to fit the concrete situation people face, but direct personal experience is the most reliable to almost everyone. Someone who would continually take the word of other people about his own experience, even when their word contradicted his experience, would seem utterly insane. One of the most shocking experiences a person can have is deciding that his own direct experience of something was wrong. Paradoxes, magical mirrors, illusions, and the like, are all intriguing to people precisely because they appear at first to contradict direct experience; but people almost always reassert direct experience in some way.

Second, we also rely upon the direct experience of other people, but less so because we have learned from direct experience that there are all the problems of lying, misinformation, misunderstanding, etc. The experience of others is used in the form of what scientists like to call independent retests or observations, but which are more commonly called independent evidence and testimony. When we see something that is hard for us to believe in terms of our past experience, we automatically turn to others and ask, "Did you see that?" We recognize in everyday life that the independence of others' observations is problematic (they may be in conspiracy); this is something we must determine, along with many other decisions about their reliability. So this test is secondary, less reliable than direct experience, but it is still important. All kinds of subsidiary ideas are related to it (such as, the more independent, the more reliable observations are). But we shall come to these.

Third, there are the abstract rules of logic or reason, which are certainly waived in the face of direct experience to the contrary, but which are generally found to be so reliable that we can use them without much thought.

Fourth, and closely related to the third, are our complex, less general, more concrete common-sense ideas about people, acts and situations; these are the many ideas about honesty, trustworthiness, and so on, that we use in deciding if someone is telling the truth or if that person really knows the truth.

For many complex reasons, but especially because of their own deep distrust of subjectivity, classical scientists seized upon the second test of truth, that of independent retest, as *the* basis of objective truth. Scientific objectivity came to mean independent retest and, as we noted, the idea of objectivity replaced any more general idea of truth. Then scientists convinced themselves that somehow the experimental and verification methods of *controlling* individual subjectivity, or bias, would automatically eliminate the individual factors. They failed to notice that independent retests still made the whole enterprise dependent on direct experiences of individuals and that placing their faith in the rules of controlling subjective factors meant they were placing their faith in abstract rules of reason, which thus either were acts of faith or were ultimately derived from direct individual experiences. Twist and turn as they would, their absolutist science was built either upon the direct personal experiences of individuals or else upon some ideas presumed to be transcendental—articles of faith.

All worldly truth rests ultimately on direct individual experience. There is no escape from this iron-clad fact of the human condition, and it is a truth which must be kept constantly in mind and must form the basis of all social research, as well as of all worldly, practical human endeavor. This does not mean our direct experience is never wrong; it does mean that when it is wrong we have decided so on the basis of further or additional direct experience, which may include the independent evidence given by other individuals on the basis of their direct experience. (If it is not based on their direct experience, we discount it. "But did *you* yourself see him do it?") Objectivity, or the independently retested and shared forms of truth, is necessarily based on individual subjectivity.

The retesting is more problematic than our own direct experience. For we must always be concerned with the questions of whether people are lying to us, how they think they know something, why they would tell us such a thing, and so on. But the complementing of our own experience by others is a partially independent addition to our practical truth-seeking efforts. It is, then, certainly valuable in itself, but secondary to the direct experience.

Controlled forms of research are generally more problematic, simply because they are based both on indirect experiences and on less reliable common-sense theories about persons, acts and situations—such as who will tell the truth about what things in what situation. For example, any questionnaire survey study of something like attitudes toward sex or money is based not only on the indirect experience or experiences told to the researcher, but acceptance of its results as true is also based on all kinds of unasked and unanswered questions concerning who will tell the truth to whom about what in what kinds of situations. Will *they* tell *you* about *their sex* on a *questionnaire?*

All of these things are as true for social researchers as for any other human beings. We begin with direct experience and all else builds on that, whether we know it and recognize it, or deny it. This does not mean that this test of truth is unproblematic; no truth is unproblematic. But it is the least so, the most reliable. The independent evidence given by others may add to our direct experience, but only to the extent we have reason to believe, based ultimately on experience, that they are telling the truth, something which depends also in good part upon our knowing what their experience is.

The most important implication of this argument for all social research is that we begin with and continually return to direct experience as the most reliable form of knowledge about the social world. But it does not mean that all social research has to be direct experience. That depends on how reliable we want our findings to be. If we want the most reliable truth we can get about the social world, which is what is commonly meant by scientific truth or data, then we want as much direct experience as possible through the direct experience of field research, followed by checking it against the independent direct experience of others, and tested out and checked out by us as being true within certain limits in terms of our direct experience and our reasonably reliable, vastly complex ideas of truth-telling in this society. But we do not always have the time or resources for that. We often need results more immediately because we have pressing practical problems. That is, we need policy-oriented or other practical data and we need it under greater practical constraints. When this is so, we naturally relax our tests of truth. We make do with less reliable forms of truth, especially those which can be done easily and produce results that will give us the big picture of the society (for reasons dealt with in Chapters 2 and 9). These forms of practical data are generally collected by survey data of some sort, but there are many alternative forms.

The researcher must always begin his research with an idea of what kind of data he wants (his research goals), what the situation allows, and what his practical constraints are. The goal of one's research is the first crucial question. Its answer has fundamental implications for all his research and its results. The goals chosen largely determine the general methods used and thus the kinds of data produced—their truthfulness and usefulness. Most researchers begin their research and end it without ever clearly formulating and answering the basic questions:

(1) What are the goals of this research?
(2) What, in view of these goals, is the kind of data I want this research to produce?
(3) What research will allow me to achieve these goals and get this kind of data?
(4) Given these goals and this research setting, what research methods should be used *ideally?*
(5) What research methods are practical in this research setting?
(6) Given this estimate of the practical methods, is it possible to approximate sufficiently the goals and kinds of data we want to make this research desirable?

Because researchers often do not formulate these questions and systematically answer them before beginning or, at least, as early as possible in the exploratory stages, they commonly use methods that do not produce the kind of data they are seeking and often only pretend to have what knowledgeable social scientists expect them to have—highly reliable truth. Because they do not clearly formulate and answer these questions for the recipients of their data, the latter must also remain in a fog concerning the truthfulness and usefulness of the data. They either reject it or wing it, or fly blindly, little realizing the hidden perils of such data.

Field researchers always understood, if only implicitly, that direct experience was the bedrock of truth in social research. But as we have already noted, the classical tradition of field research, commonly called the Chicago tradition because it was largely developed by sociologists and anthropologists at the University of Chicago, grew within the classical conception of objective science. This led them to use participant-observer methods, which allowed only partially direct experience. They remained profoundly suspicious of true immersion in the direct experience of everyday life and insisted on a form of being-with, but not part-of, the members' experience. They became secretaries or scribes to the members, not members themselves. Our analysis will show us that this too, while sometimes desirable or necessary in a concrete research setting, is a compromise in our search for scientific truth about the social world.

Our argument leads us further to see that the problems are considerable in getting the truth from others in our society. People are extremely adept at constructing complex and convoluted forms of falsehoods and deceptions to front out others, such as researchers, and sometimes even themselves, from the most important parts of their lives. Researchers have to use more in-depth and investigative methods to get at these private regions of life than they would to study the public realms which are open to almost anyone. It is precisely to get at these most important and pervasive parts of our lives that we have developed the methods of investigative social research reported on in this work.

We also find that the classical forms of individual field research are not adequate for many scientific purposes today and that they almost never are for policy-oriented studies. For these reasons we have developed investigative team field research methods (Chapter 9). These allow us to get scientific data that is also of practical value in making social policies to deal with social problems.

NOTES

1. Each of these will be dealt with in greater detail in Chapter 2 and in various sections throughout this book. There are some important exceptions to the following discussion of field research methods, but these will also become apparent as we develop the argument.

While I have rarely mentioned them directly, my discussions of these more abstract questions draw directly upon all the arguments over philosophical issues such as subject-object dualism. Those who wish to go into these more deeply may wish to look at my works and those of my co-workers in books such as *Existential Sociology* (Douglas and Johnson, 1976). But they are not necessary to understanding this work.

2. Most of my everyday life experiences are in the footnotes. They are important in seeing why and how I myself have done research, or I would not mention them. But it is only fair that those readers who find my personal experiences boring or grating should have the chance to float above them. They need only keep their eyes above the fine print at the end of the chapters.

3. I can hear the logicians and sophists among us insisting that this approach is doomed because it involves an infinite regress—it uses the very ideas of truth it is trying to analyze. Being of a more practical bent, I would simply point out that the same would be true of any ideas of truth and that, however mysterious it may be, human thought is able to be self-reflective without thereby being merely a circle. And so we get on with it.

Chapter 2

FIELD RESEARCH IN THE SPECTRUM OF

SOCIAL RESEARCH

Any attempt to typify the complex forms of social research will obviously involve some oversimplifications—which will appear to make sharp distinctions where actually there are only vague outlines, to polarize where actually there are many convoluted interminglings, and to make logical what is actually accidental or, at least, nonrational. Such typifications of research methods also easily lend themselves to professional politicking, allowing the typifier to construct straw-man types which he then uses to label—in tar—his professional competitors. Let us remember from the beginning that any analysis of research methods such as this is itself a research activity, and thus subject to the same kinds of basic problems that characterize all social research.

Having warned the reader to keep these natural complexities in mind, and not to allow us to construct polarized types of social research with which we can straw-man our methodological competitors, I hasten to assert that there has long existed a reasonably clear-cut division of social research into two natural types; that is, types which social researchers themselves would recognize as characterizing their work. These two types of research are *natural direct observation* and *experimentally controlled observation*. Each type is grounded in complex common-sense experience, and each has been recognized since ancient civilization as a distinct type. Each is represented, both in the natural sciences and the social sciences, by broad streams of research activity made up of many complex sub-types; each partially overlaps and runs into the other along a complex spectrum of actual research methods. Ideally, each can complement the other. But in fact there have been endless arguments, especially in the social sciences, over the merits and costs of each. Indeed, there has been a lamentable tendency for the arguments between the proponents of these two grand types of research methods to degenerate into ideological squabbles marked by struggles for intellectual purity, warfare over research grants, and even excommunication procedures.

Hopefully, this work will not contribute to the squabbles. On the contrary, I hope to show that the actual methods used by social researchers fall along a continuum from totally uncontrolled (or natural) to totally controlled (programmed) methods of observation (see Figure 1), and that researchers should choose their methods to deal with the concrete problems they face in any particular research setting rather than to satisfy some preconceived biases about methods. (See also Churchill, in Douglas, 1973.)

Both general types of observation are based on common human experience and both are essential to the progress of our thought about the world and our practical action in the world. Direct observation of things in their natural state (uncontrolled) is the primary basis of all truth. As we saw in Chapter 1, this bedrock facticity of concrete experience and observation pervades our everyday lives. It is this which has made the concept of nominalism, or the belief that truth and reality are to be found in concrete individuals, endlessly appealing ever since Aristotle first formulated it as an abstract idea. It is vital to remember that concrete realities (existence) come first and would go on without the abstract ideas or symbols (essences) of those realities, since animal experience would go on without human experience. But it is also important to remember that the human being is the most symbolic of animals, that he has an inherent need to symbolize or abstract from the concrete realities, that these symbolic abilities are an essential aid in his quest for survival, animal comforts, and self-transcendency, and that they become a self-generating motive in much of human activity. It is this equally necessary symbolic aspect of human experience that has made symbol-realism (commonly, but confusingly, called realism by philosophers) so intriguing since it was first formulated in concrete terms by Plato.

The gut-level conviction that truth lies in the direct experience of concrete things and events leads us to want to experience them directly, as they are found in nature—out there—with nothing between us and the concrete realities, including no mentalistic paraphernalia of abstract preconceptions about the world or how it should be observed. The opposite conviction that truth lies in abstract thought, in symbols, in the culturally inherited way the human mind goes about observing the world, leads us to believe that we can know what is going on out there by thinking about it, by the exercise of mind alone. Indeed, in its purest form symbol-realism involves a distrust of concrete, direct experience of the world. Direct experience is thought to be subjective, the product of an individual's personal relation to a concrete situation. This subjective experience, then, according to symbol-realist thought, is too individual, too situational, too temporary, to be true. Truth must be derived from thought or reason itself, independent of the uncertainties and flux of concrete, direct experience. Truth must be object-like or objective—absolute—the same for all times, places and knowing minds.

The complex interplay between these epistemological convictions, nominalism and symbol-realism, has gone on over the centuries, largely at a prereflective level, until the last several centuries. People of common sense, philsophers and, more recently, scientists, have created a vast array of natural types of social research to understand and to affect what is going on in their social world. While these types can be viewed in terms of many complex dimensions, they all fall somewhere along a dimension ranging from completely natural observation to observation totally controlled by preconceived ideas; this dimension seems to be of fundamental importance in understanding all other relations among the types of social research.

The Spectrum of Types of Social Research

Like other experts and professionals, sociologists are apt to look at the basic ideas and methods of their discipline as somehow unique to the discipline and, indeed, as the products of their own creative work. But this is far from the truth. Most sociological methods are really imports from much earlier forms of common-sense social research and from methods used in the natural sciences. Certainly sociologists have added to these earlier forms, but it is important to our understanding of the basic aspects of these methods to see their broader foundations in common-sense activities.

In the most basic sense, of course, all people are common-sense sociologists. That is, all people seek to understand their social world in order to solve problems they experience in that world. In their attempts to understand their social world, all people create and/or use complex methods of observation and analysis. Consider, for example, a universal social activity such as sex. Most human beings at some time, generally in some socially defined period of puberty, experience some problems with getting a sexual mate. (Where there exist patterns of arranged marriages, the problems fall upon parents, nobles or some other intermediaries.) These are generally important and difficult problems. As a result, there are elaborate ideas about what constitutes a good mate, how one can determine such a thing, and how to get her (him) once the determination is made. If we were to carefully examine all such practical human activities, we would find they contain the core ideas of all social research methods.

Only a tiny fraction of the information collected and social research done in our society today is collected or done by sociologists or by people who have seriously studied sociology. Most social research information is discovered by social research done by people of practical affairs, such as journalists collecting information through interviews, writers doing life stories by taping long talks with the subjects, retired politicians writing memoirs or publishing diaries, businessmen trying to determine the profitability of a new housing development or a new toothpaste, government officials trying to determine public response to a new schedule of bus fares or the amount of crime, and so on almost endlessly.

While sociologists might well wish to discard much of this kind of information because they do not feel it meets their standards for social data, it is important to realize that all these forms are there and that, as in the past, there may well be some forms used by non-sociologists that can make vital contributions to sociology. For example, I shall argue in this book that the investigative methods of journalists and some of the investigative occupations, such as detective work, are of great importance in developing all forms of field research. Sociologists should be aware of all forms of social research and should choose their own methods in terms of the value of the methods for producing the kinds of information they want in any given study, rather than in terms of some preconceived biases about what are "sociological methods." In making these choices, they should look to the full spectrum of available research methods.

All of these forms of information and research fall on a continuum ranging from total immersion in natural experience to totally controlled observations and analyses. The major forms of such information and research are presented along such a schematic continuum in Figure 1. At the top of this spectrum we have the forms of human experience least subject to any form of rationalized control, that is, dreams and subconscious experience. As we move toward the bottom, we find forms of observations that are more and more controlled, more and more the result of pre-conceived methods of observation, less and less the kinds of observation done in our everyday natural (nonexperimental) situations.

It is only when we get to the bottom that we find the observations almost exclusively those made by the experiments of social scientists. For this reason that part of the spectrum is called Controlled Experimental Observations. Though we could obviously debate the issue of where the degree of control seems great enough to warrant a clear-cut distinction, most sociologists would probably agree that when we move from interviews with a flexible checklist which are done by in-depth, conversational methods to natural experiments or interviews done with a close-ended list and by formal question-and-answer methods, we have moved to the kind of research that is predominantly preprogrammed or controlled. Field research in general would be any form of

Figure 1: The Continuum of Free-Flowing Existence to Controlled Observations

Everyday Life Social Experience and Thought

Unconscious Experience
Subconscious Experience
Dreams
Conscious Experience
Practical Thought and Action
Diaries and Memoires
Travelogues
On-Site Field Visits and Reports

Systematic Reflection

Philosophical Thought

Field Research

Participant Field Research

Depth-Probe Field Research
Investigative Reporting, Detective Work
Covert Field Research
Overt Journalism and Police Work
Overt Field Research

- -

Non-Participant Field Research

Discussion (free-flowing), In-Depth Interviews
In-Depth Interviews with Flexible Checklists of Questions

Controlled Experimental Research

Natural Experiments
Pre-programmed Interviews (statistical)
Official-data and Business Analysis Reports
Judicial Investigations (operating under Rules of Evidence)
Business Studies (statistical)
Panel (test and retest) Studies
Laboratory Experiments
Questionnaires and Polls
Computer Simulation Studies
Mathematical Models

research that comes above this, but which is still performed as a scientifically-oriented enterprise aimed at providing, by planned methods, information that is generally better than that gotten simply by natural experience of individuals acting with common sense. Everyday Life Experience lies still further up the spectrum: It too shows degrees of control exercised over observations, but it is less controlled than field research.

Field research includes all forms of study of society in natural situations by means of natural (relatively uncontrolled) social interaction. Field research might better be called naturalistic social research, since the crucial point is that it is done in natural settings by natural forms of interaction, and since some forms of controlled research (such as polls or questionnaires) are often done in the field. (Some researchers have also referred to such relatively uncontrolled forms of research as unobtrusive measures, meaning that the measures used do not significantly affect or change the natural setting; that is, the methods of observation have little uncertainty effect. See especially Webb, et al., 1972.) But field research is the name that has been used traditionally and we seem to be stuck with it.

It is important to note that field research is only relatively uncontrolled; that is, relative to the more controlled forms called experimentally controlled, and relative to the less controlled forms called everyday life experience. Also important is the fact that there are degrees of control within field research methods themselves. At the one extreme, for example, we have depth-probe field research, in which the researcher surrenders (Wolff, 1964) to the everyday experience while in the natural setting but, instead of going native, remains latently committed to being a researcher and comes back to reflect and report upon the experience as a member. Depth-probes are vital in getting at the deeper, more secret aspects of social life, those about which the members often would not talk or possibly even think. In these forms the researcher's knowledge of his own feelings becomes a vital source of data.

At the other extreme we have in-depth, conversational interviews (or discussions) in which the only preprogramming would be the use of a flexible checklist of questions, used by the researcher to make sure he covers all the things he already knows to be important through involvement and earlier discussions. Our study of drug dealers, for example, was based largely on in-depth interviews, which were really free-wheeling discussions that often went on for hours, sometimes over many sessions, and in which a changing checklist of questions was used only from memory to make sure we covered everything. They occurred wherever the dealer wanted to do them and every method, such as drinks, was used to make them relaxed, quasi-natural discussions. (See Adler, Adler, Douglas with Rasmussen, 1977.) Investigative methods in general fall nearer depth probes simply because they rely heavily on direct experiences, reading body language, being flexible, etc. The overt methods involve more controls since the researcher, whether intentionally or unintentionally, imposes the social meanings of research upon the situation.

There are two major subtypes of field research. The first, nonparticipant field research, involves little or no direct interaction with the people, acts or social products being observed in their natural setting. Nonparticipant observation is used mainly to study behavior in public places, such as we find in Goffman's well-known works (Goffman, 1959 and 1963) and in the many studies of micro-ecology by social psychologists. But it could also involve the study of private settings by the use of bugging techniques. The so-called "unobserved observer" (Goffman, 1959) is one form of nonparticipating field researcher. Nonparticipant field research does, of course, rely upon interaction or participation for its crucial data, the imputed social meanings. But it uses previous, general cultural participation and understanding, not participation with the people actually being studied.

Participant field research, the second major subtype of field research, involves some form of natural social interaction with those being studied. Since most field research involves a considerable amount of natural interaction, field research in general is often mistakenly identified with this particular subtype and called participant observation. Participant field research, in turn, is distinguished by two subtypes: Overt participant field research involves telling the people being studied that they are being studied by a social researcher; covert participant field research involves the researcher's passing as some kind of member, or in some other way keeping his research activity secret from those being studied. We shall return to these important distinctions in our later discussion of investigative methods.

As with field research, the experimental research methods involve many different types and degrees of controls. The one thing they all seem to have in common is the assumption that the controls will eliminate subjectivity, thereby increasing objectivity, and that the researcher knows enough about the research situation to know how the controls used will do this. The crucial weakness of all experimental methods, upon which we shall elaborate in the next section, is that researchers commonly do not recognize that they are making these assumptions, especially the one that they know enough about the research situation to know that their controls are actually doing what they think. All too commonly they tend to assume, with no evidence at all, that their controls work automatically and, by implication, that their human subjects are not changed by the controls used in observing them. They simply assume that people act normally when they're in a research laboratory or their preparations for dinner are interrupted with a questionnaire. In fact, experimenters often ignore any contrary evidence—they have automatic controls to screen out any criticisms of their assumption that controls automatically produce more truthful (objective) results. There is now extensive literature showing, that this assumption is unfounded and that controls do affect the results (i.e., produce uncertainty effects). (See especially the massive bibliography on these works in Sudman and Bradburn, 1974.) Rather than needlessly repeating these, we are concerned here with pointing out the major types of controlled observations used and briefly considering in the next section some of the ways in which the assumptions underlying their uses are justified.

One of the least common forms of experimental research is the natural experiment. This form involves less control than any other form we have put into the category of experimentally controlled research. It is explicitly based on some kinds of field research observations of the setting being studied, and assumes that one knows the natural setting well enough to do what members will see as a natural action. Harvey Sacks and some of the other ethno-methodologists have used this form as the basic part of their methods of studying linguistic accounts. They argue that when the researcher can generate accounts seen by members as natural or sensible in the situation, then he has an adequate understanding of the deep rules lying behind their accounts. (This is one form of the so-called phenomenological member test of validity.) David Altheide suggests that a crucial test of one's understanding of a group is being able to joke successfully (1976, Appendix on Methods). These ideas of natural experiments involve minimal controls.

Some natural experiments involve more controls. For example, in doing our study of drug crisis intervention (Douglas, 1974b), we were concerned with determining how different hot lines dealt with calls about drug crises. How much did they know about different drug problems? Did they give the same kinds of answers? Did they know much about drugs? Did they give answers that doctors might see as dangerous to drug overdose cases? So we decided, after having determined a great deal about how hot lines work and about drug overdoses from various field observations, to use a natural experiment. We had two researchers (the ones specializing in hot lines) call in to different hot lines and, in what their experience led them to believe were convincing tones, said they had a drug problem. We worked out three standardized problems which would reveal the kinds of things we wanted to know; and we noted each of their responses, including no answers and referrals that didn't work. As expected, we found that no one questioned whether these were real calls and that there was vast variability in responses, from none and dangerous "common-sense remedies" (which don't work) to detailed information.

Again, in the same study, we found that a journalist had done a natural experiment of some value on emergency rooms. He called hospital administrators and asked what they would do if he brought in an overdose. Then he called emergency rooms and asked the same thing. He got extremely varied answers, both among different hospitals, and even within the same hospital. This was clear evidence of the conflicts within one organization, especially between official policies and individual decision-making about drug cases. (The contrast was even more striking when one compared what was actually done in real cases.) In both cases the results checked out with what we found from intensive field observations, they were easy and cheap to do, and were of definite value to our study, especially in getting evidence about places we didn't have the time to study in depth.

The two most common forms of experimental methods in sociology are questionnaires and laboratory settings. There is a serious question as to which involves the more controls, is the more preprogrammed, has the least natural interaction. The reason for this is simply that there are many forms of lab settings and ways of observing and analyzing them. Some come close to natural experiments; others are rigidly controlled. In general, they seem to involve fewer controls than questionnaires, since questionnaires have preprogrammed sets of questions and, generally, preprogrammed methods of administering, coding and (to a lesser degree) statistically interpreting them. But this comparison between lab experiments and questionnaires raises the question of another basic dimension along which methods may vary—that of the naturalness of the setting.

As we made clear at the beginning of our discussion, what concerns us about controls in social research is the degree to which they affect or determine the social phenomena we observe, that is, the degree of uncertainty effects. The argument, which we shall see more clearly in the next section, is that controls pose a grave danger for sociology because, if we do not know what their effects are and thus do not know how to control for the effects of controls themselves, then we run the grave danger that as controls increase they unknowingly become more important in determining what we observe. Controls raise the danger that we are studying research procedures, not the natural social world, the world of everyday life. Unless we are concerned only with understanding research methods, we don't want this.

There are at least two major aspects to controls that seem to produce this danger. One is the programming involved in controls, which is what we've been mainly concerned with up to this point. When we preprogram our methods of observation, coding of observations and ways of analyzing those coded observations, then we run the risk of imposing a structure upon the world we observe, that is, the structure of our preconceptions used in setting up the preprogramming. But when we use experimental methods, we also are using a situation that is unnatural, not like everyday life, and one which may have its own special definitions by the members of society. Indeed, all evidence indicates that those situations defined as scientific research settings do have special meanings for the members of society. Significantly, for example, we get the omnipresent phenomena of "scientific compliance," or going along with what the scientist wants because of his prestige, authority, etc. In addition to these generally shared social meanings of social research, any concrete research setting will have concrete meanings to the subjects; for example, a research setting may look confusing, suspicious or dangerous to people because they don't know what the researcher really has in mind. (The guy at the door could really be a rapist, bill collector, narcotics agent, nut, etc.) It could also look like this because they suspect they do know what he has in mind and don't like it. It is especially common today for people to believe that the research will have some bad effects on their interests, so they lie or refuse to cooperate at all. We shall look into this more in the next section.

When we look at the spectrum of research methods in terms of this dimension, we find some important differences from those revealed in Figure 1. For one thing, there is potentially a crucial difference between all research methods done in natural guise, including covert research, and that done with the overt definition of the researcher as a researcher. As a result, we must conclude that covert forms of research fall into a different category from overt forms. This is an important distinction and sometimes proves vital in a research setting. At times it prevents a researcher getting in at all, if he's known to be a researcher. But it is not always so crucial. In some cases, just as with tape recorders, the people being studied eventually seem to get used to the researcher's presence and stop worrying about his being a sociologist; in some settings people even forget he is a researcher. David Altheide (1976), for example, found that TV news people repeatedly referred to him as an apprentice, even though he often reminded them he was doing research. This "getting used to the researcher" would rarely apply to any forms of research other than field research because other forms are almost always momentary events rather than associations stretching over days, weeks and months. When someone hits a person with a questionnaire or political poll, that person can't forget he's a researcher and he can't get used to the idea in ten minutes or an hour.

A questionnaire, while having more controls, may seem more natural than a lab experiment because it takes place in one's home or on the phone. As a result, we would expect that the uncertainty effects cut in opposite directions—questionnaires have a greater effect upon the observations because of preprogramming, but less effect because of being in more natural settings. We can't be sure of such speculation, since there has been so little attempt to determine by field research observations and other means just what effects these different methods do have on people. But it seems most reasonable at this time to look upon questionnaires and lab methods in general as having about equal amounts of effect on observations. However, we must remember that the actual methods used in a concrete setting can drastically change this evaluation. If, for example, a questionnaire is used in a setting where we already have a lot of field research understanding that allows us to anticipate and even check up on the effects it will have on answers, then we can see that it would have less effect. (We shall return to this important point.)

There is little doubt about the effects of the research methods at the extreme. Mathematical models and simulation studies are commonly built on a minimum of observations and a maximum of preconceived ideas. Since they can produce nothing other than what is programmed into them in the first place, they are the ultimate examples of studying one's own research methods. This is not to say that they are not useful in some cases; they can be useful in analyzing a mass of complex information and checking on the reasonableness of one's assumptions—*if* the information is known to be highly valid and reliable. But, in general, there is little doubt that mathematical models and simulation studies produce the extreme in uncertainty effects.

This, then, is the spectrum of research methods in terms of their degrees of control over observations and, secondarily, their naturalness. Our argument leads us to expect that as we increase controls, we must expect to increase both kinds of uncertainty effects, even if we are eliminating individual biases. But this does not mean to imply that controlled methods cannot be used without producing unacceptable uncertainty effects. These effects can be controlled to some degree, *if* we first understand the social setting sufficiently by participation methods to have a good idea of how the controlled methods are likely to affect the people involved. This leads us to propose a mixed strategy for research methods (see the following section). But we must first examine more carefully the general conditions under which we can use control methods and the questions of how useful they are in our society today.

The General Conditions for Using Field Research and Controlled Research

In spite of our pervasive dependence on direct concrete experience in our everyday lives, direct experience has had a bad reputation throughout most of Western history, probably because history so far has been largely by and about wordsmiths or intellectuals. Symbol-realism in some form or another has been dominant since the works of the early theologians, philosophers, logicians, mathematicians, and so on. This dominance has not been total or universal. Each basic mode of observing and knowing the world has always been mixed with the other, except in extreme instances of mystical idealism and know-nothingness. And there have always been some realms of experience, even among intellectuals, in which direct observation was given more consideration. Still, among the intellectual and educated (by intellectuals) groups symbol-realism has normally been dominant.

It is little wonder, then, that in the natural sciences experimentally controlled observation became the dominant method of studying the world, nor is it any wonder that the social sciences, which were explicitly cast in the mold of the natural sciences by their creators in the 19th century, should have followed the same path. Since the natural observation method of field research has always been based, whether explicitly or implicitly, on the argument that the dominant method of controlled observations is somehow wrong, or at least not as good a method for studying society, we must first examine some basic properties of the control method.

Lying behind the controlled methods of observing the world is Plato's metaphor of the shadows in the cave or some similar image degrading common-sense, direct experience. In this metaphor Plato presented the ideas of people in everyday life as being like shadows cast on the walls of a cave. We see the shadows, but cannot directly observe the realities, the things which cast the shadows. Yet it is the things themselves, not the shadows, that we want to know. The problem of gaining all knowledge, of epistemology, is thus believed to be how to get from the directly observable shadows to the realities that cannot be directly observed. The answer is found somehow in the exercise of reason, though Plato himself realized something was wrong with this view, and seems to have relied ultimately upon some form of mystical insight to jump from the shadows to the realities.

Plato's cave is one of the most mischievous metaphors in human history. Intellectuals have commonly found its temptations impossible to resist; in fact, few have even tried. Why they have found it so irresistible is easy to understand. (I well remember how enraptured I was by this metaphor when I first read it as a fledgling intellectual of 17.) If humans live in a cave where they cannot see the realities of things, but merely the shadows of those realities, and only the exercise of reason, the very thing the intellectual does, will reveal the "really real" things, then the intellectual is the only one who can reveal the really real truths. The intellectual becomes the arbiter of reality itself and his enemies, the *hoy poloy* who scoffed at his mental legerdemain, become mere cavemen unable to see reality. He becomes the one person capable of freeing all the others from their submission to the idols of the cave. Plato's shadowy cave has been the opiate and the inspiration of centuries of intellectuals.

A modicum of resistance to this tempting idea would lead one to ask: "But what in the world makes you think most of our ideas of everyday life are mere shadows? The fact is that those ideas work well in our everyday lives; they tell us almost everything we need to live well—to eat, drink, sleep, procreate, whatever. They seem perfectly fitted to how we actually live.

Those are the realities and your contentions to the contrary are mere rhetoric inspired by your intention of creating an ideology that will justify your lording it over the rest of us."

To this the intellectual might retort: "Let us not become *ad hominem* about this just because I have impugned the integrity of your view of life. After all, is it not true that you are sometimes wrong about things in your own experience? Do you not sometimes believe it is Tuesday when it is Monday, or believe you are awake when you later discover you were asleep, or think a stranger has stolen your ox when it turns out your son took him for the day? Indeed, these mistakes of common-sense observations are merely symptoms of a deeper malady. The 'truths' of common sense are in general merely apparent truths that hide the real truths from us.

"Consider, for example, the omnipresent common-sense experience of 'intention.' Each individual tends to be convinced that he knows faultlessly what his own intentions are, what he really intended in a given situation. Yet as soon as we turn the pure light of reason upon them, even intentions are immediately revealed to be confused and even deluding to the individual who has them. As Durkheim said, in obvious justification of his rejection of intention as being part of a definition of suicide, "Intent is too intimate a thing to be more than approximately interpreted by another. It even escapes self-observation. How often we mistake the true reasons for our acts! We constantly explain acts due to petty feelings or blind routine by generous passions or lofty considerations." (Durkheim, 1951:43.) What is needed, then, is some method, some form of investigation worked out by reason itself, that will allow us to eliminate from our observations all these false-hoods of (direct) common-sense observation. These methods of observation will govern all our observations of the natural world and thereby eliminate these falsehoods of common-sense experience. These methods will treat human experience and thought itself "as things, that is, as realities external to the individual" (Durkheim, 1951:38) and, thus, not subjectively determined, not distorted by the inevitable falsehoods of common-sense (natural) experience. Only in this way, Durkheim believed, can we produce a truly objective science of human society that will enable us to solve the problems of our natural social world. This simple statement contains the crux of the argument in favor of (exclusively) controlled observations. Let us briefly examine its basic assumptions.

The crucial point of our intellectual methodologist's argument is the contention that there is a fundamental dualism in the world: The world can be divided into subjects and objects, experiencing beings and objects experienced. Since our basic purpose, at least as scientists, is to know what the world is really like, our goal becomes that of separating the subjective biases out of our knowledge of the world as it really exists as objects out there. The way to do this is to control our observations of the world in such a way that the effects of the subject, the person doing the knowing, will be eliminated. That is what classical ("hard science") methods in the natural and social sciences are all about.

Much of the development of the natural science philosophy and practice in the twentieth century, especially since the development of the principle of uncertainty, has led to the progressive whittling away of the assumption of subject-object dualism and the assumption that the scientist can eliminate the subjective elements from his scientific work. Natural scientists and philosophers alike have come to believe there is an ultimate, necessary interdependency of subject and object. The nature of the mind is a determinant of the ways in which we can know the world, but the nature of the world has also, presumably through complex forms of natural selection, been a determinant of the ways in which we know the world. Therefore, the ultimate structures of mind and world are interdependent and, rather than producing a lamentable bias, the structure of the mind allows us to know the world in that way best fitted to our survival and prospering in the world.

More immediately, natural scientists and philosophers have come increasingly to believe that any method of observation affects the observations made. The only questions are what effects a given method has and how much. Natural scientists have abandoned the quest for absolutely objective knowledge, but this has by no means led them to abandon science or all distinctions between truth and falsehood. (It is not my purpose here to examine in any detail the basic questions of objectivity. I have done this in some earlier works, such as Douglas (1970c and d), and others, especially Johnson (1977), have done so as well.)

The developments of phenomenological-existential philosophy and sociology (see for example Douglas and Johnson, 1977) have led us increasingly to see that the assumption of subject-object dualism implicit in all classical methods of social research, as seen so clearly in the examples of Durkheimian methods, is even more distorting than the same assumption in the natural sciences. The basic reason for this is simple. As I and others have argued before (see for example Douglas, 1971), sociologists have found that they must know what social meanings[1] are involved in any group's activities and must use these in any attempts to explain those activities. They have also found that in determining what these social meanings are they necessarily rely, at some level, upon their own common-sense experience in society. There is no other way to understand or get at internal, meaningful experience. As a result, their own subjective experience is ultimately the basis of all their imputations of meanings to the people they are trying to understand scientifically. The subject, their own experience, is the ultimate basis for their understanding of the "external objects" and, while they can and do try to make some partial controls on individual biases, such as lying, it makes no sense to believe it is possible to ever totally separate the subject from the object. Rather than trying to eliminate the subjective effects, the goal must be to try to understand how they are interdependent, how different forms of subjective interaction with the people we are studying affect our conclusions about them, and so on. Rather than looking at research methods as a preconceived constraint that automatically eliminates subjective elements, methods now become an inspiration as well, an attempt to show how one can create and use subjective experience, gained from interaction with other people and from introspection, to understand them and oneself.

Any simple observation of how sociologists actually do research immediately reveals how they are using their own common-sense, natural participation in society and their own common-sense, natural participation in society and their own understanding of social meanings to arrive at their research conclusions. Yet the rhetorical power of the classical idea of absolute objectivity, of eliminating the subjective experience from the object one is studying, has been consistently so powerful, and therefore tempting, to sociologists that they continually use it to berate their enemies. Even ethnomethodologists, whom one would least expect to give in to this temptation, have repeatedly done so.

Early social research, such as Durkheim's classical study of suicide, generally involved the repeated insistence that the researcher was treating social events, such as suicide, entirely as objects or "things." Yet careful analysis of such works (see for example Douglas, 1967) inevitably reveals that they were "bootlegging" their own common-sense understandings to derive or infer the key (independent) explanatory variables, such as egoism. Their "objectivity" was largely based on a pretense that they were inferring meanings as if they were objects from their observations of the social world, when in fact they were using their own common-sense understandings, derived either immediately or at an earlier time from their own natural participation in society.

Again, if we look at any questionnaire study, the most popular form of "hard science" in sociology since the 1940s, it is obvious how they are using their own common-sense understandings derived from participation in society to do their studies. All of their understandings of the words used in the questions, all of their ideas about consistency and lying, all of their ideas about how to interpret the answers, etc., are derived ultimately from such natural social experience. The best questionnaire sociologists have always understood this and tried to make use of it by pretesting their questionnaires, which meant participating enough in the group to know, strictly by natural, common-sense means, how the subjects were understanding the questions, what their answers meant to them, etc. The ethnomethodologists, following Garfinkel's early work (1967), long dissected all other methods for relying on common-sense experience as the resource for explaining what they were observing in society. But as Johnson has shown conclusively (in Douglas and Johnson, 1977), they themselves were doing precisely the same thing and, indeed, necessarily so.

Since everyone must rely on his own common-sense, natural participation in society to get at the social meanings that are crucial in any sociological research or theory, it is not an interesting question to ask whether a researcher is doing so. The crucial question is *how* is he doing this and whether his particular form of participation is adequate to provide the kind of information he needs about the people he is studying.

The first crucial distinction to be made about forms of social research in this respect is between all those forms that assume, generally implicitly, that their general participation and common-sense understanding of their society is adequate from the beginning of a research project, and those who believe they do not have adequate participation in the particular group they are studying to get the kind of information they need. A sociologist who does a nationwide questionnaire study of American attitudes or voting preferences without any pretest is implicitly assuming, even if he does not realize it, that he already knows enough from his participation in American society about how people look at such questionnaires, the questioners, the ways their answers might affect the issues involved, as well as innumerable other things, to adequately prepare, administer and interpret the questionnaire. Insofar as these assumptions are met, the researcher is probably right: His general Cultural Participation (GCP) and his General Cultural Understanding (GCU) based on that participation probably allows him to get the information he wants from the questionnaire study. The only questions then are those concerning the adequacy of the information for his purposes.

Importantly, for example, a questionnaire study, even an open-ended one, is largely preprogrammed. It is hard to come up with new ideas about the world from such preprogrammed study. Consequently, if the researcher is interested in learning new basic things about the society, such as new values or conceptions people are using in their everyday lives, he probably couldn't get it from such a study. However, if he simply wants to get at something like the national distribution of some concrete thing, such as clearly defined voting preferences, or orange juice drinking, then this method is probably adequate.

The kinds of in-depth research methods used by field researchers, which are the main concern in this book, would be immensely too costly for such study, as long as one just wants something like the temporary distribution of such unproblematic, concrete actions or attitudes. Voting polls, for example, seem to meet these requirements. As long as one only wants to know how people will respond to a simple, almost universally understood situation, such as voting in a presidential election, and as long as he is interested only in expressed preferences that hold for a few days, then the voting polls are the most efficient means available for getting information adequate for those purposes.

It will take a lot more study and analysis before sociologists know under what conditions they can use their GCP and GCU to do their research.[2] But there appear to be some good rules of thumb for such research.

In general, the more concrete the phenomena being studied, the more unproblematic for the members of society, and the less subject they are to any moral disputes or conflicting interests (which make people hide things from researchers), the more the researcher can rely on his GCP and GCU in doing his research. Hence, the more he can rely on some method of research, such as questionnaire studies, that does not require his participation in the particular group and/or social situation he is interested in understanding.

While there are, as already noted, some broad areas of research in which such methods can and should be used, those areas seem not to be the ones of most importance to sociologists interested in constructing theories of our society, nor, with some exceptions, do they seem to be the areas of most practical concern to our society. Moreover, the areas in which these conditions of concrete phenomena and unproblematic aspects are met in our society seem to be shrinking. The reasons for this are relatively simple and will be thoroughly examined in succeeding chapters. In general, the conditions under which a sociologist's GCP and GCU are adequate for his purposes are commonly found only in reasonably simple, nonpluralistic and nonconflictful societies; yet American society is vastly complex, pluralistic, and conflictful and is rapidly becoming more so.

Consider a few examples of what might appear at first sight to be reasonably simple, concrete forms of data that might be needed for some simple, practical purposes. During the gasoline shortages in the United States in 1974 most people were anxious to determine how much of the different forms of petroleum there were, and where they were, and why there were those quantities of forms other than gasoline. What man/woman/child would send out a questionnaire to the people who supposedly know such things, such as oil executives, to determine the answers? Our common-sense, cultural understanding alone tells us that there are too many moral and material-interest conflicts involved and too much tendency among people to lie in such situations for us to consider using questionnaires to determine the answers.

Or consider the question of how Americans feel about their work, which is admittedly a much more difficult one. Even our GCU tells us that our feelings about our work are tremendously complex and vary greatly from one time and one situation to another. Some people have clearly defined feelings about their jobs, but generally only at the extremes of love or hate. Most people, however, have mixed feelings that vary with the situation at hand, often from one moment to the next. Often we don't know how we feel about our jobs. Even more often, we can't tell how those we know well feel about their jobs.[3] Any attempt to determine all these different feelings and their variations by a method based only on our GCU will surely result in findings that are worse than useless. They would be distortions. And they would be terrible distortions if the individuals doing the study did not have the cultural wisdom to realize that our feelings are as complex and variable as they are, and, instead of at least trying to develop some way of getting at these, imposed an index upon them that assumed they were simple, homogeneous, invariant over time and fell upon some linear scale. Yet those who do such studies, having committed themselves to their "hard science" methods before ever conceiving of what they were going to study, frequently make precisely these assumptions about *anything* they are studying with questionnaires and similar methods. When they have gone to the extreme of imposing such assumptions and methods upon such volatile and problematic values, feelings, thoughts and actions as race relations, they have taken the use of questionnaire studies to the point of absurdity. It is little wonder that, as Irwin Deutscher (1973) and others have shown, such researchers have never been able to find any significant relations between their studies of attitudes and what people actually do.

Just as we can expect, as a rule of thumb, to use our GCP and GCU to study a group under certain conditions with nonparticipatory methods, so we can expect the converse to be true. The less concrete the phenomena being studied, the more problematic they are for the members of society, and the more they are subject to moral or material-interest conflicts, the more the researcher must use natural participation in the group as the basic method to get at the phenomena.

As we shall see, there are many forms of participation and each concrete research setting and research goal demands its own form of participation to get the best results. But regardless of the particular form demanded, when we find the conditions of the above paragraph to exist (social complexity, conflicts, problematic meanings, abstract phenomena), we must expect to do our study by getting *inside* the group or groups to be studied, in order to observe carefully and systematically how they manage their everyday lives. Only in this way can we be sure of penetrating the misinformation, evasions, lies and fronts that groups use to screen out enemies in conflict situations. (These are discussed in greater detail in the next chapter.) Only in this way can we hope to see all the complex convolutions of problematic meanings and the complex, often conflicting patterns (and nonpatterns) of actions these convolutions give rise to in everyday life; and only in this way can we avoid taking a superficial and temporary patterning of attitudes, largely constructed precisely for the purpose of appearing sensible and reasonable to an outside investigator, as the whole reality of a group's social meanings.

The growing complexities, conflicts and problematic meanings of American Society (see Douglas, 1971) make it necessary for sociologists to move toward deeper involvement in the settings they wish to study, often appearing to be members, and generally using the methods long used by investigative reporters. (We shall discuss investigative methods, as opposed to more cooperative methods, in the next two chapters.) As a general rule, I suspect the problems of fronts, uncertainty effects, problematic meanings and so on, are so great in our society today that a sociologist should play it safe when he can by passing as a member of the setting or group he wishes to study. This is the way he can feel most secure, though never certain (since they may in fact have detected him[4]), that he is not being fronted-out or, worse, set up by the wily members.

But as with all social research methods, this one has its problems, or costs, and its gains must be weighed against these costs. For one thing, in many settings it is time-consuming to go through the process of becoming a member. If one is adept at acting like a member, as few sociologists are, then he might be able to pass as a member; but, regardless of one's ethical feelings, this can be risky—anything from illegal to physically dangerous. Rarely would it be worth the time involved in becoming an actual member of an organized group, such as a newsroom staff or an operating room staff. Rarely is it worth the risk to try to pass as a member by conning people. Consequently, one generally chooses to become a member only in an open public setting (i.e., one open to the general public) or an organized private setting where he already happens to be a member or can easily become one.

Another consideration is that in some situations there are things members will not tell each other but will tell someone defined as a reputable researcher. For example, in his study of the Joe Bonanno family Gay Talese (1971) reports that, as far as he could tell, the members of this mafia family told him things as a way of talking indirectly (through his book) to their family about things which they were not supposed to say to each other in their everyday lives. In our studies, we have found many instances of things members would tell us because they trusted us not to pass stories on to other members. This is especially common when the research is done by an insider-outsider team (see Chapter 9) in which an insider has become part of a team. In these cases the insider is generally trusting of his fellow researcher and will tell him all kinds of things he won't tell fellow insiders. The same is true, though less so, of research confidants or "key informants." In most organized settings, as opposed to open settings, the costs of becoming a member are too great relative to those of not doing so.

We see, then, that the rule about the value of passing as a member is subject to a more general and reliable rule. One must weigh the costs and benefits for any research method for the concrete situation he faces relative to the kind of information he is seeking. This applies not only to the general type of method (such as field research versus controlled methods) but all the way down the line to the specific questions of whether one passes as a member, reveals his purposes to this person or that, uses a tape recorder or not, etc. As a closely related general rule, we find it valuable to be flexible and use a mixture of methods.

Mixed Strategies

Since all research methods have costs and benefits, and since they differ greatly in their particular costs and benefits, a researcher generally finds it best to use some combination or mixture of methods. But since human events are commonly time-bound or historical, generally it is not possible to use just any combination in any order. It is essential to figure out early in the research, often before it begins, just what mixture can be used and how it should be used. The problem of making the right beginning, a beginning that will not get the researcher thrown out or refused entree and that will not bias the rest of his study, is especially difficult because, as our whole argument has led us to see, we must have participation in order to answer such questions as whether a given method will bias our findings. How do we participate before we begin? Actually, the problem is not as paradoxical as it might seem.

First of all, we have our general cultural participation. Most of us have some prior experience with the kinds of settings we want to study. Second, while we must be cautious in using previous sources, since they so often have assumed answers to the very questions we wish to ask, there are almost always some earlier sources that can be counted on to give some basic facts about the obvious structure of the setting. Third, we almost always can find some people, generally colleagues or their spouses or friends, who will give us some insider understanding about similar settings. We use these and any other common-sensical sources we can think of to get as good an idea as possible about the setting we're going to study.[5]

At least three other general ideas cross-cut all mixtures of methods in helping to get started. The first is a simple maxim of all entrepreneurial activity. All good field research involves many of the same kinds of activities as any successful entrepreneurial activity—creative thought, a search for opportunities, seizing opportunities, working with people to get their help, and the like. The researcher should maintain his options as much as possible in the early stages of research; that is, until he knows enough to make knowledgeable decisions about his research methods and their effects on the information he is seeking. He should make no more commitments than necessary. It is important to be as vague as possible in making research bargains to get into the setting, but he must also avoid seeming too vague or he'll probably not be let in. He might try to explain that he does not want to prejudge things, and therefore doesn't want to get too specific. He wants to maintain a low profile in the early stages, and not become too committed to any one person or group until he knows what their position is in the group and how his association with them will affect the research findings.

The second general strategy is closely related to the first and complements it. It too is an entrepreneurial idea. The researcher must be highly flexible in the early stages of any research, playing each situation by ear rather than by some preconceived plan, and feeling his way into each situation, letting the members who appear to be friendly lead him into giving the answers he wants. Any new situation is one in which one will not know clearly what is going on. Consequently, any attempt to deal with the situation in terms of rationally preconceived ideas, as the classical model would lead one to do (see further discussion of this model in the next chapter), is likely to be wrong. Moreover, if it is a complex organization, as it is likely to be if overt entree is sought, then there are many cross-currents and conflicts in which the researcher can get caught, and he must be nimble and supple in paring his story to the different levels or groups with which he is dealing at any given time.

The field researcher is the complete other-directed individual, as David Riesman so aptly called that person who is continually using his interactional radar to adjust his views to the people and situations with which he is dealing; and he is especially so in the early stages of his work. He tries to feel his way into the labyrinthine conflicts of his new situation. If he is lucky, his situation will be one in which he can create a multistage strategy of entree, such as John Johnson was able to do in his study of welfare caseworkers. He was even able to do a dry-run study; that is, he was able to study one group where he could make all his initial mistakes and learn how to maneuver in the caseworker world, then was able to gain entree into the similar group that he really wanted to study. (Military strategists use this approach to test their strength and tactics, train their men, prove their ability to defeat the enemy, and avoid putting all their chips on the line at one time. This was one of the reasons for the U.S. strategy of "leapfrogging" across the Pacific toward Japan in World War II. A research assault on a social institution is often analogous to a military assault on a nation.)

A third general idea is by far the most important of the three. Our argument in previous sections has already led us to see the use of relatively uncontrolled methods as underlying, as being more basic than controlled methods. Generally we must use uncontrolled methods to determine how we should go about using controlled methods and how those controlled methods will affect our findings in any given setting.

The obvious implication of this general argument for the specific problem of choosing the best mix of methods is that we should begin with as little control in our methods and with as much natural interaction as possible in the setting; we should go from the relatively uncontrolled methods to the more controlled, from the more natural to the less natural forms of inter-action, from those forms most likely to have uncertainty effects to those less likely.

If possible, in most settings we would like to begin as a member and then move toward overt definition of ourselves as researchers, then possibly do in-depth interviews, then recordings, then any questionnaires to get at specific details and, possibly, more representative findings (that is, information on a wider group than we were able to do with our in-depth field research). Of course, we have to continually weigh this strategy against the costs. Importantly, it seems unlikely that we will want to take all the time and cost necessary to become a member in most private settings, so we begin with an overt definition of ourselves as researchers and move from that point to more controlled methods. As we shall see later, this does not necessarily mean that the researcher loses all chance of gaining member understanding. He may be able to establish such close, trusting relations with some members that he is able to turn them into researchers who can provide him with secret, in-depth material on member experience. Moreover, as we have already seen, the researcher is often able to pass, even when he has already defined himself as a researcher, in part because the members often forget that fact.

We shall return to questions of mixed strategies later, but there are a few points of such significance at the beginning of research that they deserve some note here. Recording devices are the technological invention with probably the greatest potential use in field research. Because of this potential, they pose a strong temptation to the beginning researcher, one that can easily lead him astray. Some researchers have been almost transfixed by recording devices, so that they come to define their research settings and their theoretical interests in society as a whole in terms of these devices.

This seems to be a major reason why many ethnomethodologists, whose initial goal was to get beneath the surface features of everyday life (do phenomenological reductions of everyday life), wound up studying nothing but linguistic accounts, which are all surface. Researchers like Sacks and Garfinkel became progressively committed to the use of the audio recorder, while others, such as Cicourel and Jennings, grew increasingly committed to the even more specialized and obtrusive technology of the videotape machine. These machines seemed to offer the chance to capture all the details of the social world for total recall—total objectivity. The rhetorical power of that position was overwhelming in a discipline still dominated by 19th century positivistic ideas. More important, on the surface the devices really seemed to offer that hope.

Unfortunately, experience has revealed that recordings done overtly (as almost all sociological recordings have been done) have profound effects on the people being recorded. This is so much the case that it is common for people to refuse entree to a researcher who proposes to tape the setting, especially if the setting is private in any way. Because nearly all important settings are private, a researcher who insists on using recordings overtly frequently winds up studying only very public events and then has a considerable but unknown effect on all the information he is using in his study.[6]

Because of this, it is generally vital for a field researcher to save his attempts to record his setting until the later stages of his research. By the later stages he knows enough about the people to decide how best to approach them about recording, how this is likely to affect them, and he can feel them out about it without having to lay all his chips on the line and run the risk of being rejected. (Being explicitly rejected always builds a wall between a researcher and his people. It stands as a silent reminder that their interests are in conflict and that there are limits beyond which their intimacy cannot go. The researcher, like the wise lover, never presses his case to the point where an explicit "no" is possible—unless his situation is desperate or unless there is no tomorrow.)

In general, we have found that the researcher uses the recorder in the early stages mainly for debriefing himself, but once he understands the situation and has the trust of people, he can do selected in-depth recordings[7] to get greater detail and also as a fabulous record to which he can listen again and again in his search for further insights.

This, for example, was the approach we used in studying nude beaches (Douglas, Rasmussen and Flanagan, 1977). We began the work as a depth-probe, all of us first becoming members. (One of us, Carol Ann Flanagan, was a member before she became a researcher.) We simply interacted with people in all the natural ways, observed our own problems of interaction and the ways we solved these, and surrendered to the experience.

As a second stage we began to probe our own feelings and thoughts by talking with each other, often taping these conversations and looking for insights in the freewheeling discussions.

When we felt we knew pretty much what it was all about, and when we were sure people would see us as members, we moved into the third stage. Rasmussen and Flanagan taped interviews in the natural settings with many people, but would also alternate back and forth between natural involvement and taping, often ·meeting people in natural involvement and later hitting them up for interviews. During this stage I continued to interact with people naturally, some of them the same ones being interviewed by the other two members of the team. (This was the ideal, but was often hard to accomplish.) In this way we tried to provide a double check on the uncertainty effects of the interviews.

We also were able to combine a few other methods with these, especially a natural experiment. We wanted to do some photography in a natural way. When TV news people would come to the beach to report on the nude scene, we would tag along, acting as if we were newsmen, taking the shots we needed for the study and even at one point interviewing as if we were reporters. (This was important because there was a strong feeling on the beaches against "camera voyeurs," and any other way of doing it involved the risk of our getting stigmatized as camera voyeurs.) The news programming on the beach also provided us with an opportunity for a minimal form of natural experimentation.[8] We had already done our comparative studies of the network-affiliated news departments. Now we had studied a situation that the news media might be interested in covering. One of the researchers involved in both studies decided to call in a newsman he had studied earlier to report on the nude beaches. By doing so we were able to compare what we knew to be going on with what the newsmen reported. We found, as expected, that the newsmen were set up by the members, and they bought the fronts—hook, line, sinker and pole.

As always, there are complex exceptions to this general rule about taping. For example, in our study of drug dealers (Adler, Adler, Douglas with Rasmussen, 1977) we found that we could tape some people with whom we had trusting contacts in the beginning, so we were able to get hours of detailed talk about their lives as dealers. Other people would not even talk to us directly, but would let intermediary friends tape them, while others let the intermediaries put their own voices on tape, and some people would never allow the recorder near them, insisting that the intermediary do nothing more than take notes. (In these last cases the intermediaries would commonly put on tape what they could remember beyond the notes when they got home.)

Conclusion

All forms and tactics of social research must be continually related to and successfully embedded in the social setting being researched. Each method has its values and problems and these must always be weighed against each other. Increasingly, however, field research must be used to solve the problems encountered in getting at the most important truths about social settings in an increasingly conflictful and problematic society; and one in which social research is increasingly suspect and, thus, fronted out. But this does not mean that we simply use the well-known forms of classical field research. On the contrary, our research experience has progressively revealed basic problems with this classical model of field research. We have tried to overcome these by developing investigative field research methods and the investigative model of society that fits these. Let us examine these two major models of society and the field research models that complement them. Then we can go on with the further development of the concrete problems faced in doing field research and the specific investigative methods we have devised for solving these problems.

NOTES

1. The term "social meanings" is used throughout this work in its broadest sense to refer to any "internal experience." It refers to such experience as feelings, thoughts, ideas, values, morals, eidetic images (picture thoughts), etc. At times I shall refer to feelings and meanings to emphasize the fundamental importance of feelings as distinguished from other meanings in that context.

2. It is important to note here that individual researchers differ greatly in their degrees of GCP and GCU. Sociologists range from cultural morons, who have almost no experience of American society, to those with vast cultural experience of different classes, regions, groups. From the standpoint of our analysis here, it is obvious that a social researcher and theorist would benefit greatly from as wide and deep a cultural experience as possible, ranging across as much of our complex society and the rest of the world as time, resources and his natural abilities allow him. The good field researcher should always be poking into new groups, trying to grow rich in cultural participation and understanding. While we obviously cannot tell anyone how to gain "wisdom" about his experience, we can urge him to be continually open, observant, questioning and analytical about his experiences. (This does not mean that he should be always analyzing his social experience, since that often destroys the natural experience. Rather, it means that once he has had the experience, he should be observant, questioning and analytical.)

3. My discussions with John Bradford concerning his study of Post Office workers helped me to see how complex our feelings about our jobs can be.

4. Every field researcher can learn great humility by having his cover blown a time or two, especially by being led on by the members before they blow his cover away. In our study of nude beaches I approached two college-age women one day and struck up a conversation with them about the setting, what they were doing, what they made of it, and so on. At the time I was passing entirely as a member, so I was careful not to talk about my identity and not to act in a professorial manner (i.e., pompous and puffed-up). But after talking with them, I did want to know a bit more about their social identities so, on the basis of their sophisticated and careful manner of speech, I surmised, "You're college students aren't you?" The one who had done most of the talking said softly, as they moved away, "Oh, yes. . . ." As they walked on a bit, she turned and said, smilingly, "We're even sociology students. . . ." Then, as she was almost out of range, she said, with a broad smile, "We even took your intro class last quarter. . . ." I felt terribly exposed. I knew my cover as an ordinary member had been blown, that I'd been treated

as a research dupe (a special category of contempt in our increasingly studied world), that I'd probably been "studying" what I'd told them about the setting in class, that uncertainty effects are not restricted to questionnaire studies, and that in social research, as in all social life, the only certainty is uncertainty.

5. The present discussion implicitly assumes that the researcher is studying a group in which he is not already some kind of member. As we shall see further in the next chapter, this is not always the case. Some of the best field research is done by people who are already members of the settings they study. In those cases, however, the beginning is not that much of a problem and they are able far more easily to tell what mixture of methods is likely to work best, at least if they have prior experience with the methods.

6. An example will clarify this. A doctor in a medical school told me one evening over dinner of his experience with one of the videotape ethnomethodologists. This doctor was in charge of hiring interns for the university hospital. The videotape researcher had approached him, asking permission to videotape the interviews of intern applicants. The videotaper assumed, as they almost always do, that this was reasonable and that it was simply a matter of getting the reluctant member to comply. He was refused. He kept insisting. The doctor eventually got angry about the whole thing and seemed to feel the taper was a nut of some kind. He expressed shock at discovering the taper was a full professor, rather than an "inexperienced beginner." The doctor apparently tried to explain to the taper that their methods of interview were too informal, "not really interview methods at all." He tried to convince the taper that he should videotape admission procedures for medical students, since these were highly formalized and took place in one specific room. What the doctor didn't want to tell the taper, and what the taper probably never discovered, was that the quasi-methods were highly individualized, unrationalized and situated. As he put it at dinner, "I literally had to take one guy into the men's room to interview him because he was only going to be there for a short period and there was no other room free." (Everyone found it hilarious to envision the taper busily videotaping the men's room.) The tape machine had become the determinant of what could be studied, how it could be studied, what could be found and what couldn't, and thence, of the kind of social theory this sociologist could create and verify—yet the taper seemed unaware of these realities. Like the computer simulators, the tapers become captives of their technology and produce nothing but simulacrums of society.

7. Again, being a trusted member can make all the difference, so a member can often record from the beginning, even in a touchy situation. I saw a good example of this in a study of scuba deaths by Robert Gilmore. A young man diving with three friends had disappeared. The lifeguards had been called and had arrived, followed by a TV news reporter and cameraman. I came across the scene by accident and called Gilmore. When he arrived, the friends were standing together in a tight group, saying little to anyone. They were apparently reluctant to say much to the lifeguards beyond what was necessary to help the search for their friend, probably because they were unclear about their responsibility in the situation and he was the official. They were completely unwilling to be interviewed by the TV newspeople, especially because they did not want the parents of the missing man to hear about it on the news before they could tell them about it. (In fact, they were furious at the TV news reporter and grew even more furious when the station aired the story without first determining whether the parents knew.) When Gilmore arrived, he had to clear himself with the lifeguard, since all information now came under the official aegis, but he then immediately joined the tight circle of friends. He told them he was a scuba diver, briefly referring to some of his extensive

credentials of membership, and in every way demonstrating his insider understanding and his sympathetic understanding of their situation. He told them what he was doing and proceeded to talk with them about the situation, then was able to record the talk without much apparent problem. They told him many things they had not told the outsiders.

8. It should be kept in mind that natural experiments, like any other research method, have many forms. Just as the natural experiment involves more control over the inputs and/or methods of observation than other forms of field research, so are there variations in the degree of control exercised in natural experiments. The form discussed here involves a minimal degree. The researchers did little more controlling than to set up the situation, then watch it unfold naturally.

Chapter 3

THE CLASSICAL (COOPERATIVE) PARADIGM OF SOCIETY AND FIELD RESEARCH

"It is surprising how quickly the average person will respond to the genuinely scientific attitude of an investigator and make an effort to give accurate, revealing statements." Vivien Palmer, 1928.

Field research, as we have seen, is the most "natural" form of social research. In fact, when it is done for purposes of pure science, it often involves little more than writing notes on (or recording) one's common-sense experience and systematically analyzing it. It is not surprising that field research emerged over the centuries from perfectly natural, practical forms of common-sense activity. Nor is it surprising that it is the earliest form of systematic social research. To this day, there is probably no greater field research report than that of Thucydides' *The Peloponnesian Wars,* which was written in the fifth century B.C. (See the quote in the frontispiece.) This monumental work was based on Thucydides' years of involvement as an Athenian general in the war. He was a complete insider who observed much of what he reported and kept field notes (a diary) on it for the explicit purpose of writing a truthful account that would transcend his historical and personal circumstances—that is, that would be scientific. He was concerned with the problems of "personal bias," the problems of unreliable interview data, and the necessity of cross-checking data and interpretations which we are concerned with today in our investigative research. Many centuries of myth, moralism, and scientific rhetoric about human society lie between Thucydides and us. It is shocking to discover how much more scientific he was than most of what now passes as social science.

Everyone knows and takes for granted in everyday life that the most reliable and truthful knowledge of everyday life is that gained from personal observations and experience. If you want to know what is going on, you "take a look and see." "Experience is the best teacher." But everyone also knows that his own experience and direct observation is limited to a small part of the world about which he wants to know. Everyone relies on his family, friends, and associates to tell him about parts of the world they have seen. Rulers and businessmen came many centuries ago to depend on the reports of direct experience by emissaries and lieutenants of many kinds as their other sets of eyes, their methods of knowing about those parts of the world they did not have the time or ability to directly experience. Greater numbers of people came to depend on the reports of travelers, either in verbal form or in travelogues, as their source of information about the wider world that aroused their curiosity. The travelers' accounts of men like Herodotus and Caesar became basic forms of social data for centuries of Western intellectuals and sources of delightful curiosities for the masses. The travelogues of early adventurers and explorers, such as Marco Polo, perhaps the most famous of all, may appear "fabulous" by present standards, but they are the direct predecessors of scientific field research. Most of nineteenth-century anthropology, such as the famous works by Frazer, was based on the travelogues of missionaries and others (Wax, 1971). Some of the most important American social documents of the day, such as Olmstead's journalistic books on the ante bellum American South and de Tocqueville's classic analysis of American democracy, were largely inspired by the travelogue model of reporting. In fact, the travelogue is still a very popular and worthwhile source of information about surface, or publicly observable, social phenomena, especially about such short-run phenomena as "the climate of opinion." This method is used all the time by columnists and pollsters to test the "political climate" of everything from health care programs to impeachment. It is used by some journalists, such as Bill Moyers in *Listening to America*, to "get the feel of the nation." It has been used by authors such as John Gunther in massive attempts to provide journalistic pictures of much of the world. When done by a person of great cultural experience and wisdom, this method of observing public life can form the basis for worthwhile "guesstimates" about the deeper, private lives of a people. De Tocqueville did it masterfully in the nineteenth century. Most contemporary attempts, such as Studs Terkel's works, concentrate on doing "cameo shots" and providing insights, but there is certainly no reason the method cannot be used to even greater effect by contemporary social thinkers of all kinds. The important point, as with any method, is to recognize the strengths and limitations of the information gotten. This method is good for getting at the shifting events and meanings of public life, especially in a relatively open and friendly society such as America; but these mini-probes give only hints about the more enduring and private aspects of social life.

This, in fact, was all de Tocqueville, commonly seen as the greatest of these travelogue-ethnographers, ever tried to get from his journey through America. As David Riesman (1965) has shown in some detail, de Tocqueville really spent little time actually observing American society, had little in-depth involvement, and was interested primarily in getting at general trends of democratic society—which were largely forms of public behavior. De Tocqueville's success in analyzing those trends in American society was largely due to the fact that America was experiencing trends common to those in Europe (as is still true) and to his already developed cultural wisdom about European society.

Everett Hughes (1971:530-542) did something similar in using some casual field research on industrial relations in the Rhineland as a source of perspective on industrial relations in French Canada. This kind of *casual comparative field research* has been a great stimulus to some of my own ideas and research on the mass media news (1977a) and social economics. At the same time, my experience has also made the relative weaknesses of casual field research abundantly clear. One example of this was the difference between my casual understanding of British society and my understanding based on living in London for three months. Casual observation led me to see primarily the similarities of British society to American and to see the small villages and ancient roads merely as a shrinking part of old Britain. Involvement in the practical problems of everyday life quickly convinced me that underlying the rationalized exterior of industrial society was a vitally important realm of "feudally localized" everyday life that is basic to understanding education, shopping, union-management relations, intra-union behavior, labor immobility, and most of the other "big issues" of British life. All of my subsequent research and analysis of British life have confirmed the importance of that "discovery."

These go-out-and-take-a-look-see-and-write-about-it methods of the travelogue, including unstructured interviews, were reasonably standard methods of journalistic reporting in America by the early part of the twentieth century. It was from his work as a journalist covering the city beat in Chicago that Robert Park learned these methods. After studying abstract theories of sociology in German universities, he returned to the city beat to wed to sociological theories the basic journalistic methods of taking a direct look at things. This was a major source of the now famous series of Chicago field research reports on the city, covering everything from "gold coasts" to "Hobohemia" and "taxi cab dance halls" (see Faris, 1967:51-87; Hughes, preface to Junker, 1960; Park, 1952; Madge, 1962:88-161; and Hughes, 1971:esp. 543-549).

But there was another major source of the classical Chicago model of field research, one which is so obvious that is is commonly overlooked. This is the field research of anthropologists, especially of Robert Redfield (1930, 1934: esp. Appendix A; 1941) at Chicago. Redfield was a close friend of Hughes and even had some of his students work with Hughes in the French Canadian study (Hughes, 1971:530-542). This anthropological connection was so close that Junker's text on field research, which was introduced by Hughes and which presents the Chicago model, uses anthropological and sociological sources indiscriminately. This is in *striking* contrast to the earlier classic work on Chicago field research methods by Vivien Palmer (1928), which contains no significant reference to anthropology. It is this anthropological model which seems to have become dominant in the thinking of the Chicago sociologists and other field research sociologists. This dominance was greatly reinforced by the importance at that time of the works of W. Lloyd Warner (see especially the Yankee City series, published by Yale University Press in 1936, 1937, 1941, 1942, 1945, 1947, 1959) who was also an anthropologist.

The anthropological model led in a direction opposite to much of the journalistic model and the historiographical model which was used extensively by Chicago sociologists in the 1920s (see Palmer, 1928). The journalistic model included a great deal of emphasis on getting behind the fronts of informants (interviewees), analyzing data for internal contradictions, assumptions of conflict between news sources and newsmen, and many other aspects of the investigative paradigm we shall examine in the next chapter. This was most apparent in the famous *Autobiography of Lincoln Steffens.* Various sociologists have referred to that work's importance, but few took it as their model of field research (see, for example, Whyte, 1955:242-243).

The anthropological model led above all to a "participant-observer role" in which the sociologist is inevitably restricted to being an outsider or, at most, a marginal participant, who is studying a "small community" by gaining the cooperation of participants who are often marginal (see Junker, 1960:esp. 32-69; and Hughes, 1971:436). Just as in anthropology, the sociologists quickly came to use the "lonely observer" (or "Lone Ranger") approach in which a single researcher attached himself for about a year to a small group to report to the world how they presented themselves to him. Investigative journalists concentrated on "exposing" those they studied, and historiographers were acutely aware of all the problems of bias and selectivity in their data. Anthropologists and sociologists concentrated on "taking the side of the underdogs" they studied and "unmasking" the upperdogs in conflict with the underdogs, primarily by showing that the things the upperdogs said about the underdogs were not true in terms of what sociologists could observe in their participant-observer roles. Even in those truly rare instances when they tried to study upperdogs, they tended to take their point of view (see, for example,

Rose, in Habenstein, 1970; Dalton's [1959] study, *Men Who Manage*, is not an exception because it rejected the whole idea of the marginal man researcher; see the next chapter.) Oscar Lewis (1951) later tried to show that Redfield's methods had led to a complete distortion of everyday life in Tepotzlan (1930). In a roughly similar way, we have come increasingly to believe that the Chicago type of research led to peeling off the public layer of stereotypes about groups, but only in too many instances to replace them with the private stereotypes groups present about themselves to marginal men researchers who are seen as "spies." Even in those rare instances in which they study a group involved in intense conflict, we can almost never see beyond the group's presentational (front) work. For the most committed Chicago sociologist, the adoption of the participant-observer role generally involved as well a moral commitment not to reveal the innermost secrets of the group. Thus, even if he does discover the innermost secrets, they cannot be revealed. As Hughes wrote, "The sociological investigator cracks the secrecy, but buries the secrets, one by one, in a tomb of silence—as do all the professions which deal with the problems of people" (1971:436). It is likely that the "participant-observer bargain" is necessarily an "unholy alliance" in which the subjects are partially betrayed by revealing more than their public rhetorics, but in which the readers are also betrayed by not having revealed to them all that one knows to be the truth in a scientific work popularly assumed to be trying to tell the whole truth. But the most serious problem seems to be that the classical model of field research adopted by the Chicago school and almost all other field research sociologists is not fitted to revealing the innermost truths about groups and individuals in our society because it is built on assumptions that *might* fit a "little community" studied by anthropologists, but do not fit a complex and conflictful society like ours.

The Classical Paradigm of Society and Field Research

We should be aware from the beginning that no model abstracted from these hundreds of field research reports will cover all aspects of them. I assume that in the tens of thousands of pages of these reports it would be possible to find almost anything, except proclamations of revolution or denunciations of Chicago professors of sociology. Because they often reported raw data and did low-level analyses of that data, they were bound at some point to incorporate almost any aspect of the complex and shifting social reality they were studying. Some of their statements even contradicted the general assumptions they made. Nevertheless, there seems to have been a reasonably consistent paradigm of research methods and a largely unquestioned paradigm of the social world involved in almost all these works. It is this paradigm or model that we are interested in here, rather than a statistical study of intellectual precedents.

When we look at the descriptive material and low-level theories of the field researchers in the grand era of Chicago sociology, from about 1920 to 1950, we see much of the complex, seething, shifting, conflictful life of America's great immigrant cities, especially in Chicago. Thrasher's classical work, *The Gang* (1927) includes a lot of description of violent conflict, much of it taken from newspapers. It also includes some low-level ideas about the importance of conflict in social life. For example, he argued that street play groups become gangs in part because they come into conflict with adult society, especially the police. But this conflict almost completely disappears from his and other Chicago sociologists' bigger theoretical picture of American society. Most of their general theoretical ideas either consisted of or were inspired by the social disorganization theory, which was remarkably similar to Durkheim's social disintegration theory. In *The Gang,* for example, we find the social disorganization theory laid over the rich descriptive material. For the most part, the theory comes at the beginning of the book and is not very well integrated with the rest of it. It can literally be peeled off the descriptive material without hurting it and without even leaving a sense that something is missing.

While a theory with the word "disorganization" in it might seem to imply that they saw disorganization as a basic force in society, this is not so. To them, as to almost all of the classical European sociologists, disorganization and all related phenomena, such as conflict, were extraordinary phenomena. They were in some way failures of the normal mode of society. In fact, the Chicago sociologists normally followed Thomas' definition of social disorganization as "the relative lack of effect of social values." They believed the normal condition was for people to obey social rules, and thus to act in an organized or ordered manner. But some people did not seem to do so, at least in more urban areas. There were obviously some deviants, or "pathological" types. How could this be? The explanation was found in a failure of values, which was itself supposed to be the result of a lack of the close personal contacts which supposedly characterized the less urbanized parts of society.

These social values were implicitly assumed to be shared by all members of society, even when they had a "relative lack of effect" on someone's behavior. Moreover, these values were assumed to be institutionalized throughout the society, so that there were no significant conflicts between one part of society and another. A very important aspect of this was the assumption that values were congruent with, or in agreement with, the laws of the society so that the legal institutions of society agreed or cooperated with the various groups, such as the ethnic groups, of society. (It was this assumption that was first shown to be wrong by sociologists of deviance, beginning in the 1930s. Its rejection and the attempts to deal with the facts of incongruence led eventually to basic theoretical changes, as seen in labeling theory and the social constructionist theories. (See the discussion of this in Douglas, 1971.) Certainly the Chicago sociologists were too close to the terribly conflictful society of Chicago to completely overlook conflict. They gave it far more consideration, though primarily in descriptive material and low-level theories, than classical sociologists like Durkheim did. But even when they explicitly considered conflict in their general ideas, they wound up arguing that it would be resolved by the normal operations of society. Probably the most important example of this is seen in Park's famous theory of ethnic and racial interaction. He realized there were such things as neighborhood invasions and that conflicts grew out of this. But he also believed that accommodation and even assimilation (or homogenization) would naturally follow this conflict. Out of conflict would come cooperation. Cooperation was the natural state of society (see also Madge, 1962:125).

This theory of society as basically homogeneous and nonconflictful had many basic implications for their research methods, though I know of no place where they themselves explicitly considered the questions of deriving methods from these theoretical considerations. (One of the earliest explicit considerations is Becker, 1970:69.) Instead, they seem to have used field research methods because that was the way it was done by some journalists, by most anthropologists, and by Robert Park; because it seemed common-sensically reasonable, and because it seemed to work. It just all seemed to "hold together" and was not subjected to much analysis until it came under increasing attack from control methodologists. In fact, the "Chicago tradition" of field research methods was largely a word-of-mouth and apprentice tradition until the 1950s. Everett Hughes, recognized by almost all the Chicago researchers as *the* great teacher and user of the tradition after the Park era, wrote almost nothing about it until his brief introduction to Junker's (1960) systematization of the whole tradition (but see the earlier work by Palmer, 1928; and Hughes, 1971).

This assumption of homogeneity was the unspoken rationale for the in-depth study of one (generally) small group by one sociologist. It was all the more striking that their methods should take this turn since the community survey movement, which had such great influence in sociology and led to such important works as the Lynd's study of Middletown, preceded the Chicago work, and since some of the early Chicago works, such as *The Gang,* combined a community survey approach with field research. The survey movement attempted to cover whole communities, even big cities like Pittsburgh, while the later Chicago studies concentrated progressively on depth and progressively gave up considerations of representability. Hughes' first major work, the study of French Canadian towns (1971:530-542), did involve a study of a number of towns by a team of researchers. But studying a number of towns was intended to establish only a "baseline" which could be used to determine social change, not to get at diversity and conflict.

It might be contended that the Chicago field researchers really intended to study at least the whole city of Chicago by sending people out into all its parts, at least eventually. (This approach is what Becker, 1970, called a "mosaic" of research.) This was obviously true (Palmer, 1928), but it is also obvious that the goal was eventually forgotten, since most Chicago-type research eventually became the one-man-to-one-group type and little attempt was made to cover a wide area of society systematically. (The team works of Hughes, Becker, and Geer are noteworthy exceptions.) It might also be contended that each researcher simply assumed that other researchers would study groups similar to his own so that eventually we would have a representative view of such groups. However, if that had been their assumption, they were simply wrong. It didn't happen in more than a few areas and even in these, such as formal organizations and medicine, the pictures covered only part of each area. In both formal organizations and medicine, for example, there have been almost no field research studies of such crucial aspects as top management decisions, boards of directors, governmental relations, financing, sales, public relations, and so on. (We shall soon see that the relative lack of investigative methods contributed to leaving these vital areas out of their research, but the crucial point is that the classical field researchers rarely even raised the question of whether these should be included. Their goal was to go in-depth in the study of a union group, a bank-wiring room, a rooming house, assembly workers, etc. They did not worry about the big picture or representative findings.)

The second major methodological implication of the relatively homogeneous, nonconflictful, unproblematic picture of society was that the researcher could rely upon the cooperation of his subjects in doing the research and that they would act naturally while he was studying them. (This view is epitomized by the Palmer quote at the beginning of this chapter.) If society itself is looked at as basically a cooperative and integrated set of activities, then why wouldn't you implicitly assume that the researcher would cooperate with his subjects and become well integrated with them? Certainly he would just "fit in naturally," adopt their point of view, get along with them, be moral from their point of view (which would, of course, be the same as any other point of view in a homogeneous world), and report the findings with no great misgivings about their effects on the group studied—maybe they have some enemies, but that's aberrant and unimportant in a basically cooperative world. This cooperative assumption about research was so strong that most of the Chicago researchers adopted what Fred Davis has so aptly called the "convert model" of field research (1973).

The cooperative assumption was found at all levels of the research, analysis and reporting. While they came to realize from harsh experience that many groups did not care to be researched, and thus came to view entree as one of the problems in the life of any researcher, they often even viewed entree as not all that difficult or, at least, as almost always manageable. For example, Robert Bogdan and Steven J. Taylor (1975) recently argued that almost any group will give the researcher entree if he just keeps after them. And, of course, they assumed that "honesty is always the best policy" in dealing with subjects. After all, in a cooperative world, in which there are no basic conflicts of interest, value, or feeling, it's best to just lay all your cards on the table. The subjects will see what a decent fellow you are and help you all they can. The classical paradigm exudes the small-town Protestant public morality of openness, friendliness, and do-gooderism. Everything is open and above-board, honesty all around. (Kai Erikson's blandishments against "secret" [hence unobtrusive] research [1967] are mild compared to some of the expressions of outrage I've seen the classical researchers express over secret recordings or any similar "dishonest" methods.) Once inside, the researcher is expected to establish trust unproblematically with the members and from these relations of trust will flow the truth about what the members are up to. As John Johnson (1976) has shown in detail, the assumption was that once trust was established you kept it. It didn't wax and wane, or disappear in angry recriminations. During the research and the reporting of it the almost inevitable stance was assumed to be that of the convert—that is, one of "sympathy." If there is any conflict of interest, value, or feeling between the group studied and the rest of the society, then the researcher almost in-evitably takes the side of the subjects, as Becker argued in his famous essay on "Whose Side Are We On?" (1967). If the group is in some way deviant or stigmatized, when the report is written it tends to show the world that the group studied is not "bad" in the way people thought. So, for example, *Talley's Corner* (1967) explains that poor black males are not really shiftless and dishonest, as some outsiders might assume.

There are instances in which the classical researchers explicitly recognized the possible conflicts of interests, values, and feelings between researcher and subject. Probably the most interesting instance is Hughes' contention (in Junker, 1960) that the researcher cannot escape the fact that in some way he is acting like a "spy" by reporting on the group to the outside world. In these instances, however, the researcher generally sees these conflicts as due to the subjects' inadequate understanding of the situation. Hughes, for example, seems to be arguing that the subjects may sometimes *see* the researcher as a spy, not that he is really acting in the way a spy does, which would certainly be to the detriment of those spied upon. Instances in which the researcher accepts a real conflict between his own interests, values, and feelings and those of his subject are there, but they are rare, and generally are found in works done by non-Chicago researchers. (One such instance is Whyte's famous conclusion that the multiple voting he had participated in while working in Cornerville was contrary to his own values [1955]. Also see Thompson [1966] and my discussion on this point in 1972b.)

The third major implication of their big picture of society, and one very closely connected to the first two, was that the research could be done from one perspective within the group and the report written from the one perspective of the host group. It was assumed that, within the group, the researcher would be able to establish a clearly defined research role from which he could observe what was going on in the group. While they found from experience that any given research role tended to align them with one part of a group and to create problems with other parts of the group, presumably those in conflict with their allies, they did not often see this as creating unsolvable problems for the lone researcher. Instead, they tended to assume that as researchers they were defined by the members as outside or above group conflicts, so that the members could be counted on to tell the researcher all kinds of things they would not tell each other or any other member. This, in fact, was frequently used as a reason for not passing as a member (see Lofland, 1971:93-99).

It was further assumed, and even more strongly, that studying things from the perspective of the group would be sufficient. That is, while the social world was thought to be a socially defined reality, that social reality was assumed in some way to be uni-perspectival. Even when the analysis of the group involved implicit recognition of the conflicts in social perspectives between itself and the rest of the social world, there was no attempt to get at the other social perspectives. Only the group's social reality was presented, and somehow it was taken to be the whole reality. Relativism of social realities was assumed theoretically (in accord with symbolic interactionism), but was overlooked in concrete instances. For example, when Becker (1967) argues that the researcher should take the side of the deviant group he is studying, he is obviously assuming that there are conflicting perspectives, such as that of lawmakers and police; but he does not argue that the researcher should get all the perspectives of social reality and somehow put them together into a multi-perspectival picture of society. When this possibility is considered, it is seen as simply not possible and passed over. Again, in *Talley's Corner,* Liebow (1967) says that outsiders often look at the lower-class blacks as unwilling to work, and then he tries to show this is not so. But there is no attempt to actually study the outsiders or to study his subjects from the standpoint of the outsiders. Rather, his subjects' definition of reality is implicitly assumed somehow to be *the* reality, or, at least, the only reality which needs to be studied, analyzed, and presented. Even in those uncommon instances when the classic researchers used a group of researchers to study a number of related groups, they rarely studied the different social perspectives involved. For example, Walter Miller's studies of lower-class gangs involved a number of field researchers studying a number of different gangs to get at their "focal concerns." But when he came to contrast their focal concerns with middle-class boys in the society, he did not study the middle-class boys. Instead, he *assumed* they had certain known focal concerns and proceeded from there.

A few of the works of Becker (1970), and of Becker and Geer (1960, 1969), Hughes and Strauss touch upon the existence of different and even conflicting perspectives within the groups they were studying, and at times they used different people to get at these different perspectives, but those were minor aspects of the work. Where intense conflict was found, the normal tendency was to quickly restrict efforts to studying only one side of the conflict (see, for example, Roy, 1970) or to argue that the researcher could nevertheless "weave" his way through the conflicting groups and see their interrelations (see, for example, Mauksh, 1970).

In addition to these major assumptions following from their picture of society, the classic field researchers made a set of assumptions about their research that came directly from the nineteenth-century metatheory of scientific truth. Most importantly, they assumed that the classic ideas of "absolute objectivity" are more or less true and that sociological research methods such as theirs should generate such truth. They certainly recognized that there are terrible problems of separating the subject (especially his value judgments) from the research object, something essential to the classic ideas of absolute objectivity. But they believed this could be done by the methods they had devised. (Moreover, their considerations of this have mainly come up in recent years when the problems of the classic paradigm have become increasingly apparent.)

In general, the classic field researchers looked at field research as a set of rationalized, or rationalizable, procedures for generating objective truth in the same way other methods of social research, such as questionnaires, did. That is, the field research methods themselves could be largely controlled in the same way other methods were, so that the effects of individuals and situations could be eliminated or accounted for. Field research was different in its methods, but its view of truth and its end result, objective truth, was the same. This view was, of course, most prevalent among the "control" researchers who merely used field research for "pre-testing" or "arriving at hypotheses" that would allow them to then find the objective truth by using controlled methods (see, for example, Lazarsfeld, 1972) and those who saw it as a frequently useful adjunct to more basic methods (see, for example, Trow, 1969). But the traditional conception of objectivity was also pervasive among the most dedicated field researchers. Some of them went so far as to construct "accounting schemes," complete with numerical estimates, for evaluating possible "contaminants" in the inferences from field research data (see especially, Becker and Geer, 1960). And others went even further in constructing statistical "quality control" measures for interpreting field re-search data (see especially, Naroll, 1962; and McCall, 1969). In the great majority of instances in which they did argue that participant-observation provides "more information" than interviewing techniques, they were con-cerned primarily with the difficulty of getting at taken-for-granted meanings, touched lightly upon possible "resistances" by subjects to telling all they knew, and almost never dealt with the possibility that crucial experience might be unexpressible. (See the important essay by Becker and Geer [1969]. In their response to Trow's criticism of this essay, they give away most of what they had earlier claimed for participant-observation.)

Though the work of some of them (especially of Hughes, Becker, and Geer) at times included important aspects of the investigative perspective we shall be developing, the overwhelming tendency was to use field research as just another method that produces the objective truth of classic, positivistic science. There was something to the argument of some critics (such as Trow, 1969) that most of the time field researchers, like other kinds of methodolo-gists, just did their research that way because that was how they learned to do it—and even because there was a lot of "participant-observation romanticism."

From this theory of objective truth and this rationalized model of field research came the specific rationalized procedures of many of the Chicago researchers. The researcher was told just how to go about making contact with the "gatekeepers" of the group, how to build his case to establish entree, the kind of role to adopt once he had gained entree, how to choose "the right role" in his relations with subjects, how to establish trust, how to use this trust to get the information he needed, how to collect the information, how to categorize it, how to keep notes, how to use these in doing his analysis, how to establish and evaluate theory from his data, how to deal with the problems of value commitments, and so on. Field research came increasingly to be seen as a set of highly rationalized and even systematized techniques. For example, once you gained trust by the correct procedures (being honest, showing your good intentions, etc.), it was assumed that the problem of trust was solved and you could now go on to solving the other problems on the list. Once you used the technique correctly, the problem was solved—generally, if not always, since everyone knew that there were always some failures (see Johnson's critique of this assumption, 1976).

Having noted these rationalistic assumptions and techniques of the classic Chicago sociologists, I would hasten once again to point out two things. First, it was definitely the case that these sociologists did their research differently from the way they reported it. (The same, of course, is even more true of the quantitative researchers, as anyone knows who has ever seen a big question-naire study in progress.) Whether they did this for cynical rhetorical reasons, out of a simple failure to see the contrast, or a combination of these (which I would suspect is more the case), the fact remains that there was always a great, though highly variable, gap between the reportedly rationalistic methods and the actual methods. This is most striking in the case of some of the most important work done by this group of sociologists, including, for example, the very important work of Howard Becker on marihuana use among jazz musicians and the theory of rule use that partly came out of this (1963). The method reported as the basis of this study was even more rationalized than any of his later field research. He reported primarily on the use of open-ended interviews analyzed by analytic inductive methods (that is, searching for the universal properties of the cases interviewed) and only mentioned in passing that he had been a member of the jazz world for years as a piano player. Needless to say, it now seems clear that it was these years of highly unrationalized membership, combined with Becker's creative abilities as an observer and analyst, that constituted the real basis of his important work on the nature and uses of rules in our society. The pressures from fellow sociologists to do "hard-data research" seem to have been so great in those days that the most creative sociologists literally had to use an *Aesopian research language* to launder their data. They dared not reveal that they really knew these things through partaking of the forbidden fruit of membership ("going native" was an original sin in the sacred scripts of all those inspired by positivistic ideas of absolute objectivity), so they would use a show of respectable methods to launder their knowledge gained from membership, and, thus, *bootleg truth into sociology;* yet they were able to reveal some of the truth of their methods to those who understood the evil secrets by writing in Aesopian terms.

Interestingly enough, the Chicago sociologists commonly did the exact opposite of what the "founder" of participant-observer methods in anthro-pology did. As Murray Wax (1972) has shown, Malinowski presented a totally false picture of himself as a close and sympathetic participant in the exotic life of the Trobriand Islanders. He was actually more of an aloof, even "racist," observer of these "inferior" types. The Chicago sociologists com-monly presented a false picture of themselves as aloof, scientific observers of their exotic "subjects." The very best of them might be better described as natives in disguise as scientists. The lasting value of their work comes from their cultural (or native) wisdom, not their scientific forms. It was this cultural wisdom that led to a growing concern with problems of conflict and multi-perspectivism in the works of Becker, Geer, Hughes, and others in the 1960s and provided a vital transition to the investigative paradigm.

The second thing to be noted is that the Chicago tradition has not been the most rationalistic or positivistic tradition of field research. Indeed, I have seen many instances where the Chicago sociologists and anthropologists, such as Murray and Rosalie Wax (1971) and Becker (1970) have steadfastly opposed the extremes of rationalism and positivism found among most of the ethnomethodologists. It is the ethnomethodologists, paradoxically, who have carried this rationalism and commitment to the positivistic ideas of absolute objectivity to its extreme. This seems to be paradoxical because one of the basic ideas of the phenomenological tradition from which ethnomethodology sprang was the denial of subject-object dualism (see Douglas and Johnson, 1977). One would expect from this that the ethnomethodologists would be among the first to disown a rationalistic and positivistic approach to questions of truth in studies of the social world. Indeed, one of the subordinate verbal traditions of ethnomethodology, never actually attempted until Jules-Rosette's (1976) recent work on an African religious sect, was the desirability of becoming a member in order to see things from the members' perspective. But this data did not take into consideration another and more powerful idea of ethnomethodology. The ethnomethodologists have always remained committed, in varying ways, to the search for Husserl's transcendental-ego, more commonly called the "invariant properties of cognition," or symbolic thought. In short, they have been searching for the universal or invariant properties of mind and thence in all situations at all times for all persons. It is, of course, precisely such properties of knowledge which traditional science was seeking in the name of absolute objectivity. But the ethnomethodologists went one crucial step further and argued that these invariant properties operate to "constitute" all of the observed features of the social world and, indeed, of the entire objective world "out there." Having argued this is true of all minds and all realities, they rightly saw that this included their own realities and that of all sociologists. They thus arrived at the fateful conclusion that all scientific activity, like all common-sense activity, is simply a search for the constitutive properties of mind (or intersubjectivity) itself. Scientific research, including sociological research, is thus seen to be simply a way of "displaying" the constitutive features of mind. What we find when we do research *of any kind by any methods* is not the object but the feature or properties of the subjects. Therefore, it does not matter what we study or how we study it as long as we do so in such a way as to display, or capture for presentational purposes, the cognitive presentations of the subjects. By displaying these captured or recorded presentations, and illustrating how the invariant cognitive properties of mind are constituted in concrete presentations, we have *documented* those invariant properties we were seeking and have, thus, accomplished all that any science can do.

There are certainly complexities, contradictions, and divergent strains within the works of ethnomethodologists. But their general position now seems clearly to be that just presented (for a fuller discussion of these points, see Douglas and Johnson, 1977). It has had two direct implications for their field research methods, which is what concerns us here. First, the exclusive concern with the invariant, constitutive features of mind led them to concentrate their efforts on the study of "accounts." Indeed, Garfinkel (1967) defined ethnomethodology as the "study of accounts." Second, the concern with displaying the accounts so that their properties could be "documented" led them to concentrate on the use of mechanical recording devices, both the audio recorder and later (in the works of Cicourel and his students) the video recorder. The hallmark of ethnomethodological research and analysis became the use of mechanical recordings to analyze accounts, especially linguistic accounts, since these were the most recordable of accounts. (Body language is also an account, but it has only rarely been "attended to" because it is harder to record, display, and analyze for "documentary" purposes.)

This focus of ethnomethodology on recording and analyzing accounts has made this research the most obtrusive form of field research ever attempted. As we saw in the last chapter, there is every reason to believe that obtrusive recording devices have fundamental effects in determining what actors think and feel about the researcher (mainly, it makes them terribly suspicious and on guard) and what they do in his presence. It has also made them eliminate from consideration most of what sociologists are concerned with in the world. In fact, it makes sociology into merely a branch of post-Chomsky linguistics. And it makes sociology and linguistics into the study of only those forms of behavior which are most immediately available to public observation, since people who know they are being recorded behave in terms of public fronts. (A few ethnomethodological studies are done with secret recordings.) Its epistemology and research methods thus turn ethnomethodology into a study of front work (for a fuller discussion of these issues, see Douglas and Johnson, [1977]).

This does not bother the committed ethnomethodologist because, as we saw, he believes the features of mind are displayed in any accounts, public or private and, most importantly, because he believes we can only study accounts, or the subjective features that "constitute" our social world. Whereas the positivists believed they had eliminated the subject from sociology, or absolutely objectified sociological knowledge, the ethnomethodologists have gone to the other extreme of eliminating the object. In its purest form, ethnomethodology sees (subjective) accounts as the entire social world and necessarily sees all accounts as equally valid. When there are only accounts to be studied there can be no question, no consideration, of whether one account is more true about the world than another. The world *is* the accounts. Rarely have the ethnomethodologists themselves carried their analysis to its systematic, logical conclusion. But in the stances in which they have, such as in Melvin Polner's application of Cicourel's ideas to the accounts given in traffic courts, they wind up accepting a solipcistic position. All accounts are equally true. Indeed, all analyses of accounts are presumably equally acceptable. The question of truth itself disappears. And, in line with this, almost all "research" done by ethnomethodologists is done without the presentation of their methods. Their methods remain totally "unexplicated," "awesomely indexical." (Mehan and Wood [1976] present the ultimate expression of this view which includes such startling conclusions as "science is superstition.")

Some of the time, ethnomethodologists stop short of following their analyses of accounts to its extreme position by implicitly assuming, rather than explicitly arguing, that they are able to evaluate some accounts as more truthful than others. They do this in two ways. First, they look at documented display procedures as somehow more acceptable. For example, in his work on methods (1964) and in his analysis of official accounts of delinquency (1968), Cicourel argues that questionnaire methods are inadequate because they do not explicate the ways in which language itself constitutes a feature of their findings and that field researchers should document their methods by providing accounts of the research situation, by displaying the data in recordings, by demonstrating members' agreement over accounts and their acceptance of the researcher as competent in his interaction with them (i.e., the second form of the member test of validity).

These research methods actually contradict the theoretical arguments of the ethnomethodologists who make them. They also implicitly assume a far more rationalistic and cooperative paradigm of the social world and the social researcher (also contrary to their theoretical arguments) than did classic field researchers. And their insistence on using highly obtrusive methods of recording any setting almost guarantees that they will generally be restricted to studying carefully constructed public situations (front work) and that their studies of these will be as riddled with uncertainty effects as questionnaire studies. Their methods almost necessitate their focus on the study of linguistic accounts and thus the absorption of sociology into linguistics. Since there seems to be no good reason to restrict sociology to the study of accounts (Douglas and Johnson, 1977), and since our goal is to study society in its natural state, rather than transforming it for display, we can only conclude that the so-called field research methods of ethnomethodology have failed to benefit from the vital lessons of the rich Chicago tradition. We want to go beyond the classic tradition, not betray its strengths or compound its weaknesses.

Chapter 4

THE CONFLICT PARADIGM OF SOCIETY AND

INVESTIGATIVE FIELD RESEARCH

"It took me a long time to discover that the key thing in acting is honesty. Once you know how to fake that, you've got it made." John Leonard, 1970.

As we have noted, most field research done by businessmen, government officials and journalists has been inspired by roughly the same cooperative and rationalistic (classical) paradigm that inspired the Chicago sociologists. But for many centuries there has been a clearly defined alternative paradigm for people of practical affairs. This is the investigative paradigm.

The investigative paradigm is based on the assumption that profound conflicts of interest, values, feelings and actions pervade social life. It is taken for granted that many of the people one deals with, perhaps all people to some extent, have good reason to hide from others what they are doing and even to lie to them. Instead of trusting people and expecting trust in return, one suspects others and expects others to suspect him. Conflict is the reality of life; suspicion is the guiding principle. As those involved in using this paradigm love to put it, "Life is a jungle and all the animals in it are predators." It's a war of all against all and no one gives anyone anything for nothing, especially truth. The "do-gooders" who trust others and expect them to tell the truth are looked at as kooks, "do-do birds" destined for extinction. Sure, people tell the truth most of the time in their everyday lives, at least as they see it. How often do people bother to lie about the weather or where the salt is? But the outsider trying to find out what the truth is about the things that count most to people, such as money and sex, must look upon all their accounts of those things as suspicious until proven otherwise.

Spies, counterspies, police, detectives, prosecutors, judges, psychiatrists, tax collectors, probation officers, child protective service workers, FCC staff workers, FDA staff, NLRB staff, investigative journalists, and all others involved in the vast array of investigative occupations in modern society are the most obvious practitioners of the investigative paradigm. They share the paradigm in its most extreme and pure form. But business people of all kinds, especially business people who must deal with strangers, also share it to varying degrees. Indeed, wherever there exist important conflicts which members of society recognize, individuals use some form of the investigative paradigm in ferreting out the truth about others' intentions, thoughts, feelings and actions. Any suspicious lover can suddenly turn into a dedicated investigator, showing how available the basic ideas of the investigative paradigm are to all members of society. We shall draw upon all of these sources in developing the investigative paradigm of society and then of social research.

But it is the journalists who have developed this paradigm most explicitly and completely since the work of Lincoln Steffens, so we shall draw upon their work more than others. As always, however, their work is put into the context of our own investigative social research. We are not concerned with providing a scholarly history of their methods but, rather, with presenting what seem to be the most effective means of getting at the truth about a conflict-ridden, secretive society.

Throughout most of this chapter we shall be emphasizing the conflictful, secretive, distrustful, uncertain nature of society and the methods we have devised to deal with these problems.[1] It is all too easy for anyone to lose perspective in such a discussion and conclude that we see all of society as being like this and therefore reject all cooperative methods in studying society. This would be completely wrong, as will be clear in our later discussions of the uses of key informants, independent observations and team cooperation. But to avoid any such misunderstandings we should emphasize from the beginning that we see society as being mixed and are proposing a mixed strategy of researching it. As argued in detail in earlier works (especially Douglas, 1971), our society is a mixture of the highly patterned and the highly unpatterned, the cooperative and the conflictful, the open and obvious and the secret and obscure. Because of this, the methods of investigative social research rely upon a crucial combination of cooperative and investigative methods. While the emphasis is put on the differences between the cooperative and the investigative methods, thus making them look extremely different, in actual practice as investigative researchers we necessarily rely upon some degree of trust and cooperation at some stage of our work.

The crucial point is that the investigative paradigm is dominant. Then the important questions which will concern us are those of how we combine the cooperative with the investigative methods, in what sequence and with what priorities.

In order to see how and why we propose the methods we do, we must look more closely at the concrete problems we face in getting at what is going on in society. As we saw in the last chapter, in its most extreme form, as found in questionnaires, the cooperative paradigm of society assumed it is possible to ask the members what is going on and they will tell. Yet everyone knows when he thinks about it that only the naive, the innocent, the dupe takes this position all the time in everyday life. Rather, all competent adults are assumed to know that there are at least four major problems lying in the way of getting at social reality by asking people what is going on and that these problems must be dealt with if one is to avoid being taken in, duped, deceived, used, put on, fooled, suckered, made the patsy, left holding the bag, fronted out and so on. These four problems are

(1) Misinformation;
(2) Evasions;
(3) Lies; and
(4) Fronts.

We shall examine these in some detail and then turn our attention in Chapter 5 to three major problems which are less apparent to most people, but often of more importance to a social researcher seeking to understand what is going on and why. These are the problems of

(5) Taken-for-granted meanings;
(6) Problematic meanings; and
(7) Self-deceptions.

Misinformation

Misinformation, or unintended falsehoods, are commonly the result of the complexities and uncertainties of things to the people being studied. It is common for researchers to assume that the members know all kinds of things which in fact they don't really know. It is common for members themselves to assume they know all kinds of things which they don't really know. Anyone who has ever gone from being a work-a-day member of an organization, such as a university, to being deeply involved in its operations knows the difference between work-a-day knowledge and expert practical knowledge, and knows how blissfully ignorant he was before. For example, it is common for faculty members of universities to attribute all kinds of powers to the boards of regents or directors, and to make public pronouncements about those powers, which in fact the directors do not have.[2] Anyone interviewing faculty members about such things would get confident assertions about the facts and be misled, albeit unintentionally.

In any field research these are insiders who are convinced they know the facts and are willing to tell the researcher the "truth." A researcher has to be on guard constantly against these unintended falsehoods. Such misinformation is especially difficult to detect when it is shared by the members and when it concerns something that is obviously vital to them. These organizational myths are found in all groups and are extremely difficult to penetrate because they are shared so deeply and confidently presented as facts.

For example, in our study of massage parlors we were long misled by the massage parlor people about the way the vice laws work. They were almost universally convinced that the laws against police entrapment, combined with the word games they used to make the customer do the propositioning (described later), would protect them from the vice squad undercover agents. It was only when we had observed some actual cases and were able to observe the work of a lawyer who specialized in these cases that we learned they were wrong about this. These people had staked their freedom and social reputations on a word-of-mouth legal interpretation. It simply seemed implausible to us that they would all be wrong about something so important to them, but they were.

In fact, it is such strongly held organizational myths about the laws that commonly form the basis for official statistics and the "scientific data" based on them. In our study of drug crisis intervention, we found that emergency room medical staff commonly asserted some definite facts about what the laws were, and about how they dealt with the question of calling the police on overdose cases. These "facts" almost always proved to be organizational myths and in some cases outright lies. Fortunately, we were able early in the research to detect some hesitancies, contradictions, and confident assertions which we had observed to be based on hearsay. The following brief example reveals a doctor first asserting a policy, then apparently suddenly realizing he doesn't know what he thought he did, then a nurse confidently feeding him an organizational myth she herself had just picked up from another nurse:

> Since I had arrived after the patient had been treated and transferred, I asked a nurse if the police had been called. She said, 'No, we only do that with heroin. But they usually show up somehow, and I just don't know how they get here.' From across the room another nurse said, 'The fire department calls the police; they get the same calls.' A short while later I was asking the doctor the same question, 'Do you call the

police on overdoses?' With some hesitation, he said, 'Yes, well . . . (to a nurse) what do you do with that?' The nurse was the same one who had not known how the police arrive just a few minutes earlier. She said that they call only with heroin ODs [overdoses]. The doctor then asked, 'Well, how come the police always are here?' The nurse then told him what she had just 'learned,' that the police are called by the fire department and show up for all their calls [Douglas, 1973].

We found the same thing to be true of police, only more so. The police are responsible for knowing the laws, or so the public thinks. This is probably the major reason they are so assertive about their knowledge of the laws. When we asked them questions about the legal aspects of reporting drug overdoses they always had definite answers. We eventually determined that they merely asserted as legal whatever their common practices were. We first came to suspect this when we found that different police would give us very assertive answers that were in conflict with the answers of others. We've found in other studies as well that the police are frequently quite assertive about laws they know little or nothing about.

Fortunately for the researcher, organizational myths are rarely shared universally within a group. There are generally some people who have had to deal with the problem directly and know the facts about it, or else there are some members who are simply confused and assert varying things, or some people who simply disagree with each other. When members are found who really know the facts, they can, if willing, explain specifically how the others are wrong and how to find the truth. For example, in studying coroners' classifications of death (reported in Douglas, 1971a) I found that almost all of the coroners were ignorant of the specific state laws defining suicide and what their legal duties were in such matters, but they thought they knew what those laws were. I eventually found a funeral director serving as county coroner who knew in some detail just what the laws were, so much so that he was able to tell me how he was purposely violating one of the laws. He had already been through the legal hassle over this, learned the laws, and knew there were no legal consequences for the violation he was revealing.

Evasions

All individuals and groups of individuals also practice evasions and partial deceptions which they know to be untrue in a literal sense, but which are not out-and-out lies. Evasions are intentional acts of hiding, of not saying or revealing, rather than of unintended misinformation. They involve *not* telling, or leading down the primrose path, or putting on the send, or simply silence in the face of an obvious mistake by the researcher or, often, the statement of a literal truth as if it were the whole truth when it is known by the teller to be only a partial or situated truth. Evasions are much more common than lies and much harder to detect and pin down, so they commonly pose more of a problem for researchers.

Evasions are extremely common in our everyday lives from early childhood on. In fact, they are so common among children, who often are too afraid to tell lies because of their moral absolutism, that there are little jokes about them. The most common form is the comeback to the question, "Why didn't you tell me?"—"But you didn't *ask* me!" The humor, and the angry frustration, comes from the fact that the person asking "Why didn't you tell me?" knew he could assume the respondent was aware that he did want to be told. The evader commonly relies upon the use of literalness as his escape hatch. "Sure, you asked me if he did it; and I told you he didn't, which is the exact truth. But you didn't ask me if *I* did it!" This may make evasions sound like kid stuff, but it is exactly such kid stuff from which Great Events are made. Such evasions are commonly the grounds for loopholes in tax laws, and even more for legal defenses when one is charged with a violation. The Watergate testimonies show widespread use of the evasive defense, "But that isn't exactly what you asked me." One of the crucial questions concerning the perjury trial of Lt. Gov. Edward Reinecke of California was whether he had talked to then-Attorney General Mitchell about something before a certain date. He had answered no to such a general question and, when evidence was presented that he had so talked with Mitchell, he contended that the literal meaning of the question had not covered telephone conversations, which is what the evidence showed he had done.

While literalness is one of the first complex-forms of evasiveness learned or created and is quite common, the four most pervasive forms seem to be:

(1) Silence;
(2) Avoiding the situation;
(3) Turning aside; and
(4) Loopholing.

Silence in nonresponse to what we believe to be false or misinformed is so omnipresent in everyday lives that we take it for granted. There is no need to exemplify it from research experience. The best way anyone can be convinced of its importance is to watch himself doing it throughout part of a day. (This might be a bit traumatic if the person is used to thinking of himself as a straightforward and honest person.) Silence is demanded by the rules of tactfulness, manners, kindness, decency, and mercy, as well as by the ideas of strategy, self-presentation, manipulation, cunning, and deceit.

Even more important, partial silence is demanded by basic ideas of relevance and sufficiency (or practicalities) of meaning in our everyday lives.

That is, we rarely tell the whole truth about things as we think of it for the simple reason that it would take too long or go beyond what we think the others are interested in at the time. The demands of practicality put a pretty tight focus on what meanings are needed or relevant for the purposes at hand in our everyday lives; the rest, the so-called "fringe" of consciousness, is supposed to be left unsaid and anyone who is not silent about it is apt to be seen as having foot-in-mouth disease, being verbose, boring, smart-alecky, or nuts. (See Douglas, 1971, 1970a, 1970d.)

The researcher faces at least two big problems in dealing with these forms of silence that other people in the setting commonly don't. First, he usually doesn't yet know the people and the histories of their interaction well enough to know the meanings of silence. The members are tremendously keyed into the complex meanings of silence in a particular social context. Indeed, not saying anything often speaks louder than words for them: "I *knew* as soon as you didn't say anything that . . .," "I could *tell* from your silence . . .," "The silence was deafening . . .," "Why the hell didn't you speak up?" "No one said anything, but it was obvious what everyone was thinking."

Second, the researcher is commonly interested in precisely those things which are ruled out as irrelevant (fringe) by the everyday demands of practicality; these are often meanings that are so basic that the members take them for granted. (We shall discuss this in the next chapter.)

The researcher usually tries to overcome these silences in at least three ways. First, he uses his general cultural understanding to spot general forms of silence that might be meaningful in the particular context and then tries to draw them out if they seem important and if he can do so without appearing gauche. Second, he comes to recognize the meanings of silence through prolonged participation, which provides him with much of the necessary social context, and can probe them when appropriate. Third, he tries to develop sociable relations with the members, both to establish trust and simply to get them to talk about the general context, the fringes, of their everyday, practical affairs. People frequently talk about the unspoken things in their nonpractical moments, the times when they "let their hair down" over beer after work, when they sit ruminating around the fire after dinner, putting it all together, and philosophizing. It's at those times that the sociologist can see the "practical actor" considering, talking about, and agonizing over what he himself sees as the irrationalities, contradictions, immoralities, unfortunate necessities, etc., of his practical affairs. If the researcher only studies him on the job, he gets a truncated picture of the common-sense, practical social actor constructing rational appearances for his fellow workers and his bothersome social researcher. On the job all of these things linger at the fringe of his consciousness—"pricks of conscience," etc. In the quiet hours they are revealed to be more important, perhaps even leading him to want to change the whole society, to escape, or to commit murder or suicide. The "practical actor" is also commonly a whole human being, even in our bureaucratized, Kafkaesque world. The whole person should be found and related to the practical setting. If there is no whole person, no human being suffering and aspiring, rejoicing and fulfilling, this is a fundamental discovery in itself.

Avoiding the situation is a more subtle way of remaining silent and even of preventing the arousal of internal feelings and thoughts that might lead to anything being said or not said. The member generally has to know the situation and the people involved well, or else the situation has to be patterned throughout society for the member to be able to predict what situations will arouse what feelings and thoughts and, thus, to be able to take actions to avoid those situations that will lead to feelings and thoughts he does not want.

They come up all the time in our personal relations. For example, all intimate relationships involve painful feelings and disruptive thoughts that can lead to arguments or hurt feelings. The participants come to anticipate certain places, words, ideas, and intimations that will arouse such feelings and lead to arguments, fights, separations, or similar negative situations. So the participants take actions to avoid such things happening. They make sure that certain people are not invited to dinner, certain mail will not be seen, etc.

In field research certain people will be careful never to be interviewed (never in), never to let the researcher see certain things, and so on, that might lead to embarrassing questions or the need to take more deceitful actions. Sometimes it's a simple matter of keeping him busy looking at things that don't matter so that he won't have time to look into the serious ones. This can be even harder to handle than silence, since it involves so much understanding of the situation that the person does not even have to be silent or more overtly evasive; the situation simply doesn't arise. In-depth understanding and making sure that he (the researcher) sees as much of everything as he can are the best research defenses against such wily strategies.

Similar to avoiding the situation, turning aside is a complement to silence. It consists of the many ways in which we avoid talking about things by turning aside questions or situations in which questions might arise. They range all the way from simple pretenses of not hearing the question, to leading people down the primrose path so they won't ask about the important things, to outright lying about anything of interest being there. Most of them are simply devices like "Umm-m . . .," "Oh, nothing . . .," "Hardly matters. . . ." The researcher deals with them in the same ways he deals with silence. But they're sometimes easier to note because they are more explicitly evasive.

Loopholing is a more complex form of evasiveness than the other three, and verges into and overlaps with lying. It involves intentional playing upon the problems in uncertainties of meanings and complexities of situations, generally to avoid commitments and responsibilities for acts—"Sure, I said I'd be there, but I didn't say I'd *wait* for you." It is used in such a way as to avoid these commitments and responsibilities without appearing to be doing so on purpose or, in the case of laws, without being seen in public to be doing so. One of the most common forms is found in business dealings. The British have a lovely name for a specific form of real estate loopholing which covers most of these business forms and which I suggest as the generic term for the practice, since we have no other generic term: Gazumphing. Gazumphing involves the purposeful presentation or conclusion of a deal in such a way that the deal looks final and definite to the victim but which the perpetrator can legally get out of it if he changes his mind because of better opportunities. The crucial thing is knowing better than the victim how the laws operate, in order to be able to use legalistic terminology that provides the loopholes for the routinized judicial decision.

This is generally easy to do with contract law, because most business people know the routinized contract decisions in their areas far better than any consumers, who are merely part-time participants in that area. One of the most widespread is the hiring gazumph. It is found in the academic world in the same general form as elsewhere and is an important part of the widespread academic gazumphing. The potential employer commonly sends a letter, or, far wiser, says on the telephone to the prospective employee something like, "Would you be willing to take a job here at . . . ?" The trick, of course, is that they are trying to get him to say yes, which ties him up, while they remain free to try to hire the people higher on their list.[3]

Most publishing contracts signed by academics have a standard, obscure phrase which says the author must deliver a manuscript "acceptable to the publisher." Almost no academics realize what all publishers realize: That little phrase is the crucial legal part of the contract. As any publisher will tell someone he trusts (mainly some one who is part of his schemes), that phrase allows him legally to refuse to publish the delivered manuscript unless he likes it, whatever that might mean at the time. However, publishers realize it isn't all that open-ended. Fortunately for academics, publishers are usually anxious to avoid bad public relations and judicial and jury decisions, and therefore take into consideration far more than the literal legalistic statements. Still, many academics have been shocked to learn that the manuscript they spent years working on can be turned down with impunity when it is finally delivered. One learns such things only from the inside—or the hard way. This is just as true for researchers being evaded as for people in everyday life.

To avoid the impression that evasiveness is somehow what evil-doers do, and not good guys, and that it is always an individual creation, let's consider a few instances of well-institutionalized evasiveness from universities and police work. One of the universities in which I taught for years had a basic rule that student grades cannot be changed for any reason other than "clerical error." That's the rule and it's known to all faculty members and administrators. It's absolute. And faculty members use it all the time to explain to students why they *absolutely* cannot change their grades—"It would be against the rule unless it were a clerical error, which this obviously is not." The faculty member is telling the literal truth, the absolute truth—but not the whole truth—and that's where the evasiveness comes in.

In fact, all faculty members quickly learn, often by being told in Aesopian language by administrators, that they can change any grade they want to, regardless of the absolute rule. All they have to do is lie about it: "Due to clerical error, I would like to change the grade of X." I use the nasty word "lie." Actually I doubt that many faculty members ever look at it that way and I'm sure they never publicly own up to that foul deed. Rather, they just do it and on the rare occasions when they have to provide a public rationale for it they do complex and convoluted interpretations showing that whatever change they want to make is in fact a clerical error. But when they don't want to do it, the rule is absolutely Absolute, as the student is sadly informed.

I myself have been involved in some beautiful proceedings in which faculty members would go to great lengths to avoid saying anything about this, even though the whole proceedings were based on the assumption that the faculty could change a grade if they wanted to do so, regardless of the source of error.

We all know "the facts of life," but one of the crucial facts of our whole social life is that one cannot talk about all the facts of life in public. (In fact, one can be arrested and imprisoned for obscenity for talking about the most crucial, elementary facts of life in public settings. If any reader doubts this, I suggest he try it, maybe on a television interview sometime. This could be called the Lenny Bruce Principle.) So, in the proceedings about grades, we would spin verbal webs of obfuscation and hem and haw and circle around, and say nothing. After all, the members *knew,* so why say anything? Anyone who didn't know, shouldn't know. Forget it.

The police have a similar rule that does many of the same things for them. This is the rule of the "universal applicability of the law." The rule, which is often a law making the police responsible for obeying it, states that "Everyone is subject to the law. There can be no exceptions. All laws must be enforced at all times." (Common-sense variants consist of things like, "Suppose everyone did that, just think what. . . .") When the police give someone a ticket or arrest him, and he objects that there were extenuating circumstances (such as "I never heard of such a law") the police commonly retort, "Well, I'm sorry, fellow, but that's the law and it applies to everyone—you included." Sometimes they put it more briefly: "That's the *law,* buddy!" Yet, everyone who knows any of the facts of life knows that police have wide discretionary powers; that they can and do let off high percentages of violators they detect, probably a great majority, with no mention of it or only a warning; that there are seldom adverse consequences for them in doing this; and that, indeed, their jobs would be impossible if they tried to apprehend and arrest every violator they detected.

Anyone who has followed the police around or ridden with them has seen the extreme instances in which the decision to enforce seems so arbitrary that it can only be a matter of individual emotion. For example, I followed the police around a great deal in our study of the nude beach to see how they would deal with a new city ordinance restricting nudity to one part of the beach. (See Douglas, 1977.) For several weeks they just warned people. Then one day they were putting two little girls into their van for possession of a matchbox of marijuana when a young man, nude, stopped to watch. As far as I could ever determine, he really didn't know there was a new law and certainly insisted so at the time. But one of the police immediately gave him a ticket for it, the first one issued under the new ordinance. When he objected, and when I asked the officer if there had been any complaint about his nudity or anything, he said simply, "No, but that's the law and we're going to enforce it." After giving him the ticket, the police immediately drove over to a couple lying nude about fifty yards away. They warned them to go to the nude area or they might have to give them a ticket. The couple continued to lie there, but the police drove off. The couple, whom I knew well, couldn't give any more rational account for it than I could and left shaking their heads and denouncing the arbitrariness of the "pigs." Such are the facts of life about absolute rules.

In a closely related vein, we found in our studies of the mass media (Douglas, 1977a) that it is common for their members, especially their administrators, to assert to outsiders, such as researchers seeking entree, that "We don't make the news, we simply report it." This motto asserts that how things become news is unproblematically defined and therefore not researchable, not something that anyone would be interested in studying. In some public situations they even seem to believe this motto, yet they also know from experience that it hides the vast complexity of their work, which is why it's such a useful evasion in dealing with researchers.

In all of the above cases people are telling the truth, but not the whole truth. Rather than being the exception, I suspect such evasiveness is the common situation in field research: People rarely tell the whole truth as they see it about the most important things, but they are generally being evasive or misleading rather than lying. A field researcher must understand this and the reasons for it: Primarily a fear of exposure, of being caught in a lie, and an unwillingness to appear less than absolutely "moral" to an academic stranger. He must understand as well that people are evasive for different reasons. Sometimes they distrust the researcher, or assume that he is out to get them, and for this reason try to send the researcher in the wrong direction. But sometimes they want to help by revealing the truth in veiled terms so that they will not be guilty of betraying their colleagues or friends, or so that they cannot be specifically blamed for revealing things, or so that the researcher will not look at them as immoral creeps. This latter situation is important because it is found even in those who trust a researcher a great deal. If they didn't trust him, they wouldn't use half-truths or Aesopian language to help him. Probably the most common thing is the desire not to appear immoral or creepy to the researcher: They'd like to tell the truth, but then just think what he, the priestly academic (the professor), would think of them, the "people of practical affairs" (i.e., "dirty" and "vulgar")'

This is where the attitude of suspicion is so vital to the researcher, even in dealing with his friends. There are two general rules of thumb used by all investigators who understand this need of the attitude of suspicion:

(1) Where there's smoke, there's fire; and
(2) There's always far more immoral or shady stuff going on than meets the eye.

Assuming these rules of thumb, the researcher always probes and when he strikes evasiveness, even a telltale pause or shifty-eyed averting of attention, he expects more, so he cautiously digs for it. We shall discuss the elaborate means of guessing and asserting the truth and drawing out subjects in the next chapter, but here it is enough to note how we seize and probe evasiveness (always, of course, with the caution and indirectness demanded by the goal of not affronting or arousing fear of exposure in the subject).[4]

At a dinner party one evening I happened to be talking with some people about the widespread use of call girls in business, especially to get sales by making potential customers happy. I noticed that one of the businessmen present, a shirt manufacturer, agreed with the idea in general, but seemed intent on turning the conversation in other directions and agreed only evasively, "Well, yeah, I guess a lot do. . . ." His evasiveness made me suspect he was into it, or at least knew about such things directly. To draw him out, I took any opportunity available through the evening to say how necessary these things were in competitive business and how people who take moralistic views misunderstand the situation—they'd do the same in that situation, etc.

He soon told me explicitly how they kept a list of girls they could call on for special customers, how it was looked upon, and so on. This sort of thing happens all the time in research settings, as well as in everyday life situations (the reader might recall how often his or her husband, wife, boyfriend or girlfriend professes knowing he or she is up to something because of evading the question or averting the eyes). It's so common that people normally do not notice doing it. It's useful to the researcher to become more conscious of this and seize the opportunities it provides. Anyone who is evasive, rather than blatantly lying or just shutting up, is in conflict, either internally or in the situation, and can probably be drawn out without too much trouble.

Lies

The inevitable lies are another evasion, those untruths intended to mislead the researcher, to give him a false picture of the world. In some settings lies are so common that the members themselves *expect* to be lied to by other members, and the members support each other's lies, since lying is sometimes essential to achieving the shared goal of concealment. For example, in any casual sex scene, such as a nude beach or pick-up bar with lots of casual sex and widespread danger of exposure, the members themselves assume and support widespread lying about last names (in the rare instances where any last name is given), occupations (or anything bearing on identity or prestige), addresses, etc.

In one instance, after a year of day-to-day interaction with one of the pick-up artists on the beach, we learned from another source that he had even lied about his *first* name. The members often joke about the widespread lies concerning anything that would allow people to discover their nonbeach identities. Contrary to what Garfinkel (1967) and others have contended, perfectly enjoyable and satisfying social relations can take place without any general sense of trust about such cognitive matters. The people there are primarily doing a body thing, not a thinking and talking thing. One's body and the physical setting are the truths that count most, so who cares if he lies about his name, or about everything else? (The one person I saw in agony over being lied to was the girlfriend of the pick-up artist. But her agony was either short-lived or contained, for she then went to great trouble to join him in deceiving his wife and her family in order to continue the relationship.)

As usual, there may be some sanguine readers who scoff at examples from nude beaches and pick-up bars, insisting that such deviant settings are highly unrepresentative of the rest of society. This might seem to be a peculiar view in a society in which most of the officials closest to a U.S. president, who was elected by a historic majority partly on the basis of one of the most intense "law and order" campaigns in our history, were convicted and sentenced for felonious lying and other crimes; yet it is certainly a widespread view and one that people defend aggressively. They often assert that all these lies were told only by a "small group of evil conspirators," yet this contention is as ridiculous as all the rhetoric that the President had used in his early days about the "evil group of communist conspirators." We shall see further reason below to believe that these men were just doing what members of our society generally do in their situation. (I have also argued this before in Douglas, 1974c.) But even casual observation indicates the "other guys" were doing the same sorts of things—some of them too were caught in complex lies about campaign funds; the first vice presidential nominee of the other party had to resign when it was discovered by investigative reporters that he had either lied or evaded the truth about his mental health record; and a leading contender for the other party's nomination was a man generally portrayed in media reports to have lied about his actions and intentions in the death of a young woman. Peter Manning (1974) has shown in minute detail how and why police systematically lie to the public, their superiors, and each other.

In the face of such obvious indications of the pervasiveness of lying, these defenders of purity commonly assert that it is only those "corrupted by power" who do such things. While I believe it is true that those who cannot stand to lie and conspire tend to lose the competitive struggle in our society, falsehood knows no class lines. In keeping with the general finding that, in such a complex, pluralistic and conflictful society as ours, one man's deviance is another man's absolute morality, we find falsehood is omnipresent in our society (and probably universally). Certainly people do not lie much of the time. Only hotel owners lie about the weather, or cooks (and tactful guests) about the meat. Unfortunately for us researchers, people tend to lie precisely about those things that matter most to them and us, such as sex, money and power. What varies is the frequency and the things lied about. Some groups and individuals lie about one thing, others about different things. Some groups probably lie more than others, but then those others commonly indulge in more evasions for purposes of avoiding situations where they have to lie. (For example, I suspect from my own experience that fundamentalists in our society lie far more about things like sex and drinking than do libertarian academics, but the latter lie more about money, politics and work standards.) From the researcher's standpoint, either one misleads him.

Consider some examples that can be taken from probably anyone's experience. Does anyone doubt that lying is a common practice of business people in their advertising? That lying is a standardized practice of business people and union officials in contract negotiations? That lying is a standard political tactic? That lying is a standard investigative practice of the police? (If so, we shall try to convince that doubting reader otherwise in our consideration of some modern police methods in the next chapter.) Most people might at least consider the churches to be free of lying. On the basis of the ministers and, especially, the ex-ministers I've known well, I would conclude that people who believe this simply don't know their ministers and priests well enough to know how evasive and/or lying they have to be in their personal lives, especially their sexual lives.

But let's look at a less important area where there is some better evidence--church statistics. Sociologists now commonly understand how and why police, coroners, welfare workers, etc., purposefully create false reports and statistics (i.e., they lie in "hard numbers"). (See for example Douglas, 1967, 1971, especially Chapters 3 and 4; and Johnson, 1973). But it is less well-known that churches have been deeply involved in the same numbers game (as members in-the-know commonly call it).

I first learned about these church practices from a sociologist who had formerly been a minister at the national headquarters of one of the major denominations. He said it was standard practice to "pad the numbers" by doing things like never dropping people from the rolls, even when they died, simply because money and reputation were partially tied to the number of members.

But the ultimate verification came from a natural experiment performed by Altheide, Johnson and Snow (1977). Using Altheide's member under-standing of fundamentalist religions, they attended meetings of the world's most famous and publicly esteemed evangelist (Friend of Presidents). At the proper time they came forward as possible converts and were interviewed concerning things like whether they had ever been converts before, were they church members, had they "declared for Christ" before, etc. They found that the interviewers invariably listed them as first-time converts, even when they explicitly looked at the official form and told him he had made a mistake; nothing could change his mind. They were added to the official rolls, which the evangelist used to show church groups that he could "deliver" new members. These statistics are used in getting his bookings, in which the local church groups are asked to guarantee so much money in advance. So the purpose of the "dirty statistics" seems reasonably clear, even without a randomized sample of linguistic accounts by the members concerning their own motivations.

The truly sanguine reader might still hold out with the contention that at least the Boy Scouts could be counted on to be honest. I have long had some suspicions about this, based on some casual observations of "merit badge awards" among Brownies and Girl Scouts. These suspicions were fanned by the insistence of another ex-minister that his mother secretly did much of the work that made him an eagle scout. But they could always be seen as "the few bad apples that don't make a barrel"—i.e., unrepresentative deviants.

Recently, however, my suspicions have been confirmed by the national leader of the Boy Scouts, who publicly admitted, *after* an investigative report by the *Chicago Tribune* revealed it, that some of their professional staff, both at headquarters and around the country, had been "cheating" in reporting the number of Boy Scouts. As is common with dirty official statistics, the purpose was money. The federal government's model cities program paid the scouts money and this, as usual, was pegged to the number of scouts. The *Tribune* reported that some of the scouts' staff in Chicago estimated that only about 25-50 percent of Chicago's registered scouts existed. That meant the official statistics were only wrong, by lying, by about a factor of two or three, which is probably par for the official statistics course.

It is also true, and of vital importance for all social researchers to understand, that all competent members of our society assume that friends (those of our private lives) should and will protect each other from strangers, or those of less friendly feelings (the public realm), and that this protection will include all forms of falsehood. (How far out on a limb one will go for a friend depends, as everyone knows, on how strong the feelings of friendship are. This is such a strong relationship that people will sometimes test the strength of friendship or love by seeing how much lying will be done for them.) Certainly it is true that these feelings, assumptions and actions are in irresolvable conflict with our absolutist, universalistic values and laws, such as the laws against perjury. But that is merely another of the omnipresent instances of such irresolvable conflicts that pervade all parts of our social lives as a result of the laying of an absolutist public and legal life upon the more basic, concrete, intimate, body-feeling relationships.

We all know from personal experiences how we lie to protect our friends as well as ourselves. All of us who have had any significant contacts with legal authorities also know from experience how pervasive perjury is in our society. Consider a few examples. All of us assume that it would generally be ridiculous to ask someone's friend to tell us about the private life, especially the inevitable "immoral" aspects of that life, unless we were also a close friend—and probably not even then. Consequently, we generally wouldn't ask because we'd be asking someone to commit treason. ("My love, right or wrong.")

A few simple examples of the absurdity of such a request come to mind. When I was 16 one of my younger brothers shot an uncle of ours (under what we considered to be justifiable, if unfortunate, circumstances) and was sentenced to detention on a church ranch in Oklahoma. He fled the ranch and came to live with us. Naturally, we lied when asked if he was there. After my freshman year in college a probation officer came looking for this same brother on some new charges. He came up to my two brothers and me and inquired where the one brother was. We realized he must be from the law and obviously didn't know what my brother looked like, since he was standing there. We constructed an impromptu, unspoken conspiracy. I told him the brother hadn't been around in a long time, that we had heard he was someplace far off, and gave him some details on how to get to that far-off place for inquiries. My brothers gave supporting testimony, all in sincere tones, apparently trying to help this poor stranger. As soon as he left we roared with delight at the absurdity of the whole thing and the way we'd put him off. It always seemed so strange, and funny, to us that legal authorities would bother asking us such things. Rather than feeling guilty about such acts of perjury, we always felt euphoric over the success of our conspiracies and the reaffirmed ties of kinship.

These same feelings, ideas, and actions are apparent in any famous conspiracy, such as the Bay of Pigs coverup conspiracy or the Watergate coverup conspiracy. In the Watergate coverup almost every person approached for a major part in it went along, in spite of the dangers. How could anyone in that situation refuse to cover up for his friend, even if he wasn't in favor of what his dumb friend had done? Anyone who has ever attempted to create or run an organization, especially a political organization, knows that personal loyalty is one of the most vital ingredients, that this loyalty must go both ways, and that everyone covers for everyone else, as long as they don't do something heinous.

All political parties, big or little, are conspiracies of friends and colleagues. (If the world could be run by morality and law, there wouldn't be political parties.) And all such conspiracies involve covering up for each other when the enemy attacks, unless he gets one in such a way as to endanger the whole conspiracy. The people who uncovered the Watergate conspiracy and attacked those conspirators did the same thing, of course. They refused to divulge who leaked legal documents against all congressional and legal rules. Bernstein and Woodward, the *Washington Post* reporters most responsible for getting the news story, admitted that they had violated the laws concerning the secrecy of grand jury proceedings (1974). They illegally sought and got secret information from jurors. When this was uncovered and revealed to Judge Sirica, he denounced the practice but covered up for the reporters by never mentioning their names in his attack on the practice, though Bernstein and Woodward knew that he was aware they were the culprits. The prosecutors never prosecuted the reporters, no doubt largely because they were part of the same informal political team.

These same practices of perjury and obstructing justice are endemic throughout our society; nearly everyone does both in support of the things he believes in. On nude beaches almost everyone willingly, without any question, tells newcomers how to violate the law without getting caught and few would tell the police the truth about instances of law violation they knew of. Lawyers have legal protections allowing them to do the same sorts of things with no legal responsibility whatsoever. Doctors rarely report unnecessary operations performed by colleagues and normally "evade" testifying about their knowledge of it. University professors gladly hire on the basis of race (in order to help the minorities) and none would think of bearing legal witness against others for doing this, regardless of what federal laws say. (Besides, who knows or cares what they say?)

In research settings in which the members face possible dangers from the research there are sometimes well-patterned forms of evasions and lies. (Melville Dalton, 1959, was the first sociologist to explore the basic importance of this for sociologists. See also Becker, 1970; Webb, 1928; and Wax, 1971, especially pp. 370-373.) Indeed, the researcher's understanding of the ways these lies allow the members to protect themselves from dangers he may pose for them can be crucial in getting them to talk. For example, in studying drug dealers (Adler, Adler and Douglas, 1977), most drug dealers willing to talk with us claimed to have quit the business absolutely and irrevocably about a year before the study began. Checking out these stories revealed that some probably had quit, and this was one reason they were willing to talk about it, but that probably in most cases it was just a protective lie. While they clearly trusted us a great deal to be willing to talk at all, they were generally retaining that ultimate bit of distrust, holding back on the most dangerous information—that concerning their present drug dealing. It was important in this research that we aid and abet this lie, rather than challenge the lie and try to force the truth out of them.

We've found similar forms of understood evasions and lies in every research setting. In studying drug rehabilitation programs, such as methadone maintenance programs, we found some officials who would anonymously give us important information about how methadone was leaked from the programs almost universally. The obvious implication was that the same was true of their program. We could get some indirect confirmation of this from what they said about their own programs, but it would generally be ridiculous to ask them specifically if it was true of their program as well. That would invite a lie that would be disruptive of the research relationship. On the nude beach we found that many people would talk, even joke roundly, about how much *other* people were into casual sex, including the ever-creepy body display, but would say nothing about themselves. We felt immediately and continually that it would be a disastrous affront to ask if that included them. About as close as anyone would get to including himself in such statements would be to say, "I don't think people would come here unless they enjoyed seeing others' bodies and showing their own."

In studying the uses of zoning rules in environmental politics it was apparent that they all would invoke rules which even they considered absurd to use as bargaining tools and for other political reasons. Indeed, a few would even tell how they did this. But to ask them, "Do you mean you'd act as if you're enforcing a rule you don't believe in?" would have been quite insulting. Altheide (1976) found in the TV newsroom that reporters and cameramen would often make allusions to their contempt for the news director, without saying whom they had in mind, since that bit of information could be damaging if it got back to the director. When Altheide asked whom they had in mind, they would assert with outrage that he'd been around long enough to know whom they had in mind—if he didn't, there was something wrong with him—both incompetence and immorality. In *All the President's Men* (1974) Bernstein and Woodward report that they found repeatedly that people such as "Deep Throat," would confirm or deny their findings only so long as the reporters did it indirectly or in such a way as to protect them from feeling like traitors.

The sociologist who tries to have put into words for his "verification procedures" ("just say it once for the recorder, please") what the members assume should not be put into words, especially what could be dangerous or stigmatizing for them, demonstrates incompetence both as a common-sense actor and as a field researcher. Any researcher who understands such settings knows what evasions and lies *should* be told and accepted. If he doesn't accept the lies, he's not only an impolite s.o.b., but a dangerous one. (This is analogous to the way members will cooperate in constructing lies about stigmatized identities, but it is generally only a legal protective device, not some desire to "disavow their deviance," which implies sharing a value they don't.) In all other research settings I've known about in any detail, lying was common, both among members and to researchers, especially about the things that were really important to the members.

Fronts

Finally, in most settings there exist some socially shared and learned lies about the setting itself, just as there are shared and learned lies about persons. These are social fronts (and personal fronts). It is the fact that they are learned and shared that differentiates them from simple lies. (A drug dealer's lie about being out of dealing is a personal front but is not learned and shared with drug dealers generally, so it's not a social front.) There are many different kinds of fronts.

Simple fronts are learned and shared specific lies.

Conspiratorial fronts are sets of lies that people specifically agree among themselves to tell other people.

Physical fronts are physical props intended to communicate lies to people, to make them think that what goes on inside the physical setting is something other than what the members know goes on.

Different research settings involve different kinds of fronts. Some involve all kinds at once and in varying combinations. For example, John Johnson (1973) found at least one major instance of a conspiratorial front in the construction and use of some official statistics in a welfare agency; but there was no kind of physical front involved. The traditional bookie joint commonly involves a physical front and a conspiratorial front. A researcher generally has to know someone well enough to get in on the conspiracy. Once he knows it's there and is acceptable, he can walk through a bar, barber shop or whatever, into the back room. The bar is the front, the bookie joint the more important reality. Physical fronts are so convincing to people that they have been worked into most of the really successful big con games (Maurer, 1962).[5]

Massage parlors (Rasmussen and Kuhn, 1977) involve all forms of evasions, lies and front work. The parlors themselves are physical fronts, made to look and sound like traditional health-spa massage parlors. Most important, the owners, receptionists and masseuses are involved in complex conspiracies to make the parlors appear to legal authorities and the public who are not potential customers to be health spas, not sex parlors. These conspiracies vary greatly. Some are open and honest within the group itself: The owners teach the masseuses how to do their front work and often their sex work as well by testing them out. (Some of them will even tell prospective employees on the telephone how much they can get for each sex act.) But some of them involve fronts within fronts: The owners may lie to the girls, telling them that sex is completely forbidden, but at the same time giving them hints that it's a sex parlor, by telling them that they have complete privacy to do their own thing, and later letting them see that those who don't do sex don't stay around. In addition, the girls play complex word games with customers to let them penetrate the fronts while, hopefully, avoiding a bust by "the vice" by "fronting them out." They literally have convoluted layers of fronts, such that they can successively fall back from one to the next as each is penetrated. Roughly, these fall-back fronts consist of the following steps: "We don't do any sex here;" "Well, you can get feels;" "Well, we do hand jobs;" "We do blow jobs;" "We do out-calls for anything more;" "We ball." Girls may stop at any position, depending on complex factors, or they may even go beyond these. Anyone who doesn't understand what it's all about can easily be fronted out and go away convinced that it's all one big health trip.[6]

Some sanguine members of our society might like to think that such highly developed front work is found only in the highly stigmatized realms of society. This is ridiculous. The truth is the opposite: The most highly developed and successful forms of fronts are found in the most respected realms of society, in business, politics and legislative bodies. Sometimes they involve the actual establishment of a physical setting, such as a place of work for a political front organization. But in the vast majority of cases they involve nonphysical conspiracies to evade public scrutiny, mislead people, and lie to them. Most of them are in no way illegal. Indeed, those of power and respectability have provided themselves with complicated forms of legal front work so that they may hide potentially embarrassing activities from the eyes of strangers—i.e., the public.

One of the most common of these is "blind trusts," which can be used not only to avoid conflicts of interest but also to hide ownership. This, for example, was revealed by some investigative reporters to have been the major device used by Mayor Daley of Chicago to hide his apparently legal ownership of real estate, in order to appear more "humble" to the voters of Chicago. Multiple-staged corporate structures have been used in the same way, again according to investigative reporters, by people like Hubert Humphrey to contribute money to their own campaigns without appearing too affluent to their liberal and poorer constituents. (Probably everyone is aware of the complex, and partially illegal, laundering of funds that was used in the payoffs of Watergate defendants.)

Legalized fictitious names, pseudonyms by authors, and numbered bank accounts are used in the same ways. Millions of couples live together without getting married, but present a common front of marriage to the neighbors and others. Universities establish whole colleges in which certain students are allowed to "earn" the same degree as other students without meeting the standards the other students had to meet, largely so that these students can look the same on paper (i.e., in credentials) to the unknowing public as the regular students. Teams of research scientists, including sociologists, create complex fronts of "practical applicability" of their potential findings to justify what are really basic, far-out research projects and they are aided and abetted in this by government officials who agree with them that the basic research is more important in the long run. (Some academics aptly call this "Bootlegging the basic research" because the basic work has to be "run in" under the guise of practical research, the same way moonshine liquor must be run in under cover of legitimate cargo.) University departments, businessmen and government officials often set up special "independent" committees to reach predetermined decisions but with such a front as to legitimate that decision in the eyes of the ignorant public. Administrators, for example, frequently set up or use pre-existing "dummy committees" to fire people so that there won't be anyone such as themselves to get the heat: "The *committee* has decided that it would not be justified to renew your contract."[7]

The front work done in universities is pervasive and beautifully complex because academics share, to immensely varying degrees, an ancient set of absolute values (truth, etc.) but have to work in the very sensate setting of modern America and because academics are skilled wordsmiths. (I suspect many readers will guffaw at this and assert the truth and respectability of universities. But that is precisely because academics are so good at front work.) One of the nicest bits of front work I've ever been directly involved in was engineered primarily by politicians who had been academics, and was gladly embraced as beautifully cunning by us academics. These politicians were being pressured by some local members of their own party to do something the politicians didn't want to do and which we didn't want them to do. They needed some party justification not to do it, which meant getting some counterpressures within their own party which they could show the other side. They secretly set up an ad hoc front group of important party members and arranged for me and others to (knowingly) give talks to these people to get them to pressure the politicians. We did and they did and it seemed to help prevent what we didn't want.[8]

A major aspect of our appeal to this ad hoc front group consisted of our ability to present ourselves as the elected representatives of a large group of faculty members. But this "large number" was a partial fiction, so that in an important sense our group was a political front group.

This came about partly by design and partly by playing it by ear. In the beginning we (an ad hoc executive committee) had tried to get as many faculty members as possible to come to a meeting and give us a card signifying their membership. We did not tell the members our whole program. We told them the parts that would appeal to the widest group—i.e., academic ideals. (I don't think we ever said, "Now, let's not tell the others that. . . ." We largely understood and felt what was needed in the situation. Anyone who bugged us would not have heard such things, especially because we did not yet know each other well enough nor have enough dirt on each other as hostage commitments to open up.) The people who got them to come were old-timers and friends. For the most part they were not willing to undertake the dirty work that was needed, so they turned to me and a few others. (Some of them were wily bureaucratic politicos who no doubt saw us as front men to take the heat—i.e., the patsies. But we had our own reasons for playing the game.)[9]

As we proceeded over the months with our program we moved more toward the goals we always wanted and expected many of them didn't or, rather, weren't willing to admit wanting. We never again called a meeting because we figured we'd get few live members. As they fell away, we found we could successfully present ourselves to the journalists and officials as the elected representatives of this large group of members, and we became more independent. One of the inner group of three (which in turn was part of a group of about a dozen active, trustworthy people, which in turn . . .) put it this way: "I wonder if those guys out there know that this group is really just three guys with a hot typewriter?" Everything indicates that some people suspected so, but that outsiders (i.e., nonuniversity people and faculty members not deeply involved) didn't really know because all they could "see" from the outside were conflicting assertions. (We ourselves were uncertain of who would support us in what ways in what situations. My own strong belief, based on the direct experience, was that support would vary greatly with the immediate situation.) [10] To that extent the front group worked and helped achieve some of our goals. But it also got bad labelling, as did its leaders, so as our final act we created a new front under a new label with new front men and merged it with a statewide (front) organization. The inner core looked at this new front group as almost entirely front (we called it a "shell") created for the purpose of lying dormant in case new situations arose in which the same kind of group was needed.

We've observed the same kind of front groups created and operated in roughly the same way in some of our other studies. In our study of nude beaches Rasmussen worked closely with a group called "The Committee to Save the Beach," which consisted primarily of three inner-core people (or maybe only two) and a floating group of a dozen or so. The inner core were the official, journalistically-anointed spokespeople (one spokeswoman and one spokesman) for thousands of people who didn't know anything much about the whole issue. The very name of the committee was chosen to make it look like an environmental group ("Save the Beach!"), but the only big issue was nudity. The real, insider motto was "Save the *Nude* Beach." (Actually, everyone knew that nudity had produced a population explosion on the beach that was bad for the environment.) This group was able to get such good news coverage of the story the way they wanted it told that the opposing property-owners group decided to go undercover.

In my study of environmental and zoning issues I found that an official group called the Town Council was also largely a front group. The council, which had official status as an advisory group to the city government and journalistic status as an official community group, consisted of both commercial members (many of whom were nonresidents) and residential members. However it happened historically, the commercial members were a distinct minority but were by far the most active group. They had come to control most major positions and, very important, the making of rules that would keep it that way. They used the Town Council as a front group, pushing political programs as community programs when they were actually just merchant programs. When an insurgent environmental group (with which I was working) tried to make the public aware of this by publicizing what went on in the crucial zoning committee hearings, such as showing how the merchants voted for things the general membership was against, the merchants who controlled the board of trustees voted to close the zoning committee hearings to the public "so that the deliberations can be carried on freely." When the insurgents argued that this was inconsistent with the openness of all other committees and proved the merchants were afraid of letting the public know what was happening, the merchants insisted on closing *all* committee hearings to show how consistent they were. This sort of policy helped greatly in their use of the council as a political front group.[11]

The four major forms of falsehood that we have been considering shade into each other—misinformation into evasions, evasions into lies, lies into fronts. As everyone knows from his own experience, people find it highly problematic to deal with these distinctions and the vast number of related but less important ones, like understood myths (Santa Claus, Easter Bunny), private lives (parents doing sex only in great secrecy, children masturbating only in greater secrecy), white lies, etc. Moreover, socially competent individuals are generally tremendously adept and cunning at constructing different interpretations in these terms. By the age of four or five children are often able to construct complex rationales in favor of "white lies" or evasions. Any competent adult is able to manage evasions in such a manner that outsiders can be expected to make false inferences, yet he will never feel he has lied because he did not really say what he secretly hoped the person would infer from his evasive answer. And any intelligent wordsmith, such as politicians and academics generally are, can purposefully play on the uncertainties and complexities of language and human situations to set people up for cutting them down.

Academic philosophers, theologians, lawyers and politicians are remarkably skilled at this, since they receive training in Socratic argument, rhetoric, apologetics, adversary proceedings, and debate from the beginning of their careers. From high school on they join debate clubs and similar groups to learn how to argue people into any position they want, and nothing delights them more than being able to convince people of something they themselves do not believe, or don't think they believe; because their verbal legerdemain commonly leaves them uncertain of what they really do believe, or whether they believe anything at all. (There are no doubt some secret solipsists who adopt solipsism as a device to allow them to take *any* opportune position without feeling any guilt about dishonesty.) In addition to such well-recognized and vital parts of our "high" culture, we find that almost everyone delights in "putting people on," especially their enemies, with no sense of dishonesty about it; and that everyone agrees in some contorted manner that it is necessary to tell white lies, to be evasive, tactful, to avoid talking about things that hurt, and so on.

These convoluted forms and layers of falsehood would certainly be enough problem for any researcher to unravel. Yet these problems are superficial compared to the deeper ones a sociologist faces in grasping, understanding and communicating the truth about the social world. All of our discussion so far in this chapter of the problems a researcher faces in getting at the truth has assumed that at least some members somewhere know what is true *and* can tell him about it. His problem is finding them, establishing trust, then separating out truth from falsehood—all using methods we shall discuss further in the succeeding chapters.

But this assumption by no means holds in all situations. Some of the things that matter most to us in our individual and social lives are not known to us, or at least are not verbalizable in any form that we can communicate to a researcher. It is certainly not the case that the things which researchers, or members themselves, want to know about society are always residing out there in some member's consciousness and that they simply have to be laid bare and reported by the researcher.

There are at least three major, well recognized phenomena which force the researcher to rely on something other than members' conscious experience and knowledge to get at what is important to them. These are the taken-for-granted understandings, problematic meanings and self-deceptions we shall consider in the next chapter.

But we should also note that these conscious forms of falsehood run into, merge with, and overlap with those less conscious, deeper problems. It is especially important, for example, to note that lies and fronts easily become self-deceptions. It is common for lies to eventually become accepted as truths by the perpetrator. People are adept at marshalling all kinds of interpretations, lapses of memory and misremembering to reconstruct into self-deceptive "truths" what they once experienced as lies. (We shall explain this further in the next chapter.)

This whole process can be telescoped into very short periods of time, at least within specific situations, when individuals are moralistically attacked by other people. When Americans are attacked moralistically, they tend to become instantaneously moralistic in their counterattacks. In the process they often come to believe, at least during the heat of their counterattack, and possibly without total conviction, in their own lies or front work.

We shall return to evaluate what the researcher should do with such highly problematic phenomena. For now, let us simply note how convoluted and problematic human experience can be, how the researcher tries to avoid playing the dupe to the wily members, and thereby provides all the members of society with a more truthful picture of themselves and their world.

NOTES

1. The methods presented in this and the following chapter for dealing with these problems are generally concrete methods. We shall return in Chapter 7 to deal with the general research strategy involved in using such concrete methods.

2. In fact, I once got myself deeply involved in leading a faculty group to get such a board of directors to exercise a special procedure of appointment which I and other faculty members thought they had. It was only once I was in over my ears that I discovered they didn't have that particular power. And the way I learned it was by listening to one director explain to another one why they didn't. No one was deceiving anyone, but almost everyone involved was "misled" by his own beliefs and unintentionally by the others involved.

3. As should be obvious to the reader, I learned all these kinds of things through personal experience. In this instance, for example, I learned as a young and desperate job seeker. I had just been fired by an exclusive Eastern college for young ladies, had no job late in the season, a family to support, and no significant savings. I received a letter from a well-known sociology department seeming to offer an attractive job: "Would you be willing . . .?" I was tremendously ignorant of the facts of bureaucratic life, and almost all practical life, because I was on a "superintellectual trip"—and, of course, intellectuals *must* be ignorant and inept about practical, business things. But I'd already gotten myself into a mess because of my idealistic commitment to ignorance, so I decided to compromise with high ideals. I called an advisor, a wily old veteran of years of bureaucratic warfare, and asked what he thought. He asked me to read the letter, whereupon he told me the facts of life. "Well, boy, they haven't really offered you a job. They're just trying to tie you up, while they. . . ." I recovered from the shock and, hoping to get an even better offer from another department, we devised a simple strategy for trying to gazumph them in turn. I wrote them immediately, saying something like, "If you were to offer me that job, then I suspect that. . . ." Meanwhile, I wrote the other department to tell them I had been offered a job (no "ifs" mentioned) and "had to make a decision immediately and, since I would prefer a good offer from them . . ." They made a firm offer and I accepted.

4. We might note here that we certainly do not believe that people hiding something or being evasive always show some external signs, such as pauses, or shifty eyes. On the contrary, the more people have hidden or evaded, the more adept they are at presenting smooth appearances—no pauses or shifty-eyedness. The hard-core evader and liar is ready with his self-presentations, so he does not inadvertently give body signs of being evasive or lying. "Oh, no, no, I never ball guys in the parlor. Only hand jobs. If I balled them, my boyfriend would surely find out and raise hell. Besides, I just never feel that way about guys in the parlor. To me it's just a job and I never get it on with the customers." This was a continual lie we faced in dealing with masseuses. We almost never saw any signs of evasiveness. Indeed, their presentations were especially convincing to the researchers who observed them directly. It was the cynic who did not directly observe the sincere and straightforward looks who could confidently assert that more was going on than could be seen or was being told: "Horse-piss! Check 'em out. Keep

digging." We had to use direct observations of key informants, drawing them out, and sometimes noticing self-contradictions (forgetting themselves) to find the almost inevitable.

5. I always remember how impressed I was at the age of 12 when I discovered my first such physical front. My mother was working as a barmaid in Miami, Florida. As is almost universally the case in bars, this one had a small back room where stock was kept. But in this bar the back door in the stock room opened into a huge room (which had originally been an illegal nightclub, the infamous La Paloma Club, with a string of whorehouses behind it, during Prohibition). This huge room was rigged as a bookie joint, complete with loudspeakers. I marvelled at the ingenuity of the whole thing and relished the sense of conspiratorial closeness it gave us, that sense of being behind the fronts, seeing the things that were really important to the people with whom we lived. I came to relish this particular front a little less one day when the owner (the ex-gangster who had spent 20 years in an Atlanta federal prison for "white slavery") came out the back door and, not realizing who we were, took some shots at my brother and me. But in retrospect that too was an interesting experience, reminding the field researcher that people who go the trouble to construct physical fronts to screen out people who might put them in prison are serious people, with little scholarly detachment. (They have a bad case of the "natural attitude.")

6. I was continually surprised to find how many people, including such interested and experienced people as lawyers and sociologists, were effectively fronted out by the parlors or, at least, kept uncertain by the front. The most common view seemed to be that the police views, as reported frequently in the mass media, were probably partly correct; that is, people thought some of the parlors were into sex. But they also thought there must be a lot ("Maybe 50 percent") that did only massage. This public uncertainty was vital to the parlors. They were able to contend in legal suits that they were being unjustly stigmatized, while at the same time holding out the prospect to new customers that they have at least a good chance of getting some action. There were many cases of men who went to a parlor to get sex and came away convinced the fronts were the truth, simply because they didn't know how to negotiate and weren't aggressive enough to proposition the girls. Fronts almost always work on some people, especially because a high percentage of people in our society are indeed "suckers," innocents who trust other people to tell them the truth and not to do evil deeds. And physical fronts generally give another large percentage the feeling that they must be "real" in some way—they *look* so real, and many people never learn that looks, self-presentations, are the easiest to manipulate by those experienced in lying. In sociology we even find the Goffman sociologists and the ethnomethodologists declaring that we should take self-presentations and linguistic accounts as *being* the reality for sociologists. As we argued in the last chapter, this would largely turn sociology into the study of fronts. That is academic naiveté carried to its logical conclusion.

7. As a young instructor I was fired by such a committee without even knowing who the committee was. I was enthralled by the beauty of this bureaucratic political device precisely because, as far as I could tell, I was fired largely because I had spent part of the year denouncing such hypocrisy—evasions, lies and fronts—in the college as a whole. It was really through such personal experiences that I learned the basic importance of the differences between public and private and the tremendous problems in determining what is going on in social life. The important methodological point about this sort of thing is that the sociologist must look at such experiences as learning devices, as social facts to be collected and thought about from all angles. This theoretic stance toward one's personal experience should come only after one has first surrendered to the

natural reactions, such as anger and resentment. But that it does come and that one learns from that experience, rather than simply becoming some irate and moralistic prig denouncing the world as hypocritical (and all the time using the same devices as those one denounces), is the important thing for sociological work.

8. Having read this far, the reader may suspect a certain amount of laundering of the data is going on here. In fact, if he's reading carefully, he may feel certain of this. It pains me to admit that he is right, but it also delights me to be able to provide an internal example of academic front work—i.e., laundering the data. But the only laundering involved is that necessary to protect the identities of the other people involved, some of whom are still actively involved in such politicking. I would add emphatically that all of us felt justified in our activities of this sort because we firmly believed from what we could see that the other side was doing far more dishonest front work than we were. I also believe they felt the same way and that this mutual or symmetric self-justification is a vital reason why evasion, lying and front work are so pervasive in our social life. The reason why I report on our front work instead of theirs is because I know from direct experience what we did, but necessarily remain uncertain about what they did because I could never directly participate in their activities.

9. When I look back on this I realize it makes our involvement look like it was the result of pretty rational calculations. As nice as it might be to look at it that way, since no one likes to be a patsy and even less to look like one, it wasn't all that rational. We were rationally estimating our own expected costs and rewards in the beginning. But our relative ignorance of the people we were dealing with led us to underestimate how intense the heat (costs) would be and to overestimate our chances of success. Part of our overestimation of success was based on our sharing of a widespread organization myth about the power of the regents of the university, to which I referred earlier. Even more, we did not realize how our situational involvements would come to dominate our feelings, thoughts, actions and returns. As the heat grew intense, our feelings of anger, outrage, desire for revenge, etc., grew correspondingly and came to dominate us. It became a war of attrition in which beating the other side was the crucial goal. This is the case with almost all hard-core people ("red hots") and is a basic reason why it is ridiculous to argue with their ideological moralisms. Their ideological rhetoric is a mask for more basic, intense, overwhelming commitments—hatred and the lust for revenge. To argue with them merely labels one as being of the hated enemy, which fans their hatred and desire for revenge, rather than eliciting rational considerations.

10. A major reason why we were so uncertain of who would support us, when and how, was that we were convinced that many of our fellow faculty members were often anxious for the same things we were but rarely wanted this known to anyone and often would hardly admit it to themselves. We shall return soon to the big question of self-deception.

11. Political sociologists have often shown that Michels' "Iron Law of Oligarchy," or the tendency of large groups to become dominated by a small group (oligarchs) who do the day-to-day work of the group, holds true in America's ostensibly democratic groups. But they have almost never been concerned with the more important matter of the ways in which oligarchs construct and use political front groups, always giving top priority in our "democratic society" to maintaining the appearances of *mass* participation.

Chapter 5

INVESTIGATING SUBCONCIOUS AND

SELF-DECEPTIVE EXPERIENCE

The worst problems facing the researcher trying to get beyond the surface appearances of our everyday lives are:

(1) Taken-for-granted feelings and meanings;
(2) Problematic feelings and meanings; and
(3) Self-deceptions.

The first two are subconscious forms of experience. That is, members do not ordinarily think or talk about them and are therefore not apt to tell researchers about them; but once in a while they do come to mind, and members then think and talk about them, such as during training of new workers and during moments of reflection ("philosophizing"). They are not normally *in* consciousness, but can become so without too much problem. However, problematic feelings and meanings shade off into and overlap with the most difficult problem of field research, that of inferring self-deceptions. These involve feelings and meanings which the members think and assert they have, but which are actually in conflict with deeper feelings and meanings that are usually more important in deciding what they do. When the field researcher gets into this realm he will generally get almost no help from the members. Instead, he will get resistance and animosity. He may get screams of denunciation or worse. They are the most problematic inferences he can make, and yet are some of the most important contributions of research to be made to the human quest for self-understanding.

Taken-for-Granted Feelings and Meanings

Taken-for-granted meanings are the least problematic for the researcher because they usually lie so close to consciousness among the members and are least subject to resistance. These are the meanings which are so much a standard part of the day-to-day life of members that they are forgotten and everyone is assumed to know about them. When the researcher comes to recognize and verbalize them, members will usually look astounded and say things like, "For God's sake, I thought everyone knew that. . . ." The researcher often feels like saying, "For God's sake, why didn't you tell me that six months ago? Think of all the time you could have saved me!"

The existence and latent importance of taken-for-granted meanings are obvious at the extreme. For example, if someone were to approach a sociologist in a classroom and say in all seriousness, "I've noticed that everyone in this room is breathing," it would probably frighten the sociologist. He or she might suspect he was faced with the ultimate survey researcher, the Martian researcher (as Fred Davis, 1974, called them), one who is so removed from human involvements that he does not know the things that all human beings know and take for granted about all human beings. Even more likely, as Thomas Scheff (1965) and others have suggested, the sociologist might think the person was insane because he did not understand and act in accord with the "residual" (which simply means taken-for-granted) understandings.

All established groups have particular taken-for-granted feelings and meanings (also called background feelings and meanings). The longer the group has been interacting together, and the more they have established some kind of shared *modus vivendi,* even if it consists simply of agreeing to disagree, the more they take for granted basic feelings and understandings about their group lives. (Old married couples commonly say little to each other, whereas new acquaintances are remarkably voluble.) If the researcher is studying a group that has any significant history or shared meanings to it, as he generally is, he must always expect these taken-for-granted feelings and meanings to be there. He will find some of them difficult to get at because the members have simply become inexperienced in expressing them. (If they ever were experienced in expressing them it was probably as novitiates or when they were being created, or whenever some conflict over them arises.)

For example, in American TV newswork it has been almost universally taken for granted that the news must be "entertaining" or else they'll lose their ratings. But it is also taken for granted that entertainment is secondary to the journalist's goal of getting and communicating the news. Largely because it seems so obvious, and because entertainment is not wholly in keeping with the public ideals of journalism, news people rarely think to tell a researcher these vital facts. Consequently, sociologists studying TV newswork first learned this the hard way, piecing together their experience in the setting until they finally understood what was obvious to news people.

In the last year, however, this has changed drastically. Suddenly the TV news people are talking a great deal about "entertaining news," simply because some newsrooms have successfully reversed the old taken-for-granted ranking and made entertainment more important than news. Now any researcher going into a TV newsroom would almost certainly hear all about the basic issues and find it a great opportunity to get some nice talk about them.

But there remain the other, far more unchallengeable and inexpressible (for the members) feelings and meanings of the work. It is just such taken-for-granted feelings or meanings that McLuhan and others have tried to grasp and communicate in their ideas about media. While I think their ideas are oversimplified and partially wrong, I also think there are some other background feelings and meanings about the socially defined medium shared by its workers. For example, anyone who has ever closely observed or worked with filmers or TV people knows, and probably takes it for granted, that they always do certain things in their filming or taping, such as eliminating most forms of movement, sound and light which are normal and natural in our everyday settings (by using sound studios and directional mikes, using carefully controlled lights, and by instructing people to stop movements). I believe all of this adds up in general to putting a *tight focus* and *rigid focus* around reality, very tight and rigid compared to our everyday settings. This has great significance for a vast amount of what goes on in filming and TV work, and for the effects their products have on our society; yet it is so taken for granted in each of its particulars (if not in its general ideas) that the members sense these things and act in accord with them without thinking about them and without saying anything about them. Their words tend to be things like: "Christ, look at that!" or "Get that, George!" A simple expletive may send a whole crew scurrying, but leave the researcher wondering what in the world it's all about.

This difficulty of researchers to get at background meanings is considerable, but it often poses a worse problem. The background feelings and meanings are part of the members' "natural attitude" toward their world. To them these feelings and meanings are natural and normal, something anyone knows, at least anyone who is part of that world. They may allow a novitiate to ask questions about them in the same way a child does, but even this holds true only for the less certain, less taken-for-granted ones. In many settings a researcher is trying to present himself as just another member and any discussion of these background meanings is apt to blow his cover. It is also true that in almost any setting many people (but never all of them)[1] are so "trapped" or encapsulated by their situational feelings, rules, ideas and so on that anyone who doesn't know the more taken-for-granted aspects of these appears "funny" or "dumb." It is common for members to make fun of outsiders (foreigners) precisely by depicting their ignorance of the most obvious, natural, background feelings and meanings of everyday life. Surfers poke fun at the inland tourists by saying things to each other (generally in a mock-squeaky voice) like, "Young man, does that board have a motor on it?" or maybe "Sonny, do you wear your hair long to help you float?" On the nude beach I could always get a laugh out of the regulars by telling them about the young marine who came across the rocks drinking a beer, looked around wide-eyed, and said to me, "Hey, man, are there any rules over here? I mean, like, I know you can't go up and touch people and all, but what *can* you do?" Or about the university administrator who told a reporter all the nude beachers were "perverts watching perverts watching perverts." Or the people who would tell TV interviewers in dead-pan expressions that "I've been coming to this beach for 25 years and I've never seen any sex here," or about the middle-aged tourists sitting in the gay area who said to me, "We heard there were a bunch of homosexuals running around nude over here, but we haven't seen one yet."

Researchers should also remember that it is only a short jump from this kind of joking to a hilarious (and vicious, as we researchers see it) form of putting-the-researcher-on. (See Wax, 1971, pp. 370-3.) Any researcher who is successfully put on about important matters, especially if it is a conspiratorial put-on, might even be blown out of the place. John Johnson (1975) reported on an instance in which a single member appeared to be trying to put him on. He found deeply upsetting the mere experience of having someone try, unsuccessfully, to put him on, because it meant that that person was probably out to con him, something he hadn't realized earlier and something he couldn't make any sense of:

> Also had a talk with Buzz this afternoon. I began by asking him what had happened recently with the kids at the Young foster home, where we were last week. Buzz began his account by saying, "Oh wow, JJ, you wouldn't believe how bad I blew it," and then he proceeded to describe the details of what he called his own ignorance, unprofessional conduct, erroneous judgments, sentimental and sloppy thinking, bad

social casework, and so on. Now, I'll admit that I don't know all there is to know about social workers or social casework, but I sure as hell know enough about it to know that all the example he cited from this case wouldn't be similarly defined by *any* other social worker, that there isn't a social worker in the world who would see that as unprofessional conduct, or anything else. The account would've been implausible from nearly any worker, but it's (especially) implausible coming from Buzz. He's one of the brightest guys I've met so far. . . . It's fairly obvious he was giving me some kind of short-con this afternoon, although I'll be damned if I have any idea why. The thing today really got to me. After taking leave of the situation, I walked out of the office and over to the parking lot whereupon I proceeded to break into a cold sweat, felt weak-knee'd and nauseous. . . .

Sometimes the members react moralistically to an interviewer who tries to get them to talk about these "obvious" things. This is especially true of those who are his friends and key informants, because his appearing dumb by asking such dumb questions plays into the hands of their enemies, making them look dumb by association with a "dumb-ass sociologist who doesn't know which end is up." As Altheide (1974) has stressed in his study of the TV newsroom, his attempts to verify his inferences by getting the members to talk about these background matters were very upsetting to his friends and they let him know it.

A close friend of his who was a key informant in the newsroom was often at odds with him because Altheide had a theoretical interest in precisely some of the matters the members took for granted. The friend kept insisting, "But why are you interested in *those* things? They're *obvious!*" It seems likely that his position in the organization was partially undermined by his association with friends dumb enough to ask such questions and, worse, to spend time studying them. As we shall emphasize in the next chapter, the researcher generally has to get at the background feelings and meanings by his own experience and, if he wants to get people to talk about them, he usually should wait until the end of the research, in case he winds up looking awfully dumb.

Problematic Feelings and Meanings

In addition to these background feelings and meanings, there are problematic feelings and meanings in any social setting; that is, there are always feelings and meanings which vary from one situation, person or part of the setting to another. Unfortunately, the members commonly are not aware that this is the case. When they proclaim, "All people are created equal" or "Everyone should be treated equally" they do not recognize that in their everyday lives they interpret equality one way in one situation (such as education) and another way in other situations (such as employment or marriage). They use the same terms in different situations to mean different things. It is easy for a researcher to overlook these problematic meanings, to assume that the same terms always mean the same thing, and to present false pictures of the complex, problematic setting. This, in fact, is what sociologists did in studying such things as "suicide". They thought the same word meant the same things to the members, whereas in fact the same word has a number of different meanings in different situations (Douglas, 1967).

The difficulty of getting at these problematic feelings and meanings was strikingly brought home to me in our studies of drug crisis intervention (1974b) and nude beaches (1977b). When we started studying drug crises we took it for granted that the medical staffs we would be studying in emergency rooms, free clinics, and the like, would share our conception of drug crisis. Drug crises were obviously things like overdoses and bad trips. In our initial research forays this seemed to be true. We talked to them about drug crises and they talked back about drug crises. It met the member test of validity: We were able to communicate "effectively" with them about drug crises.

But we then came across some less docile members who, instead of adapting themselves to our terminology and letting any problems of meaning pass, assuming that we must know what we were talking about, asked us things like, "What do *you* mean by a drug crisis?" As soon as we let them take the initiative and do the defining of things, we found that different groups had different distinctions, that many made important distinctions among things like drug problems, addictions, crises, emergencies and so on. Some of the medical people and other workers had come to believe that drug emergencies (e.g., overdoses) were experienced by drug users, but drug crises (defined as psychologically experienced panic states) were experienced primarily by parents and friends of drug users, which was something we had not even considered.

In our study of nude beaches we found that there was a consistent use of ideas such as "being natural" to talk to outsiders about the nude scene, especially by people who used the beach as a sex scene for things such as promoting swinging orgies. We concluded from all our evidence that this was clearly an instance of personal front work that was increasingly being transmitted and becoming shared by people who were into the nude scene; therefore it was increasingly becoming a social front. But as we got to know some of the regulars even better it also became clear that many of them seemed to be feeling an increasing commitment to these ideas of naturalness. As their sex trips cooled, their commitment to the naturalistic ethos appeared to grow. We also came to see that the very people who were into a sex trip could be those most sincerely (as far as we could tell) moralistic in attacking "straights" (non-nude bathers) for their lack of naturalness. We also found that when one asserted it was a sex trip in the face of an assertion that it was a naturalistic trip, the people generally would accept this, even when they had just been asserting the naturalism of it. (In the next chapter we shall look into how this was done, and its effects.) In this way we came to see the commitments to the naturalistic ethos as a very complex, situationally problematic thing. People were often unsure of how they felt about it; they could feel highly naturalistic in one situation, such as when confronted with TV cameras, and very much the sexual predator in another, such as when there were no outsiders watching their attempts to pick up girls or do body-display. Individuals clearly changed in their feelings about the scene and in their ideas about the scene; and the social lives of the members, such as the things they felt, did and said to each other, changed over time. What appeared at first to be a reasonably simple case of front work proved to be a complex, convoluted, changing, problematically situated scene.

As we have said, members ordinarily are not aware of these problematic feelings and meanings; some of them are outside of the members' consciousness most of the time because of the pressures or fears that lead to repression and self-deception (discussed next), but most such problems are unrecognized simply because the members feel no great need to be rational, systematic and ordered in their lives. The obsession of philosophers, scientists and academics with the "rational ordering" of the world and of peoples' accounts of their world is not shared by many other people (nor by these people themselves outside of their professional lives).

Most people are concerned with appearing to be rational, systematic, ordered, and so on, almost entirely in those public settings in which they may be attacked by enemies for not being those things. And one of the public settings in which they most commonly fear such attacks is precisely that situation in which they are being studied by religiously rationalistic, systematic and ordered academic scientists.

One of the first things they reach for when the social scientist approaches them is the front of rationality and order.[2] As the wily, irrational and disorganized manager of a network-affiliated TV newsroom told us when we were trying to study how they did the newswork: "Well, that's no problem. It's all set out very clearly here in the TV news policy handbook. It tells you what the news is and how to report it." It couldn't be clearer, simpler, more rational or more ordered. But, of course, he didn't believe this any more than we did. It was simply the obvious front work to deal with potential enemies who might be bent on doing an exposé of TV news people. One of the first steps of this manager in investigating our request was to send a memo to his subordinates asking them to check me out to see if I was a "radical," which would have meant I was bent on doing an exposé, or worse, regardless of what we might find. Having learned the answer to that, he then sent it up to the station manager with a note saying I was not a radical and using this fact as justification for his decision to let us study the station. We were then able to observe through our involvement all their convoluted, conflictful, situated and problematic feelings and meanings about what the news is and how to do it. (See Altheide, 1976.)

While members usually are not directly conscious of all these problematic feelings and meanings, there are times when they are acutely aware of their problematicness, and times when they must deal overtly with the problems. This is most common during periods of acute transition, such as when they are trying to start a business or liquidate one, start a romance or learn to live with a divorce. A serious mistake of sociologists is in concentrating their research efforts on routinized and non conflictful activities, those which are well-established, ongoing and ordered. As I have argued about the ethno-methodological studies of "rational accounts" (1970d and 1976a), this leads to a truncated view of the social world. One aspect of this is not seeing those times when members are most aware and willing to talk about the problematic aspects of their lives–the conflicts between and within their situated activities, their doubts and anxieties. Indeed, today there are almost always some members who are able and willing to talk rather abstractly about the necessarily situated nature of our lives and the conflicts that make it worthwhile for them to lie.

In fact, Jim Stingley, a staff writer from the *Los Angeles Times,* demonstrated this by a simple device (reported in the *Times* August 19, 1974). He went to a Los Angeles beach with a tape recorder and talked with young people about honesty and lying in the modern world, including some well-publicized examples in which the police had lied to people holding hostages in order to free the hostages. He found that most of them believed lying to be essential in some ways in the modern world because telling the truth all the time hurt people too much and could get one into too much trouble. The statements ranged all the way from simple, concrete statements like, "Let's put it this way . . . When your parents ask where have you been and what have you been doing, well, all of a sudden you've got to come up with a fast one. I don't want to hurt them. I just don't want to get caught . . .," to "The story about Lincoln (always telling the truth) was supposed to have taken place when he was a child . . . and most children are honest. They've got consciences and morals. They're taught that–until they get out and learn it doesn't work much . . .," to abstract statements like that of a 22-year-old man, "It's a matter of situation ethics. Whatever's necessary for the moment. . . ."

When members are aware of problematic feelings and meanings they are usually most aware of and willing to talk about the problems in the form of differences between the members. For example, news people will sometimes disagree overtly over what constitutes a good news story, just as professors will disagree over what constitutes good teaching. This conscious experience of the problematicness of their activities almost always involves an implicit assumption that the problem is the result of someone's "mistake" or "immorality"—e.g., he just doesn't recognize what *really* constitutes good news or good teaching, or else he doesn't *want* to recognize it. The assumption of absolute meanings is preserved; that is, they continue to believe that lying behind the problematic aspect is an absolute set of "right" feelings or meanings, so the problem can be resolved by getting at them or simply invoking them.

But there are rare occasions when members themselves recognize the problem to be the result of fundamentally different feelings or meanings. For example, a professor might decide that the very idea of good teaching involves conflicting or uncertain meanings (such as holding students to a high standard vs. being liked). I have in fact heard professors make such comments on rare occasions. However, I know of no instance where news people have explicitly recognized any fundamental problems in the idea of good news stories. Moreover, John Johnson made an explicit search in his studies of welfare caseworkers to see if he could find any instances in which they explicitly recognized any fundamental problems with their own ideas, such as what constitutes good casework. He found instances of ambiguous differences, but none where he felt sure they were making such a distinction. (I would point out that our examples have involved ideas rather than feelings. People seem to recognize and accept fundamentally different feelings far more often than they do ideas. The realm of reason, of ideas, is considered absolute almost universally, while feelings are less commonly so.)

Our discussion of problematic feelings and meanings has basic implications for field research. First, it is up to the researcher to make these problems conscious. He can rarely rely on the members to tell him about them, primarily because they are not generally conscious of them, but also because they are commonly anxious to appear to researchers to be rational and ordered (nonproblematic) in their lives because the researchers are "scientists." Indeed, if the researcher relies on the members to tell him about such problematic feelings and meanings, he may be misled, as the ethnomethodologists have been, into thinking members are always concerned with appearing to be rational and ordered to each other.[3]

Second, the researcher can expect that in certain settings the members will tend to misinform him, evade him, lie to him and front him out concerning these kinds of problems. This would be true in organized, ostensibly rationalized settings, like bureaucracies. And it is precisely those who are most knowledgeable about these kinds of problems, the managers and organizational entrepreneurs, who will do most to keep him from learning about the conflicts, contradictions, inconsistencies, gaps and uncertainties. The reason for this is simply that they are the ones responsible for making things rational, organized, scientific and legal. They are also the people who deal with the organizational life in terms of words, which are always immensely more rationalizable and organized than the concrete realities, so they themselves are often unaware of the vast problems experienced in going from their words to the concrete products.

This desire to maintain the unproblematic appearances of things complements their desire to prevent the researcher from seeing the "dirty work" that inevitably goes on, such as the massive amount of "winging it," "playing it by ear," "flying by the seat of one's pants," "guessing," scheming, lying and illegal activities. The two together lead those in power to almost universally exclude the public from the inner, secret realms where concrete power decisions are made.

This means the sociologists will also be excluded, so there are almost no instances where sociologists have been able to actually observe the inner workings of the organizations. (But see Dalton, 1959.) If he is able to, his reports on it will be resisted, perhaps violently. He must be prepared for this, but it will certainly make it harder, often impossible, to get any support from others for his findings. He will have to stand alone in the face of concerted "evidence" from "independent observers," the "guilty" members, opposing his work. Since much of the revelation of problematic feelings and meanings consists of analysis comparing different phenomena and situations, his statements about these problems are necessarily more problematic, thus more attackable. Inference of these problems, then, has to be done cautiously, with great concern for detail and evidence *whenever possible.* Assuming this is done, the researcher then simply has to have the courage to go beyond the observable facts into the crucial, secret realm of innermost feelings and meanings—and then take the heat.

While it has been implicit in our whole discussion of problematic meanings, it should be made explicit that the feelings and meanings of things are necessarily more problematic to a researcher. Indeed, the crucial first step of all explicit research, as distinct from simply experiencing things, is the active cultivation of the sense of the problematicness of things. (This is not in conflict with our argument that much of basic sociological research should involve, as a second crucial step, the de-focusing that enables one to experience things almost as a member. In this case the sense of the problematicness is intentionally postponed to the later stage of looking at, questioning, analyzing and presenting one's experience. If the sense of the problematicness is never achieved, cultivated and managed, then all one presents is an insider account, a member's evocation of his experience.)

Needless to say, researchers have generally been all too aware of this. But what they have commonly failed to do is communicate this to the readers of their reports. As John Johnson has argued (Johnson, 1975, especially Chap. 6), in their reports researchers have almost always presented only "rational appearances," making it look as if their research was done with no significant sense of anguish and doubt. When they have told of their doubts, they almost always tell how all the problems were solved. But this is ridiculous. As in almost any other realm of life, many of the most important problems one experiences in understanding any research setting are never solved. The researcher winds up guessing that such and such is the case, or feeling that it is, but not being at all clear about it. He should communicate to the reader these doubts, these tentative feelings, and the certainty that he never solved a particular problem. The researcher must have the courage not to do the front work of pretending to be always rational and successful in solving the terrible problems of research—and to bear the heat he will get from academics for being honest.

Self-Deceptions

Problematic feelings and meanings merge with the most difficult problem of understanding a researcher, or anyone else, has to face—unconscious experience and the closely related self-deceptions. It is the self-deceptions which pose the big problem, for they are the result of fears that the individual must protect himself from by denying the underlying, largely unconscious experience. The self-deceptions are actually conscious feelings and ideas, which are readily available, easily expressed, well-verbalized, and advertised to the world: They are the verbal accounts, the self-presentations, that the individual gives to the world about things which are vital and fearful to him; but which are in conflict with those deeper, generally unconscious fears. They are also the things he himself believes—he insists on their truth and holds onto them tenaciously, though there are also times when he doubts them and temporarily grasps the underlying fear that inspires the self-deception.

Probably everyone, except the most repressed, is aware from his own experience of times when he has deluded himself. These are situations in which he has suddenly realized that the things he has been telling himself and others are merely covers for feelings he had not consciously recognized before. One may come to realize he has been advising a friend that he would be better off giving up a girlfriend because he himself wants the girl. Or he may look back at his adolescent attacks on adults and successful people, and realize the attacks were due to his deep fears that he could never succeed in the ways they had.

The problem is that we are also aware, and probably more acutely so, of many situations in which our enemies have accused us of being self-deluded, or of not knowing what we really want, or of secretly wanting the very things we attack. Moreover, how can we trust our own "realizations" of earlier self-delusions? If we were not really conscious of them at the time, how do we know now that our earlier thoughts were delusions, rather than our present ones about our earlier ones being delusions? For example, might it not well be the case that thoughts in middle-age about the delusions of adolescence are themselves delusions born of an unrecognized envy of the young? It is this sort of thing which has made the idea of self-deception, and of unconscious experience in general, rightly suspect among social scientists.

There have been many abuses of the idea of self-deception in politics and so-called depth psychology. In politics the idea has been found primarily in the form of "false consciousness" or some variant thereof. (They have been noted primarily in the thoughts and proclamations of those of the political left, presumably because, for some unknown reason, those of the right have preferred to see their opponents as intentionally evil and lying, rather than deluded.) In its baldest form the idea of false consciousness sees the enemy, the bourgeoisie and even more the misguided proletariat who should be on one's side but isn't, as suffering from "false ideas." The false ideas are believed to be the result of some external forces, such as the mass media and liberal government programs intended to inspire greed and bribe consent. This idea does not generally involve any use of the specific idea of internal forces, other than one's own greed, that delude people. It seems to be based on an implicit idea that greed (or maybe fear) blinds one to what he would otherwise see as the truth, but there must be external forces to inspire and support the greed (or fear).

The important thing for our purposes is that the imputation of false consciousness is always made to one's enemy, never to one's allies, even when they are found to be in the same external circumstances as the victims and the imputation is almost always made with no specific evidence of the internal states of the victims. They are seen to disagree with what the politician thinks is true of their condition, so they are obviously wrong, and there must be something to cause their being wrong—i.e., forces causing false conciousness. Only fanatics can accept such absolutist proclamations.

The uses of the idea in depth psychology have almost all been in the form of the "unconscious," "counteraction" and "resistance." Most of these ideas are traced in some way to Freud's ideas about the unconscious and almost all of them assume that sexual fears are causing repression of experience that would otherwise be conscious. The more serious ones generally involve the idea of counteraction, that is, that the defenses against the repressed fears must themselves be emotionally maintained and that these emotions will be intense. (It is often said that the two emotions are as if on the ends of a seesaw, so that for one to go down the other must correspondingly go up.) Such repressed fears, then, are inferred from the emotional counterattacks, such as the intense hatred one expresses for "dirty sexual acts" or the violent anger with which one resists any suggestion that he might secretly want the same thing. These ideas were used by Freud and most other great psychoanalysts in a cautious manner. They systematically related inferences to the meticulous details of individual case reports. But any sociologist who has observed ordinary psychiatric and analytic work in recent decades knows they are now commonly bandied about with abandon, and that any opposition to them is resisted with such force that one is tempted to think of that resistance in terms of counteraction.

It is this sort of thing that led to the massive and abusive practices, such as "looping" or "turning one's ideas back on him," which Goffman and Szasz have so rightly attacked. That is, psychiatrists came to look routinely at any disagreement from patients with their off-the-top-of-the-head interpretations as instances of counteractive resistance. (We should point out, however, that a whole new wave of psychiatry has drawn on the ideas of humanistic psychology, existential psychology, Daseins analysis, and so on, so that these old abuses are being phased out.)

There is another form of this general idea that comes close to what we are talking about when we use the common-sense term self-deception (or self-delusion). This is the idea of "bad faith" found in the works of existential thinkers, especially those of Sartre. (See Fontana and Vandewater and Warren and Ponse in Douglas and Johnson, 1977.) Bad faith is thought to be some belief that springs from or is founded upon a profound feeling, such as a profound fear of death. The emotion, the fear, is dealt with or managed by the beliefs, which may in fact be a whole complex set of ideas, even a whole religion or political ideology. And these beliefs are generally, but by no means always, defended emotionally.

In these ways the idea is roughly like that of counteractive resistance. But there are at least two vital differences. First, the beliefs manage the emotions. They do not necessarily repress it, so they do not always force counteractive measures. They may, or they may not. The relations between the ideas and emotions are more complex. Sometimes the ideas allow the progressive changing of the underlying emotions, though this is probably rare. Second, and important for any research on such things, the protective nature of the belief, the way it is held precisely in order to protect one from the emotion, is in some way consciously experienced by the individual, however fleetingly, however much it may be only on the *fringes* of consciousness. It is this which makes it "bad faith," in some way dishonest, rather than merely repressive counteraction. The individual knows or grasps, though usually not in a verbalized form, that his belief is a self-deception, a way of hiding from his emotions. And he will sometimes reveal this guilty perception by averting his eyes and using other body language.

This is what we mean here, and roughly what we mean in common-sense discourse, when we talk of self-deceptions or self-delusions. A few points should be stressed and amplified.

First, there is a whole continuum, or continuous multidimensional universes, of experience involved here. At one end self-deceptions merge with and overlap with what we dealt with as evasions and lies. Evasions and lies are more conscious, more intended, more subject to conscious self-controls, more manipulable. At the other end, self-deceptions merge with and overlap with more repressed, more unconscious, more totally counteracted and resisted experience.

Second, self-deceptions are probably far more common than highly repressed, almost totally unconscious experience. There are generally times when any individual has fleeting grasps and even, less commonly, understandings of underlying fears or other emotions that lead to, inspire or support such deceiving beliefs. Doestoevsky and many others have described these times as moments of doubt, even panic, which reveal underlying emotions and from which we generally flee. This is especially the case in a pluralistic and conflictful social world such as ours in which almost any set of beliefs worked out to protect us from our fears are challenged by others, often with charges of self-deception. It is because of these pervasive instances of self-awareness of the deceit involved, or more commonly, the possibility of deceit involved, that individuals can look back upon earlier experience and, now being free of those emotions, "remember" their self-deceptions.

Third, it is very important for our sociological research purposes that most of these fleeting experiences of self-doubt, and grasp of the self-deceit involved in the beliefs, is largely unverbalized and usually unverbalizable. Pangs of doubt, pangs of guilt, twinges of guilt, or whatever, best describe these semi-conscious experiences. A vital part of cultural wisdom, though one too often overlooked by sociologists, is the fact that talking and linguistic categorization make things different. Human beings have devised immensely complex ways to avoid saying exactly what they see or grasp, of rationalizing and valuing these activities, and even to avoid thinking symbolically of what they're doing in terms that would make them feel dishonest, cheap, and so on.

For example, all successful forms of seduction probably involve the basic strategy of doing something without talking about it. Talk makes values and all our symbols relevant to the immediate, concrete situation: "The native hue of resolution is sicklied o'er by the pale cast of thought," so people use complex devices for avoiding verbalization in their own minds and, even more, in interacting with others.[4]

When we remember all of these things about human beings, about ourselves, how can we expect social research that is done primarily through talk, especially talk with academic strangers, to be a truthful picture of what people find their everyday lives in our complex society to be? The members themselves are often hiding from the verbal truth of what they may suspect or fear to be true. What could be more ridiculous than to assume they can tell it to some scientist who's going to publish it? Instead, in research settings they commonly add to their usual uncertainties, evasiveness, lies, fronts, and self-deceptions an extra layer of situated evasiveness, lies, front work and self-deceptions to hide themselves, to protect themselves from themselves and from researchers. (We shall return to this point in the next chapter.)

But, fourth, even these unverbalized, fleeting recognitions of underlying emotions that contradict our expressed beliefs are not always hidden from others. Body language and anomalies of verbal behavior are crucial for inferring them. The simplest and most abused are so-called Freudian slips, by which people reveal ("give off") their deeper feelings. More important and trustworthy are the pauses, shows of embarrassment, and eye motions. In general, they lead us to infer doubt and possibly some searching of one's fringe consciousness.

The researcher's initial idea that self-deceit is taking place is often a direct and spontaneous response to such body language. This idea is often an excellent hunch, an idea based on the semi-conscious grasping of what others are experiencing. But imputing self-deceit, even in oneself, is highly problematic and should always be done only with caution and systematic consideration of evidence.

Fifth, while the highly individualized forms of self-deception can be inferred only from observations of the individual and his situation, and are thus highly problematic for the researcher, most of the self-deceptions that interest social researchers are found in situations where there are clearly emotional conflicts. In the same way that lies and other forms of conscious falsehood abound in situations in which there is fundamental conflict between an absolutist, or merely dangerous, social world and private feelings and intentions, so do conflicts between our underlying feelings and our conscious thoughts abound in such a world. For example, one common way in which this happens is the result of so-called "cultural disjunctions."

The most obvious and patterned one in our society is adolescence, the period of disjunction between childhood and adulthood. As children we learned to see sex and many other things as evil. As the body comes to have intense new sexual feelings, and the social world begins to make new demands on us, we often go through a period of profound struggle to repress and hide from the sexual feelings and actions: "Not me!" "I don't really . . ." "I would never . . ." The counteraction involved in repressing these intense feelings, the expressions of belief and actions intended to absolve us of the guilt we feel for the almost inevitable sexual acts, such as masturbation, and the simply dishonest front work intended to deceive others, lead to many of the grandiose proclamations known as "youthful idealism."[5] In an era like our own in which sexual repression is reduced among the young of the upper middle classes, this same "youthful idealism" arises in the area of new cultural disjunctions, that of money and worldly success. Other age periods, such as middle age and retired age, show similar but possibly less patterned emotional conflicts and self-deceptions.[6]

There are several major realms of American society in which emotional conflicts are so intense that self-deceptions and all other forms of problematic meanings and falsehoods are pervasive and constitute crucial sociological aspects. First, there is the whole realm of death and dying. Heideggar and others who have seen the dread of death as the one crucial, pervasive, overriding motive in social life today have probably suffered from too much introspection. But there is little doubt that it is vital, pervasive and strong in much of our social lives; that is intrudes into the everyday concerns and actions of a large percentage of us; and that it is covered and hidden by convoluted layers of deception and problematic meanings.[7] Any sociological study would have to take these as crucial information, if it was to have any hope of understanding what the members were experiencing and what they were doing in hospitals, funerals and similar situations.

Another realm in which self-deceptions, combined with other deceptions, are crucial in understanding what is going on is that of economic success, status, class and social prestige in general. In a society as intensely competitive as ours and in which so much in our lives is determined by our success in economic and general status striving, yet in which many must be losers by the very nature of the struggle, it is certainly to be expected that this will be an area of intense emotional conflicts; and our expectations are fulfilled by any in-depth observations. Rather than having any clear-cut patterns of caste or class conflict, such as we find in societies in which these conflicts are between groups, rather than between and within individuals, we have convoluted, complex and individualized forms of social and individual emotional conflicts. Therefore we get all kinds of secret, often self-deceptive hatreds and resentments that pervade our economic, political and private lives in complex ways.[8]

Another area of our lives in which emotional conflicts and resulting self-deceptions are rampant is that of sexual feelings, meanings and actions.

Actually, this is one area in which people are now quite aware of *some* of the conflicts and the deceptions, at least the deceptions of others. But this awareness only goes so far. In a sense we can say that Americans are currently peeling off one layer, or a few layers, of conflicts and deceptions; but have yet to rid themselves of deeper layers. In this Freudian age they have become aware of the sexual desires and the deceptions associated with them over the centuries, but they are barely beginning to discuss the deep emotional conflicts over fears of sexual failures, and to realize the falsehoods and deceits that come from these fears. We found these conflicts and deceptions to be rampant and crucial in our study of nude beaches.[9] A consideration of how we inferred such conflicts and deceptions in several instances will show how such inferences are made in general, their problematic nature, their importance in understanding what people are doing and not doing, and their practical importance in making any effective social policies.

First, the researcher's general cultural experience and understanding and his personal emotional makeup are of vital importance in any attempts to get at such problematic in-depth feelings and meanings. It is essential that a researcher not have deep emotional hang-ups, that is, absolute commitments, about the area he is trying to study. This does not mean that he does not have conflicts, fears, excitement, and all the more normal feelings and thoughts. On the contrary, if he does not have these, he becomes an uninvolved researcher (a eunuch-researcher), one unable to feel the things the members do and therefore unable to grasp their feelings and meanings. The crucial thing is that he must not be *closed* to the situation; he must be open to it, able to experience it with some flexibility, lability, changeability. If he is too deeply committed to a feeling, ideology or pattern of practical action, his research will merely be a projection of his inner commitments.[10] One should have feelings, but not passionate and well-entrenched commitments. It's one thing for a noncustomer to study massage parlors. It's another for a nun to study them, or a politically ambitious city attorney.

Second, it is of tremendous value to a researcher to have the help of other researchers with complementary but different kinds of experience, commitments and feelings about the things to be studied. In some settings this may be a necessity. This will be clearer after our discussions of team field research, but it should be made clear here that this was important in our work on the nude beaches. The three team members covered a wide spectrum of cultural experience and understanding and personal feelings, beliefs and commitments; but none were at the extremes of being monkish or political partisans of sexual freedom.

Third, regardless of how much general cultural understanding a researcher has, he must always have a great deal of experience in the particular setting or the particular phenomena before he can begin to seriously infer such problematic feelings and meanings as self-deceptions. Certainly his general attitude of suspicion will lead him to wonder and suspect in many ways in the early stages, but he cannot reliably infer anything so problematic until he has had considerable experience and has made many preliminary attempts at inferences which he has subsequently tested out.[11] Without this, his inferences become nothing more than the omniscient assertions of the penny-dreadful novelist: "She could see from the way the stranger momentarily averted his eyes that he did not really believe what he had said."

The three examples of inferences I shall use all depend on prior in-depth experience and testing out of such inferences. It is this prior experience which had led us to understand that nudity is a very emotional subject for people (which almost anyone knows) and that those who purport to be unemotional about nudity are often, but not always, operating under some form of falsehood. We had learned this, for example, by watching people involved in the dispute over the nude beach move from quiet opposition to the beach on various "rational" grounds to screaming denunciations of the nudity, all in the space of brief meetings. We saw the nude beachers do the same kinds of things. This background understanding led us to be on the lookout for specific forms of falsehoods, including the self-deceptions so common in highly emotional situations. Our three examples are reasonably typical of the inferences we made from such observations.

First, let us consider an example of an inference I consider to be reasonably unproblematic, or reasonably reliable.

I had casually observed Phil's actions for months before I talked with him.[12] He was powerfully built, in his late twenties and, as he eventually told me, a successful salesman and part-time junior college student. He was very uptight about the scene. He came alone, sat alone in an isolated spot, talked to no one for months. If no one was near him (closer than about one tenth of a mile), he would slip his suit off while sitting down near the cliffs and when young women walked past by the water's edge he would walk in front of them to enter the water. I knew from our observations that this was a common pattern of body display, which generally involved sexual exhibitionism of various degrees as well; but newcomers did not realize it was so common as to be well-recognized by regulars. Over time he grew more bold—kept his suit off more, would get closer to women, watch their eyes, etc. I'd been talking with him for several months when he came up one day and started talking with me and another regular about the whole nude scene. "Hell, a lot of people think of it as such a sex scene that they're really uptight about it. My sister's visiting me and is thinking of coming down. I think she can handle it, so I was telling her that she just has to realize it's just natural. It's not some kind of sex scene, though there are bound to be some creeps around." The other guy mentioned he'd recently seen some people doing sex on the beach and couldn't understand why they didn't see that it would "ruin the beach for everyone" because of possible political repression. Phil warmly agreed and reasserted the need for naturalness. I soon walked on, but about an hour later saw him ahead of me, near his old isolation spot. As some young women came along he entered the water. I sat down near his things, pointedly looking elsewhere, since I figured he would be concerned with my seeing him. Some other women came by and he came out of the water. He came over, waved to me, exchanged a few remarks and said, "Some people really are uptight about the nudity. Did you see how those women turned their heads aside as I came out of the water?" I said simply, "Yeah, but I also noticed that they kept watching you until they got close enough for you to see their eyes." (This was a common voyeur pattern of concealment, especially among women.) I talked with him a bit about sex on the beach, hoping he might open up, but he soon turned the conversation aside.

My inference was that this was clearly a case of evasion and lying (personal front work), but probably with some situated variations in feelings and thoughts. He knew very well what his sex trip was and was using the strong assertions of naturalness and moralistic rejection of "creeps" to deny any ideas I might have had about his own actions being sexual, since he knew that I had seen him over a long period of time (though almost certainly not realizing how much I'd seen him). He was assuming what Laud Humphreys (1970) has aptly called the "breastplate of righteousness."

I consider the inference to be reliable because of my long observation of his actions. The repetition of them immediately after our talk means he could hardly have repressed the memory and his mentioning the women's actions shows a clear recognition of the meaning of the whole thing. (I wouldn't have doubted this anyhow, since the body communications were clear.) I believe he was simply feeling somewhat uptight about his sex trip, but that with some prolonged building of trust and drawing-out he will talk more openly about it, though never with complete honesty.

The second example is one provided us by our reliable teammate Carol Ann Flanagan about some roommates of hers.

I'd been going to the beach for quite a while and had a pretty good all-over tan. It looked real nice and my roommate Ellen decided that she too wanted a good tan to excite her boyfriend. Chuck had been sort of living with Ellen and me for a few months. Ellen was pretty free-spirited; but Chuck was almost a prude. I found out later that he objected to my occasionally answering a late night phone call nude or not bothering to cover up to come into the kitchen for a minute or two. That shocked me! There I was—naked on the beach all day in front of God and everybody—then to come home and have to put clothes on. In my own house! It was, to say the least, a bummer.

Well, Ellen wanted to go to the nude beach with me and told Chuck so. He put his foot down. He said absolutely and unconditionally, "No!" Ellen and I talked to him later about it. We wanted to find out his objection and get around it if we could. Ellen and I told him two girls would be safe—we could protect each other. Ellen said she would even keep on her bathing suit. But Chuck still said, "No!" Then we asked Chuck if he would go down with us—clothed or unclothed. Ellen for sure would be safe then. Ellen and I were puzzled. We really couldn't figure out Chuck's hang-up. He wouldn't even let her go down clothed, with two clothed chaperones. Ellen's last try was to promise not to look at any naked guys. Chuck looked embarrassed at this but still said, "No!"

I moved out soon after all this happened. I doubt that Ellen ever did get to the free beach. Last I heard she was doing a furtive topless trip on an isolated part of the South Del Mar beach, near where we lived. Ellen and I never really did figure out Chuck's objection. The only thing we came up with was that Chuck was a true-blue prude and was embarrassed at the thought of anyone looking at "his girl" or worse yet, of his girl digging looking at any naked bodies. Ellen and I desperately wanted to prove to him that the beach was really a mild sort of scene—nothing to get uptight about—but Chuck's mind is closed and he'll most likely never know the freedom of a free nude beach.

We came across many cases like Chuck, among both men and women. There was a clear pattern of moralistic refusal to let the loved one go to the beach combined with the heated assertion that their refusal had nothing to do with body fears or hang-ups—"It's just immoral." Chuck didn't say this last part, but we'd predict it because it was a basic pattern which we inferred in most cases to be self-deception. I would infer the same here, but obviously with little reliability. We did not carefully observe this concrete case and Carol Ann, who did, was uncertain.

The third case is a simple one we often faced.

I was walking along the beach one day when I spotted Jerry ahead of me lambasting some innocent with his moralistic preachments against the "Evils of Nudity and Fornication!" (Jerry was our self-appointed missionary from the Jesus movement.) As I came up to him and his victim I smiled and said "Be ye as the lilies of the field, brother," and walked on. Like most people on the beach, Jerry seemed to me interesting and okay. Then a young woman with her top off and bottom on came up to me and said heatedly, "Did that old nut attack you for being nude?" I told her he always did but he was okay and sincere. She said, "He might be sincere, but he's still nuts." She was really mad at him.

I inferred from all this that she was new at the beach (bottoms on), still felt uptight about it, and for this reason angrily and moralistically attacked Jerry. I suspected she was suffering from self-deception, but looked at this only as a suspicion to be checked out if she continued to come. She did not.

Conclusion

We have seen in the last two chapters that the problems facing a field researcher, especially in a setting where people are in conflict with other important parts of society or with themselves, are formidable. It is these problems and their growing importance that have led us and others (Dalton, 1959; and Humphreys, 1970) to develop investigative research methods. We shall now examine the major strategies for trying to solve these problems and then examine some more specific tactics for dealing with them.

NOTES

1. It was a basic mistake of the phenomenologists to assume that people of practical, common-sense affairs always have a natural or absolutist attitude toward their everyday lives. While there is commonly a willing suspension of disbelief (faith) in their everyday working activities during the work hours, simply because this is essential for getting much done, most people have their doubts and fears and are quite able in proper circumstances to bracket their world. Field researchers can get whole new perspectives on social life by getting at those people who will communicate about them. But we shall return to this in our discussion of friendly trust in the next chapter.

2. It is obvious in the case of Garfinkel's (1967) well-known lab experiment on rational accounts that this is the case. The subjects were in a lab, faced with academic scientists, and asked to deal with linguistic inputs controlled by the scientists. The subjects all insisted on finding some "rational accountability" of these inputs, even when they were randomized. They didn't think scientists would play games like that and they didn't want to be dumb or impute dumbness to the people providing the inputs. In natural settings where people are dealing with real-world, practical problems they make use of the ideas of absurdity, disorder, irrationality, unorganized, ludicrous, hilarious, insane, nutty, far-out, unhinged, all-messed-up, screwed-up, meaningless, dumb, beyond-me, random, off-the-wall, for-no-reason-at-all, nonsensical, and so on, with great frequency. For example, on the nude beaches the people were concerned with figuring out what the police were up to, especially after the passage of a new local ordinance making them subject to arrest for being out of the legally nude area. They watched the police and talked about what they were up to, trying to figure out their best strategies for dealing with them. People had many different ideas, simply because the actual police

practices, while being somewhat patterned, also had a great deal of variety and conflict in them. Some people would assert that it was all carefully planned this way. Others, who knew more from long experience with watching them (which was generally the gays) would often assert that "They like to keep you uncertain, to keep you guessing. That's why they do things that don't look sensible." I think there is a degree of truth to this. Police realize that keeping people uncertain, always guessing about their activities, will have more effect in "keeping the lid on" than if people can predict their actions. The same strategy is widespread—and, for example, is common in romantic strategies. But some of the police actions were most likely due to mere contingencies—being held up elsewhere, not seeing what someone thinks they do, etc. The gays were reacting roughly like the people in the lab. But there were also the people who simply asserted that "It doesn't make any sense at all," or "I can't figure out what they're up to," "What the hell do they think they're doing!?" and "Who knows what's legal?"

3. Ethnomethodologists often even define ethnomethodology in terms of studying the procedures by which the members give each other the sense that their actions are rational and ordered. (More simply, they often say they are studying everyday, common-sense rationality.) Even here, it is important to note that they have focused their enterprise on the study of the "sense" (or feeling?) of rationality. This is important because the sense of rationality is different from demonstrated or proven rationality. The sense of rationality is merely the feeling that it's organized or reasonable, which is generally experienced even when all kinds of unreasonable things happen, and when everyone knows that one couldn't demonstrate things rationally if the question were raised.

4. It's interesting that academics almost universally fail to see the need people have *not* to examine their own lives. We seem to take it for granted that "the unexamined life is not worth living"—and certainly not worth writing about. But this not only fails to note that this ancient maxim was perpetrated on Western Culture by one of the most dishonest, if lovable and well intended, rhetoricians in our history, Socrates. It also imposes a rationalistic straight-jacket on people's lives, something most people would abhor. Probably everyone, to varying degrees and in various ways, *must* lead a partly unexamined life, must live in "bad faith" because that's the only way life can be lived. Anyone who has ever had his everyday life assumptions suspended and faced the dread of death knows that life is impossible in those circumstances, that the joyful and creative forces of life are paralyzed and that we would probably all die without those protections, those evasions, those distractions, those hopeful half-beliefs-half-myths. Many people have peered into the bottomless abyss and understand this need. My Grandmother used to insist, quietly and patiently in the face of my youthful rationalism when I would argue over the apparent absurdities of her religion that "There are some things we should not think about." In reviewing all the evidence, who can truly assert that anyone has ever had the inhuman courage to live without his own protections, his own partially willing suspensions of disbelief. Consider, for example, the powerful thrusts against "bad faith" launched by the youthful Sartre. Youth is apt to agree uncritically with those arguments. Yet that same man later dedicated his life to the nineteenth century ideologies and programs of Karl Marx; and exalted "political commitment" above all else. If he should continue to attack "bad faith," which he may not, we would have to assume that he is either more dishonest or less wise than so many of the simple people of this world who have learned their own limitations, accept them, and embrace creative faiths grounded in real human experience.

5. The same social accounts of innocence and idealism serve the dual purpose of deceiving others and *partially* deceiving oneself. This is common and in any group where there is patterned deception some people will be doing it as self-deception while others

are doing it more as other-deception (front work), with all degrees and shifting back and forth of particular individuals in different situations.

6. I suspect, however, that old age, with its increasingly profound fears of loss of power (impotence, poverty) and fears of death will become our newly recognized age of senescent idealism. Perhaps the main thing working against this is that those who have been through intense self-deceptions previously, such as during adolescence, find it hard to be *that* deceived again. Older people thus far experience too much conscious self-doubt to attack the world in a fit of fiery, self-deceiving idealism. But human beings have always shown immense inventiveness in overcoming such rational problems when their fears are great. In a world in which the consolations of religion are increasingly in doubt for everyone and in which the old are precipitated into insignificance, those fears are immense. So far they have been dealt with largely by drugging the elderly who develop signs of "deep personal disturbance." High percentages of elderly people are addicted to high dosages of barbiturates, tranquilizers, methaqualudes, and dozens of related prescription and over-the-counter drugs. Their angry idealism is literally sedated, with drugs given such lovely names as Placidyl. It seems unlikely that this will always be true. (See Douglas, 1974b.)

7. All of my understanding of these deeper feelings and meanings of our everyday lives come from my own direct experience in our society. They are partly a matter of introspective self-observation. But they have also involved somewhat more detached, meticulous observations of others in natural settings where I was a member, but not deeply involved in the emotional events. But all of these others have necessarily been people with whom I am on intimate terms. Otherwise, I would never have known them well enough to grasp and understand their feelings and thoughts, which were almost always unexpressed by anything other than body language, if that. I would never have been able to persuade them to talk about their feelings and know if they were telling the truth later; and I would most likely not have been able to be involved in the natural setting. These observations and personal experience are the kind that are most reliable, but by that very fact the kind that cannot be reported because the reporting would involve too much betrayal of intimate relations. Someday I may report them in detail and analyze them under a pseudonym or in a novel where they can be dealt with as if they were not personal experiences, which is a common device for laundering the data. Sociologists more commonly report these as findings about other people and hide the ways their own experience has been crucial in understanding them. (They use the simple evasion of silence about how they know such things.) I can point out that this was partly true of my own first work, *The Social Meanings of Suicide*. The crucial stimulus to my concern with suicide and my whole approach to thinking about its problematic meanings, including whether a death is a suicide, came from the death of my brother. Yet this was only vaguely alluded to by dedicating the book to him, the significance of which only a few intimates could be sure.

8. Here, as in my other treatments of such in-depth observations, I have experienced this first hand as well. I came from a poor family that was also highly disreputable in many ways ("disorganized" in the extreme)—including breakups, work status (my mother supported us by working as a barmaid), sexual deviance and police problems. These did not involve great emotional conflicts as long as we lived within the world of people who lived the same way, though certainly they involved emotional conflicts; everyone's life does. (These emotional conflicts had to do primarily with sexual matters, rather than anything economic.) But when I began to aspire to a different social world, for which economic matters were more relevant, I began to feel resentments and even hatreds, though I fought against these and tried to deny them. I became an idealistic democratic socialist in high school and remained so through graduate school.

9. We found the same conflicts and self-deceptions in all other sexual scenes observed. For example, masseuses, who tend to hold rather liberated views of all sexual matters, were often involved in such conflicts and deceptions with their boyfriends and others, even when the boyfriends knew all about the job. (They generally did not know all about the job from the girls, since the girls often lied to the boyfriends.) We concluded that the conflicts and deceptions were roughly the same and just as intense in any setting. What varied was the substance of conflict and deceit. For example, a straight couple might argue bitterly over a partner's showing interest in someone else, while a masseuse and her boyfriend would lie and argue bitterly over whether the girl went beyond oral sex—oral sex being okay, but intercourse constituting betrayal.

10. The best sociologists have always recognized this and refused to study what was too close to their hearts. As one sociologist told me, "I've never studied race in any way and never will, because it's something that I feel too deeply about." He could not have been open to the experience and would surely have "found" the things he already believed. If all sociologists had the honesty and self-control of this man, we would not be faced with the great problem we have now of sociologistic ideology disguised as sociology.

At the same time, they recognized the need for some involvement, but not too much, in the distinction they made between empathy, or the ability to feel with the subjects, and sympathy, or allowing one's feelings to effect one's thoughts or analyses of the subjects. I think earlier discussions of this important point (including my own in *Research on Deviance,* Douglas, 1972b) were too simplified and made too sharp a distinction. I have thus avoided using the terms here.

11. Testing out should not be confused with checking out (which we shall discuss in the next chapter). Testing out involves a careful evaluation of inferences or ideas to see how much it helps the researcher to understand what is going on. It is a more abstract, theoretical activity than checking out, which generally involves comparing something (such as a statement about what one does) with something more reliable (such as secret observations of what the person does).

12. I casually observed and collected information on at least a few hundred people in the same way over more than a year. I patrolled the beach each late afternoon all year long. As I ran, walked and, once in a while, sat on a rock, I could see what different people were doing as far away as a half mile, especially in the off-season when there would be relatively few people on the beach. Anyone who has never bothered to look at what people are doing at great distances may find this hard to believe. I don't think I knew it before. But with practice you can spot people by their walk, the fuzzy outline of their hair, and so on, the same way someone who is suspiciously watching for information given off by body behavior and subtle forms of linguistic communications can "see" or grasp a great deal more than those who are "letting it pass," merely doing interaction for the practical or sociable purposes at hand.

Chapter 6

THE GENERAL STRATEGIES OF INVESTIGATIVE
FIELD RESEARCH: DIRECT EXPERIENCE

In the last two chapters we have seen the most difficult problems a field researcher encounters; and we have shown how he deals with these problems. We can now return to our discussion of the general strategies of field research begun in Chapter 2, where we were concerned with the choice of methods, the mixing of different methods, and some problems of timing. In this chapter and succeeding ones we shall be concerned first with the overall strategy and then with some more specific tactics used in face-to-face research situations, all of which make use of the more general strategies.[1] (We shall assume throughout our discussions in this chapter that scientific truth is our primary goal. If one were seeking information with more immediate practical goals, he would modify these ideas in terms of our discussion in Chapter 1.)

The overall picture of the general strategy is simple enough. *Direct experience* is the primary goal and generally the first part of the research. In the process of gaining direct experience, and as a means to more of it, we establish *friendly and trusting relations* which provide us with key informants to tell us about things we have not directly experienced ourselves. While we always try to establish personal, friendly, trusting relations with informants, this is not always possible. Sometimes we must use *interview situations* because this is the only way we can get at some situations; it is less reliable than direct experience. Consequently, we always try to *check out* information received in this way. Checking out consists of getting direct experience, if possible. When not possible, it involves a number of other steps, such as the well-known method of getting *independent confirmations* from members and *independent retests* from other researchers.

In all of these situations it is possible to use a number of clearly defined *interaction tactics* to establish friendly trust (intimacy): fish and catch out, draw out, open up, set up, tie them up, string along, and blackmail. All of these strategies and tactics involve complex and artistic uses of common-sense theories of persons, truth-telling, and lying, such as how to tell whom to trust or when someone is telling the truth or lying, something the researcher must be aware of as part of his or her taken-for-granted methods in evaluations of his findings.

We shall examine some of the further aspects of each of these major strategies and tactics before going on to consider the uses of team field research.

Our discussions of specific strategies and tactics must always be put in the general context of the overall research goal and plan; and each strategy, and even more each tactic, has to be seen in relation to the others. Obviously, for example, if we have already decided that our general cultural understanding is adequate for the practical policy goal we have, and as a result we have decided on doing a questionnaire study, then all of these strategies may be irrelevant. Again, when we are talking about the reliability of the findings being directly dependent on the degree of direct involvement, this has to be weighed in relation to the other factors. If, for example, he has a wealth of independent retests by other researchers, then those retests may raise serious doubts about any contradictory findings from direct experience of his own.

We shall be considering the whole question of how one is to weight factors throughout our discussion. But it must be remembered that this is an artistic activity; some wise recipes can help, but none can eliminate the necessarily problematic nature of social research. All strategies and tactics must be artfully applied to the concrete situation the researcher faces.

The Major Issues Concerning the Use of Direct Research Experience

Direct experience is the most vital basis for all of the researcher's further methods of getting at the truth. All other methods rely ultimately, though in different ways and in varying degrees, upon his own direct experience or at least that of fellow researchers whom he knows intimately, trusts, and with whom he can communicate well. In general, the less direct his own experience (or that of fellow researchers) of the things he is reporting about, the less reliable his report must be considered to be (until proven otherwise by independent research reports). When he relies upon trusted informants to tell him the truth of what is going on he is relying, knowingly or unknowingly, upon his experience, however direct or indirect, to talk about the setting, to determine how much he should trust the informant in general, and to estimate how truthful this particular report of the informant is. (Someone who is truthful about almost everything may still be totally dishonest about one specific thing.) When he relies upon checking out what one person tells him with others, he relies upon his own experience in each case; and so on down the list of methods we shall consider in succeeding chapters.

This does not mean that the researcher will report only on those things of which he has direct experience. As we said in the beginning, there are all kinds of situations in which we are willing to accept less than perfection in social research, just as in anything else in life. But it is important for us to know whether research information is based on direct experience or on some other form of information, so that we can weigh the information accordingly and estimate how much we are able to rely on it for scientific or practical purposes.

There are all degrees and extents of direct participation and involvement. The classical field researchers were generally concerned only with the degrees of participation or involvement, ranging from casual interview participation to going native, and the effects on the findings. Certainly this is a vital dimension.

But there is the partially independent dimension of the *extent* of participation. One can be deeply involved in a setting without being extensively involved. The question of extension involves two major aspects. It involves the traditional questions of representability, or how adequately the findings represent the larger universe of people and similar settings. But it involves as well the question of contextualizing one's findings; that is, telling us what the larger context is and thus telling us a lot about the in-depth findings as well. For example, in studying TV news people it is one thing to tell us how representative a particular practice is of TV news people generally, but it is another thing to tell us about the larger context of their work, that is, the relations between the news people and the production, the sales and managerial people, their dependence on professional activities, and their involvements in society generally and the relations of this to newswork (e.g., political influences on their work).

In his study of news work, Altheide (1976) was concerned both with different kinds of news people and their work (representability), and with the more general context of their work, which he considered in terms of "zones of relevances," or the ways in which different external factors affected what went on in the newsroom.

In line with their almost exclusive concern with the degree of involvement, the classical field researchers generally failed to consider these two major aspects of the extent of participation. But even those researchers who have understood the necessity of getting such representative and contextualized information have rarely been able to do so for two reasons.

First, and most important, in-depth involvement often precludes extensive involvement. This is due primarily to the fact that in-depth involvement generally gets the individual identified with one group or setting and intra-setting conflicts make him suspect in other parts. There are also other reasons why an individual may not be able to get involved in other parts of the setting, such as the unsuitability of his particular characteristics. His age, sex, financial status, personal characteristics and so on may be unacceptable to members in other parts of the setting. And it is sometimes due partly to the problems of over-involvement which have concerned classical researchers, though they greatly overestimated these problems. We shall return to these two problems shortly.

Second, in-depth involvement generally makes it practically impossible for the individual to spend enough time in other parts of the research setting. These extreme difficulties are the major reasons we have developed team field research methods to replace the solo methods. We shall leave most of the methods of dealing with problems of extensive field research until later chapters, and concentrate now on the methods and problems of direct experience.

The classical field researcher's view of direct experience was always ambivalent. Sharing the positivist view that personal, subjective involvement necessarily produces bias, they were anxious to avoid too much involvement ("over-rapport") with their subjects. They assumed that involvement and bias varied directly, so involvement and objective findings varied inversely. But they also knew that many settings could only be penetrated by direct involvement. So they took a compromise position: The researcher should become as involved as necessary to establish the trusting relations necessary to get members to tell him what was going on and to be able to observe some things directly; but he should not go beyond this and should never become a member. "Going native" was a primordial sin, and "being native" to begin with was unspeakable (and thus hidden). Since this compromise inevitably opened the door to bias, it was generally assumed that the researcher would be sympathetic to the subjects, would be "on their side," but it was hoped the report would be only partially biased.

In Chapter 2 we argued that research situations today demand more in-depth methods to penetrate pervasive falsehoods and evasions. In Chapter 5 we saw that there are deeper and more important reasons to become deeply involved in a research setting. Let us examine in more detail the ways in which in-depth involvement allows us to get at otherwise unavailable aspects of our social lives and examine whether this does necessarily bias our findings and reports.

The most extreme form of in-depth involvement is natural, everyday experience with no significant thought of analyzing or using the experience for scientific purposes. The most extreme form of in-depth involvement we can have as scientists doing research is what we call depth probes, which involve de-focusing, deliberately allowing oneself to simply experience the setting as much as possible like any other new member, but retaining the background commitment to being a social researcher and later returning to more systematic observation, description, and analysis of the setting. Either one of these gives the individual one overriding advantage over all other forms of social research. Both allow him or her to feel the way members feel and to grasp the sense of (intuit) the setting the way they do. In this way they provide the researcher with direct access to the crucial information about people's lives, the raw material (phenomena) of their lives, out of which he can construct his own scientific understanding to communicate to others. If he does not have that direct experience, he is forced to rely upon the members to communicate it to him, which makes him dependent upon their honesty and their abilities to symbolize their experience.

In certain settings there can be little controversy, other than "moral" ones, over whether we should study them by becoming members. These are settings which allow *only* the initiated, the members, to enter. The most obvious instance of this is the absolutist, exclusivist, secretive religious organization. For some of these religious groups, secrecy, especially in the form of *sanctum sanctorum,* is itself a crucial part of the religion and only the totally committed are allowed to penetrate the secret. Robbins, Anthony and Curtis (1973) encountered this situation in studying a Jesus group and eventually withdrew from the study. They felt they could not honestly accept the faith and did not wish to lie. Jules-Rosette (1974) and Hayward faced the same situation in studying a Christian group in Africa, but they did become members and reported on it from the inside.

Unfortunately, most other forms and instances of depth-probe research have been the subjects of controversy in the social sciences for the past century. We must deal with each of these major controversies and show that they have been based on misconceptions of research generally and of depth-probe research specifically. But at each step let us keep in mind what we have emphasized from the beginning: the obvious basis in all our experience for trusting direct experience over all other forms of knowledge. If someone wanted to write a book about the Alps, would he or she do so without going to see them? If he wanted to write about the behavior of lions, would he write a book without having direct experience of lions? If he were writing about a famous political figure, he might feel forced to do so without ever being able to communicate directly with that person, but he would have no question about the desirability of direct communication. When one's concern is the experience of people, the way they feel, think and act, the most truthful, reliable, complete and simple way of getting that information is to share their experience. All other methods are indirect and are therefore compromises, to be accepted only when made necessary by practical constraints. This truth is so obvious that it has rarely been challenged, nor have questions even raised by classical field researchers or by those committed to more controlled methods. Instead, they have argued that the compromise of controls is necessary because direct experience involves some inevitable and unsolvable problems of its own. I believe when we examine each of these in detail we find that, while each is directed at some real abuses, they are really based on misconceptions of the ways direct experience can actually be used. They have mistaken the inadequate and abusive uses as necessary aspects of direct, member experience.

The argument against the use of natural experience and depth-probe experience as scientific data arose historically because of the 19th-century use of "arm-chair" methods and the similar empathetic and introspective methods of contemporary philosophers, including phenomenologists and linguistic philosophers. These methods involved looking at one's own internal feelings and thoughts about something and using that as data about the experience of the members. This practice was picked up by functional sociologists who, generally unknowingly, used their own ideas about social class, suicide, delinquent acts, political corruption, and so on, as "data" about the internal states of the members. (See the discussion of Durkheim's *Suicide*, in Douglas, 1967. Also see Douglas, 1971.) Looking at one's own direct experience as basic information came to be a primal sin, and any classical field researcher who used his own account of his feelings or thoughts in the situation as data would have been excommunicated. (They did sometimes tell a bit about their initial thoughts in the situation but, as John Johnson argued, 1976, they seldom mentioned their own feelings in the situation. They became the omniscient third person narrator so well-known from novels.) The crucial difference between depth-probe research and introspective methods is that the depth prober immerses himself in the actual situation and then, at least once he has reached the stage of active research, observes concrete instances of his feelings and thoughts in the situation. He does not think of "what it might be like," but rather, does concrete, situated self-observations. In general, the depth-probe field researcher performs self-observation, not introspection.[2]

The second major misconception of the nature of depth-probe research has been based on the assumption that direct involvement will lead one to experience the setting in a biased manner. This idea is a simple extension of the common-sense idea that "the lover sees the loved one through rosy glasses." Like most clichés, this one contains an important truth. There are certainly incorrigible romantics who insist on seeing only the most beautiful, most ideal, most everything splendid about their crowd, their families, their things, their selves, their anything. These are the people who "could never believe" or "never think such things." But the rosy-glasses argument is counterbalanced by the common-sense idea that "familiarity breeds contempt," and the two are put together in the popular idea that young lovers see each other in rosy colors but come to have little respect for each other after years of marriage. In the common-sense view, rosy appearances are maintained by ignorance and secrecy, not by direct, prolonged experience.

It is those who look at the world in the abstract—the abstract theorists, theologians and functionalists—who hold rosy idealized views of our social world, making it all look like the unfolding of abstract values or ideals. People who get deeply involved in a society seldom have such rosy views.[3] Those researchers who try to study the world by means of questionnaires or other methods which allow them to avoid all "vulgar contact" with the realities of the world are the ones who are more apt to maintain their rosy views—from the university office high above the "maddening crowd."

There is a third and more serious argument closely related to the rosy-glasses one. This is the argument that one who becomes deeply involved enough to feel the way members do will wind up being biased in his understandings—that is, he will suffer self-deceptions. As we have argued at length in the last chapter, self-deceptions are a pervasive part of our lives. But we argue that these occur primarily when one feels deep emotional conflicts, so that one part of the experience has to be repressed, for the most part pushed out of conscious experience. We have already tried to show that this can be dealt with partly by choosing situations in which one does not have deep emotional conflicts, or getting out of those where he finds he does, and by using team members to counterbalance one's own conflicts and self-deceptions. But even more important, those who have no direct experience also have deep emotional conflicts. Indeed, a major reason why some sociologists choose library or questionnaire methods is because they have deep emotional conflicts about all involvement in their society. These conflicts lead to self-deceptions far more easily when they can use methods that never force them into direct contact with the concrete realities. Abstract methods allow far more self-deception than direct experience, since one can use abstract methods to avoid seeing facts that disagree with his self-deceptions. One can, then, argue that the prevalence of self-deceptions in human life means that social research and social thought remain necessarily more problematic than the study of stones or trees; but it is ridiculous to argue that one can avoid such problems by using abstract methods which actually compound them.

Another form of the direct-experience-breeds-bias argument is that direct member experience leads to special pleading, that is, to insider accounts which are *intended* to hide the politically disadvantageous aspects and reveal the politically advantageous. The world is full of special-pleading books, news stories and magazine articles glorifying everything from the Black Panthers to Richard Nixon. Anyone who has studied social problems, crime, and deviance is aware of this (see Douglas, *Research on Deviance*, 1972b). I have little doubt that there are people who deliberately hide things they have learned through research because of their political commitments to the group they studied.

Indeed, at times I have made this a subject of study in itself. For example, in our study of nude beaches (1977b) we came across one "social researcher"[4] who knew about the sex on the beach but thought we should not report it. He himself did a questionnaire study of the beach in which no one told of the sex. His report failed to reveal what he knew to be true and important because it would be politically harmful to the nude beach. But we did report on it, although we had used depth-probe methods and one of us had been a member long before she became a researcher, and though we were indeed sympathetic to the cause of the beach and against the use of police power to restrict it. Also, being involved and against police power did not make us see the police as "fascist-pigs." Rather, we came to see most of the police as against the law, but a few (mainly one) as using it and other laws to hassle the people. Nor did we come to see or report on the property owners or politicians as "evil repressors." It is true that the property owners probably look "unsympathetic" from the standpoint of most people, but this is because of their own values as judged by most readers, not because of our "doing a job on them." I would also point out that this "unsympathetic picture" was presented in spite of the fact that I had (and hopefully still have) much closer friends among the property owners than among the nude beachers, and that my personal interests are far more tied up with the property owners than the nude beachers. As my team members are aware, I was sorry that many of the nude beachers would inevitably be upset at our reporting on them, but I was even sorrier at what I expected from the property owners who were friends and colleagues. (We tried to evade the whole thing, and to avoid any political effects, by keeping the work secret from both sides as long as possible.)

Rather than seeing or reporting on "good guys" (control agents) and "bad guys" (deviants), we saw and reported complex and changing conflicts of many different kinds, with falsehoods, problematic meanings and self-deceptions all around in different ways and to varying degrees. Similar things could be said about most of the better field research reports in sociology: Becker's (1963) member involvement with jazz musicians; Dalton's (1957) member involvement with men who manage; Marvin Scott's (1969) involvement from childhood with jockeys and trainers; Johnson's (1973) close and sympathetic involvement with caseworkers; Altheide's (1976) close and sympathetic involvement with TV news people; and Warren's (1975) close and sympathetic involvement with a male gay community. All of these and many more report illegal, shady or deviant activities (from the standpoint of the middle-class public) which the members would prefer were not reported, which could be used against the members by political enemies, and which the authors might prefer did not exist.

No doubt there are lies and coverups done by field researchers, though most of the ones I know of consist of the evasion technique of silence (not studying, and leaving unsaid, certain things about their own methods of study). They launder the data about their own involvements, but protect the members by anonymity or else by not studying them in the first place. Any forms of political bias that one finds in field research, such as choosing what to study and not to study, almost always comes *before* the study, not as a result of the involvement. (See also Becker, 1970, pg. 43.) And the same things are just as true or more so of any other method. In fact, in many ways it is easier to be silent and lie with questionnaire data than with detailed facts of field observations. How easy it is *not* to do certain studies, *not* to ask certain questions, *not* to report one's findings; how easy to juggle the data and analyses. In fact, the one blatant instance of data juggling to which I've been privy in sociology was done in a big questionnaire study of prison recidivism. The researchers had done their analysis and found the initial hypothesis of the whole study and the program to be false. The director of the study insisted that the analysis must have gone wrong and instructed them to "reanalyze" the findings of the research. They understood what he meant, reanalyzed it to find that the program worked, and it was accepted as true. It's really much easier to lie with "hard numbers" than to lie with the detailed observations of natural settings—though that too can be done, especially if one does it alone and just carefully takes statements out of context. (Decontextualizing statements in order to change the meanings is the major device used by political journalists to "knife" people. See Douglas, 1977a.) As Alvin Gouldner (1968) argued, honesty is an independent variable in social research.

A fourth objection to in-depth involvement is that one comes to take the meanings for granted, so he cannot observe them to report on them. This is no more of a problem for one doing field research, even a depth probe, than for any other method, because he is *becoming* a member, he is not a member of long standing. But it is a problem for someone trying to turn his long-standing membership experience into data for observation and analysis.

This problem, however, is the same one faced by any sociologist trying to turn everyday life itself into an object of study. Looking at what one has normally taken for granted and analyzing what before has been only sub-consciously grasped is the crucial step I would call "taking the sociological perspective." (It has also been called "taking the theoretic stance," "topi-calizing," "thematizing," and so on. See Douglas, 1970d.) It is a difficult perspective for most people to take, and impossible for some, simply because they find it hard, or uncomfortable, or impossible to observe themselves either during natural experience or just after. There is nothing startling about that. Everyone knows some people are more self-conscious and reflective than others and that everyone is more so in some settings than others. Those who are more able to do self-reflection are more apt to make good analytical field researchers, though some who are not particularly self-reflective might be extremely good at some field research tasks (such as gaining entree, or building friendliness and trust). This is the same as saying that some people find it distasteful or impossible to look at the world as something to be recreated in art, so they will not be good at naturalistic painting, or that some people do not like to think numerically, so they aren't likely to be good at mathematics.

The first important point, then, is that one who is not good at observing his own experience is not well-suited to doing the second most important thing a sociologist must do, regardless of his method. (The first thing a research sociologist must do is be able to *do* social life.)[5]

The second point, however, is that most people can learn to become more self-reflective by trying, by practice in observing and carefully describing their experiences in concrete details soon after they have happened. A field researcher needs years of experience in interacting as a researcher, learning to allow himself to flow freely with experience at one time, soaking up observa-tions, then turning reflectively upon that experience to make and describe self-observations and observations of others, grasping the sense of the setting, and finally trying to systematically understand and report the setting to outsiders. This experience will make those especially adept at such things more skilled at them than they would ever have imagined possible. As the Chicago sociologists have long maintained, even the ability to remember discussions is vastly improved through such experience. Like composing or painting or doing mathematical calculations in one's head, field research is a specialized task, demanding special abilities, but those abilities can be greatly improved by experience. Just as musicians watch for those special abilities that make great performers and composers, so must social researchers watch for those special abilities that make one a great field researcher and then help to develop those people into superb performers.[6]

Even if one can observe himself and others and report on those observations in this way, there remain two further questions concerning whether this in-depth involvement will allow him to experience the situation in the way members do. The major objection to this approach has been sharpened and advanced by the ethnomethodologists, but it is shared by many others in somewhat different forms. Following the phenomenologists, the ethnomethodologists look at meaning as the crucial factor in individual and social life and they define meaning, either explicitly or implicitly, as symbolic or cognitive (and rational), especially linguistic, experience. They argue that individuals in any situation construct the meanings (accounts) of the situation, and thus project or present their actions, in terms of these symbolic meanings. Most of them believe that, while particular constructions are certainly contingent upon the situation at hand, ultimately all such constructions are done in terms of previously learned symbols and invariant properties or rules, commonly called interpretive procedures, deep linguistic rules, etc. (See Douglas, 1970d.) The result is that, while there may be vast variability, even apparent "creativity," in concrete, situated constructions of meanings, these meanings inevitably wind up being "displays" of the previously learned categories and invariant deep rules. Ethnomethodologists then argue that, since sociologists are seeking these deep properties lying behind the appearances, the research findings of sociologists are really themselves symbolic displays of previously learned symbols, or categories of experience, and theoretical ideas which the sociologist may use to "document" his ideas.

The model of research they present, and one actually pursued by some of them in the form of qualitative computer simulations, is that of a sociologist-computer with built-in, pre-established categories and category relations (invariant procedures for combining categories) which the sociologist-computer uses to categorize and analyze his scannings of the social setting and then to display as documentation for other people-computers.

The upshot of the whole complex argument, which is even more complex than this, is that the field researcher necessarily perceives the research setting in terms of his categories and theoretical ideas, so he should make these explicit and try to see how it is they produce or constitute the description (account) of the setting.[7] Many of their field methods are aimed at doing simply that.

This rationalistic, close-ended model of human thinking, like all earlier rationalistic models, fails almost immediately because it doesn't fit the obvious facts. If it were true, human beings would all think in the same ways and individuals would not change basic ideas. While it is probably true that there is something mentalistic shared by us all, which does not change for any (normal) individuals, it is not now known and is not of any significant concern to those who are interested in the concrete realities of our social worlds. The question that concerns us as researchers is whether we are able to experience things the way the members do when we get deeply involved or whether our particular theoretical ideas as sociologists lead us to distort that experience—does our sociological experience prevent our experiencing it the way they do? Let us consider three forms of evidence.

First, we can note our experience in research settings compared to what we expected it to be. Like other people, we find that our experience, especially our feelings, are different in the setting from what we expected them to be; they are definitely situated and not predictable in any way from our being sociologists. We found this to be true from the beginning of our nude beach experience. From the abstract point of view of the sociological theorist, joining a nude beach doesn't seem like a major undertaking. Who hasn't gone skinny-dipping (private nude bathing) or been through medical exams? Besides, it's "only natural" and a researcher has the mantle of research to cover up any feelings of creepiness. That's more or less the way we thought of it.

But it was wrong, as we discovered immediately. Let any researcher try it. Let him go to a real nude beach, with lots of strangers running around nude, unprotected by any official religion, and take his clothes off. Unless he's one of a very small minority, such as those who have been into lots of casual sex, he'll quickly discover a concrete reality. It's *very* emotional, very conflictful, confusing, hard to grasp in words, slippery. He'll probably find it hard to think. Yet this is the opposite of what one might expect, or conclude from watching newcomers, before he's had that personal experience. Most people look stringently unconcerned when they first take off their clothes. ("Oh, how natural. Excited? Scared? Creepy? Who, me? Oh, man, look how natural and unconcerned I look! Notice how I keep looking you straight in the eye, steadily, unremittingly, unflinchingly.") A few males are betrayed by their immediate erections, but most people look overnaturalized, kind of like corpses, only the nuances of overnaturalness aren't apt to be spotted until experience demonstrates that the natural look is not true. One must *grasp* the experience before he knows how to interpret the new body language he's seeing. Someone doing team research, as we did, can get help from fellow researchers by having them describe their grasp of things. But even this can be problematic in unusual settings and the researcher needs the same kind of experience they've had to be able to communicate with them most effectively.

For example, one of my fellow researchers was quite verbal about her feelings of being uptight about the whole thing. But the other researcher didn't tell me for months how mind-blowing his first experience had been. I'd been into the scene for some time when he came down with me for the first time. I assumed he was feeling uptight to some degree, both because of my own earlier experience and because of his sudden discovery of the virtues of taciturnity. He kept saying "Uh, yeah. . . ." But it wasn't until several months later at a dinner party that his wife revealed that he had told her the first evening that he could hardly follow what I was saying and kept worrying that he would say the wrong thing. *Then*—months later—he opened up about it. This kind of experience illustrates that the sociologist is open to new and unexpected experience in the setting and that this is vital to understanding the setting from the member's standpoint, especially when the member prefers to deny the whole thing.

The second form of evidence to show if sociologists can be open to the situation, if they choose to be, is finding if initial ideas they did have are wrong, or misconceived. (See Becker, 1970, pg. 43.) If one has adopted a closed stance, such as that of a controlled researcher who insists on making all decisions before the research begins, then he will probably never discover if his initial conceptions are wrong or not even understood by the people he is questioning. If, on the other hand, he is open, he looks for these differences in those cases where for some practical reason he has not been able to de-focus in the beginning. When he finds them, he changes his research. This, for example, is what we did in policy-oriented research on drug crisis intervention (Douglas, 1974b). When we found that our initial formulation of the crises was not working in talking with the members we changed our terms and our whole research plan. We wound up studying drug problems in the streets and in the ambulances, something we had not thought of doing before the research began. We were open to the new experience even in a policy-oriented study with considerable time constraints.

Another obvious bit of evidence that seems to support the critics' contention, but which also fails to do so on examination, is a common observation of field researchers that the notes they make in the beginning of research later turn out *not* to have included much of what they later grasp as being crucial about the setting. This seems to be directly related to the use of earlier ideas to make sense of what is going on in the new setting. In the new setting the individual is continually making conscious sense of it in terms of earlier categories and ideas. It is these conscious categorizations that he remembers best when he writes them down at the end of the day. But at the same time he has been subconsciously experiencing fleeting perceptions, feelings and ideas which are particular to the new situation. As he experiences these more, he becomes more conscious of them and begins to consciously categorize them, either in terms of the members or, if they have little language to describe them, in terms he himself creates (this will be discussed later).

The crucial point of the argument is that individuals, especially rational-istic academics, often do try to make symbolic sense out of new settings in terms of old ideas and that this causes them to be less aware of new things they are experiencing in the setting. Certainly the tendency is to do this anyway, since the individual tries to use learned experience that has worked in the past, but it is made all the worse by conscious attempts to do just this.

For this reason we have adopted the opposite strategy. Rather than to relate the new experience to old ideas, according to our strategy the re-searcher tries to de-focus, to stop thinking of his new experience in terms of prior categories and ideas. Instead of approaching the new setting with the idea that somehow the members' linguistic accounts are going to be situated or occasioned, or with some other preconceived sociological concept or idea, the researcher goes in wide-eyed, like anyone else. ("Wow, what's going on here?") He flows with the experience—he lives it, does it. The only reason he would even think about it enough in the beginning to describe it in words would be to analyze his methods. Trying to do this while learning to get along in the new setting, to be like others there, is tremendously difficult, calling for the ultimate and most agonizing form of self-reflection, something which is best left to the most experienced specialists in field research. (John Johnson, 1976.)

Another objection typically made to the in-depth field research aimed at getting at the experience from the standpoint of the members bears on this point of de-focusing. Some sociologists argue that the researcher can't forget being a sociologist, that he can and will return to the office, so he can never really de-focus that identity. I suppose there may be people who are so completely committed to being professional sociologists that they can never escape the thought that they are Sociologists. If so, they shouldn't be field researchers, any more than someone with a tin ear should try to compete with David Oistrakh. I suspect the professional hang-up is really something felt mainly by young sociologists, especially graduate students who are going through anxious years of initiation and identity crises.[8] But over time they learn to separate their existential selves, their real inner selves, from the external roles, in the same way doctors or masseuses, or almost anyone else dealing with the public, learn to separate their own feelings from their activities.

This, of course, does not mean a sociologist can walk into a slum and feel what it's like to be poor all his life, anymore than it means a college president can work over the summer as a common laborer to feel what it's like to be a common laborer all his life, or that a senator's family can learn what it feels like to be poor by eating on the same amount the poor eat for a few weeks. All of these are presently popular forms of political pseudo-information used to dramatize political programs[9] and make it appear that the individual has a form of direct experience from which to say the things he always said before he had the experience. Nor, most emphatically, does it mean that a researcher can stage pseudo-natural experiments, commonly called role play in contemporary social psychology, to get at the way members think and feel.[10]

Any such ideas share a common fallacy: They implicitly assume that experience is or can be made totally situated. Whereas the classical methods of field research, and even more the controlled methods, make the opposite mistake of assuming that a person can step into someone else's situation (or shoes) and thereby have his experience. They fail to see that most experience is both situational and transsituational. In particular, they fail to see that each person's experience in a situation has a biographical context.[11] Someone who has lived in a slum all his life has very different feelings and thoughts about it than what a middle-class or upper-class sociologist might have.

Psychologists have dealt with such differences in terms of adaptation levels. They have found, as people often find from common experience, that even the smell of places is different over time. A slum may smell terrible to an outsider, but within a matter of weeks or months an inhabitant no longer notices the smell. This can be even more striking in the case of people going from urban to rural areas or to different societies where sewage and night water are pervasive aspects of everyday life—to an outsider. A modern American or European would probably have found even royalty of the Middle Ages unbearably smelly because of different habits of personal hygiene and adaptations to smell. The same is true of other aspects of life as well, including such things as the standard of living. No doubt the mass media and political actions have led to some widespread sense of "differential deprivation" among the poor, but their comparison standards are still different from those of the middle and upper classes. More important, even when they talk middle-class rhetoric, they may have very different feelings about the terms.

The implication for field research is simple and direct. We never ask a method to do something it cannot. Short-run depth probes cannot provide a biographical context that takes years or a lifetime to establish. They cannot, therefore, provide us with immediate experience of what it's like to be an inhabitant of a slum all one's life, any more than they can tell us exactly what it's like to be a Samoan adolescent chasing bronzed bodies under the palms.

But longer periods of in-depth experience do provide us with the best form of direct experience we can ever hope to have and they provide us with the experience we need to be able to establish friendly and trusting relations with those who do have that biographical context and to be able to check out and test out what they tell us as best we can. They do this only to the extent that we can approximate that situated and biographically contextualized experience. Living for three years with the people being studied (as William Foote Whyte did) is immensely more reliable than driving through the slums or role playing by eating the same food they do for a few weeks. (Eating "soul food" doesn't give one "soul" any more than eating the tongues of humming birds makes one an aristocrat.) And living with the people as one of them, as one able to immerse himself unself-consciously in their everyday concerns, pleasures, anguishes and activities shows the researcher far more of the experience they have than does running around with a tape recorder strapped to his waist or a notebook hidden in the restroom.

While the lack of biographical context limits the natural experience a researcher can have in depth, it allows him to have another form of experience that is important for the research, and one which the members are not apt to have precisely because of their biographical context. The lack of biographical context allows the researcher to experience the setting more freely, more extensively. In the stage of depth probing the scene, the one way the researcher should be doing things differently from the member is by *extending* his experience. Members are sometimes extremely active in extending their experience, as we see in the case of salespeople and politicians, but their extensions of experience are bound by practical concerns, not aimed at experiencing it the way the others do: He's using them, not being like them. Most people, however, do not do this. They find a comfortable niche for themselves in a setting and burrow in. In fact, most people are anxious to maintain their privacy and deliberately shut others out. The social researcher is different. He wants to experience as much of the setting as he can without making himself a traitor to his primary source of group support. We have already noted that he is generally bound to one group or perspective because of the conflicts within settings, and must generally have team members to get at other cliques or perspectives within the setting; but even within one group or perspective there are typically variations and conflicts. The researcher tries to extend his experience to the point where he endangers his relations with those he must have. The researcher tries to be friendly, open, charming and sociable—within the vague boundaries of loyalty.[12] He is a sociability gadfly. In an emergency room his research status commonly allows him to associate with nurses, patients, doctors and administrators. On a nude beach, even as an ordinary member, he can and should associate with as many people as possible, rather than cultivating a few friends and trying to shut others out, as most people tend to do in such public settings. Unlike most others in the setting, he deals with heterosexuals, gays and straights. But he cannot go riding around with the police, or be seen hobnobbing with property owners, or walk around the beach in coat and tie with a camera. (Of course, all such boundaries are partially negotiable, but the researcher must figure out an effective negotiation strategy before he crosses them.)

There are many practical reasons why one may not choose in-depth, member-like experience, as we discussed in Chapter 2. In some settings, such as a nude beach, we can immerse ourselves as much or even more than almost all other members, because almost all of them do it only occasionally and it is an open setting with no biographical requirements or technical training. But in some others, such as drug dealing, we may be tightly constrained by practical and personal considerations (such as an aversion for taking legal and/or moral risks) and will use minimal forms of direct experience. But we must always be aware of these as compromises with the ideal of immersion in the natural situation; we must always make up for this compromise by other means as best we can; and we must always weigh the effects of these compromise solutions on our findings.[13]

Grasping the Research Setting

The stage of de-focusing or immersion in the setting has achieved its purpose when it has allowed us to successfully *grasp* the situation. Grasping is a semi-conscious, largely presymbolic perception of the overall nature, inter-relatedness, and truth of the setting; it is what St. Augustine had in mind when he noted that everyone knows what time is and how to use it, but no one can tell us what it is. Grasping a language is what leads those who have used it for years to say that some constructions are right and some wrong, that they "feel it is right," but cannot say why or how. When a researcher, or anyone else, has successfully grasped a situation he is able to sense what is right and wrong, effective and ineffective, in dealing with others. He will, like anyone else, make mistakes, either in his grasp of the setting or, more commonly, in executing his momentary intentions. But in general he is able to navigate his way through the setting without thinking consciously or symbolically about it. The ultimate grasp of a setting, probably never achieved, is the Zen ideal of being able to subconsciously or "automatically" react in complex, artistic ways, as in a sword fight or an athletic game where one reacts physically without thinking much about it. Anybody who takes the time to think out in words how to fight with a sword is dead, just as anyone who has to think out how to dribble or shoot a basketball is going to lose, and just as any researcher who has to think out what is funny about a joke in the research setting before he laughs isn't making it—he doesn't grasp the setting.

There are many so-called interaction-effectiveness tests[14] of whether a researcher grasps a setting. The basic form is to be able to pass as a member, to not arouse thoughts in others' minds that he is merely doing research.[15] (I find that it's always reassuring to have them express shock when they learn I'm really a researcher. It's even more reassuring if they refuse to believe it.)

Altheide has suggested convincingly that the ability to joke with members about the setting is the best test. But there are other ways in which one gets the feeling he grasps it effectively as well as many other general and situated rules of thumb.

A sense of what fits and what doesn't fit is another one. For example, on a nude beach one cannot walk around nude with his shoes on without seeming weird. It is unlikely that anyone would say anything if he did, although I have heard that it happens. But it is something he would sense or feel: Doing this doesn't fit. When a researcher has such feelings and they work, and when the other effectiveness tests work as well, he has grasped the situation.[16]

The next goal, after grasping, is to *understand* the situation, to be able to put it together in a conscious, symbolic, rational totality. (This does not necessarily mean that it should all go together. Any setting contains many contingent and personal factors that are irrelevant to understanding the setting and some relevant ones that remain mysteries to be puzzled over, perhaps eventually to lead to a whole new kind of understanding.) At this stage it is vital to be able to talk with others about the setting, both insiders and outsiders. This forces one to symbolize his feelings about the setting and forces him to consider the setting from various perspectives, especially if some of the people he talks to are critics of the setting. It allows him to get others' understandings for consideration in arriving at his own. In-depth discussions with fellow team members are invaluable. If one has passed as a member of the setting, he can get insiders to talk by using methods of in-direction, which do not blow his cover. This is easily done in the setting by casually talking with the members about the setting at appropriate opportunities. When the researcher observes an event with a member he can point it out and say things to draw the member out, like "Say, what do you think he's up to over there?" Or, to get a more abstract response, "I've seen people do that a lot; what do you think it means—I mean, why would people do that sort of thing?" In sociable gatherings over a beer, especially if there are just a few individuals, it's easy to draw people out when they begin "philosophizing." Most people are anxious at such moments when they are not constrained by practical demands to talk about their views of the setting and are glad to find someone willing to listen. (Needless to say, this kind of talk can be just as laden with misinformation and falsehood as any talk in the setting, so all the usual precautions and methods must be used.)

Understanding and Reporting on the Research Setting

The first stage of understanding a setting is what Glaser and Strauss (1967) have called grounded theory. It is the development of a systematic understanding which is clearly recognizable and understandable to the members of the setting and which is done as much as possible in their own terms; yet it is more systematic, and necessarily more verbal, than they would generally be capable of expressing. It uses their words, ideas and methods of expression whenever possible, but cautiously goes beyond these. It is grounded in their modes of expression and their ideas, but is not the same as any member's account. The necessity of going beyond them is obvious. Even the most articulate members almost never symbolize their experiences in the setting to the degree necessary to be able to write an essay or book about it.

The researcher must often create words in order to communicate to others what the members themselves actually experience in the setting. These created words generally will be immediately understandable to the members, because they are made as much out of their own words as possible, and communicate their feelings. Often these are words which some few members have themselves created and shared, but which others don't yet know about. A few examples from the nude beach study might help to see what I have in mind here. Our work made extensive use of the word "nude beach virgin" (a new member of the nude scene) in talking about those who were new to the scene. This was a term we ourselves made up, but we could later use it in natural conversations with the members without having to explain it. Other terms, such as "vultching" (meaning the practice of some males of sitting around nude women,) were used by at least one member, but not by others. (In this case, for example, we ourselves had created another term for the practice–"buzzarding." But when we told Carol Ann Flanagan about it she immediately said "Oh, you mean vultching." So we used her word.) After that we could say to people things like, "Hey, look at those guys vultching that chick," without having to explain what we meant.

If he does this well, like a great naturalistic novelist or poet does, the researcher-author creates symbolic meaning of the setting which expresses what the members have felt and grasped but have not been able to say; which evokes in the audience of outsiders the experience of the setting; and which makes more reliable, rational sense of the setting than the members do.

Three significant, partially independent goals are involved in this enterprise:

(1) Maintaining the integrity of the experience of the members and communicating the setting in terms understood by them;
(2) Evoking the setting in the audience of outsiders; and
(3) Making low-level sense of the setting, again in terms understood and natural to the members (though by no means necessarily acceptable to them).

Doing all three is difficult. Sociologists have almost never achieved the second, the evocation of the setting for outsiders, and in doing their grounded theory they often move to a language that is already so oriented to the abstract, preconceived ideas of sociological theory that the members have no interest in it and may not even understand it. Evoking the setting for outsiders, while remaining true to the members' experience of it, involves the communicative skills of the novelist or poet.[17] The form is difficult and so new that sociologists and other researchers, given their preconceived ideas about sociological books, find it strange.

Once this stage of the work is completed, the researcher may find it useful to let some of the members review it. But the purpose of this is not to let them "validate it" by a member test of validity. If the investigative research work has been done well, and the report done truthfully, there will commonly be much in the report that members would prefer were not revealed to the world. This is especially true of settings that involve conflicts, since their enemies can then use it against them. And it is especially those involved in the political conflicts who will denounce the researcher's work as a lie. Contrary to the cooperative model implied by the member test of validity, this very rejection is a *prima facie* validation of one's investigative work. If it is a highly conflictful setting, with some members on each major side committed to political action, then any good investigative report will normally be publicly denounced by the political leaders of each side. The reason for this should be obvious. In all conflictful situations in which there are public political activities there is misinformation, dishonesty and generally self-deception involved in the moralistic positions of each side. Any good investigative report penetrates these on *all* sides, and thereby endangers the public credibility of all sides.

This, of course, is only a rule of thumb, since it is obviously possible for everyone to attack it because the researcher did in fact miss the truth. His belief in the truth of the work rests on all his forms of evidence. It is merely reassuring to have the political figures on all sides denounce his work, for this indicates he may indeed have gotten to the heart of things and have been relatively even-handed in his treatment.[18]

Fortunately, most members of any group being studied, other than political action groups, will not be this political, nor this monolithically committed to upholding the political position of the group. There are almost always some members whom the researcher can expect to be open with him about his work and who may be among the best possible critics of parts of the work. Our own experience has taught us how predictable the anger of politicians can be in a setting. But we have found that most members find the works interesting, and even enjoy them, without being able to contribute much in ideas or criticisms. (This is probably because the works I am talking about, such as those on drug crisis intervention or nude beaches, have been done by a team of researchers and the reports include far more than any single member knows, or has ever thought, about the scene.)

During the stage of understanding the scene in a grounded manner, the researcher is continually returning to the scene, always checking out reports and testing out ideas (see below). This is the stage of active search and testing out, and is distinct from the period of immersion and flowing with the experience. Classical field researchers commonly concluded the field research and returned to their offices to construct their theoretical understandings of the scene. A depth-probing, investigative researcher should first work up his grounded understanding in the midst of the scene. As he begins putting it together symbolically, he will begin to see things he had not thought of, he will be able to test, retain and discard various ideas.

It is at this stage that he can best use personal relations in the settings to test out his ideas through indirect discussions of them with the members. By this stage he is also able to indirectly get members to talk about those things they do not normally talk about and even now will probably not talk about directly. As we have seen before, in depth probes the researcher's own body and mind become crucial research devices. But since individual experiences may vary greatly, considerably even in one setting, he should not take his own experience as *the* experience. (This, in fact, has been one of the faults of the novelistic forms of the so-called "New Journalism.") Rather, he should take his own experience as a vital source of insights, as a means of grasping and understanding partial truths of the setting; just as he is safe in assuming his own experience will not be the whole thing, so is he reasonably safe in assuming that what he experiences will be like that of many other people in the setting and probably somewhat like that of everyone. He is now able to test out the relevance and limitations of his inner, unspoken experience by getting the members to talk, at least indirectly, about their experiences. (He uses all kinds of methods of drawing people out, etc., discussed below.)

The final stage is that of *understanding* the scene *more abstractly.* This is the time when the researcher tries to see the general significance and implications of his work. Just as he tries to de-focus in the beginning of his field research, the researcher should now try to de-focus in this, the initial stage of theoretical understanding. Rather than asking what theories make sense out of his findings, he should first look at his understanding of the setting as the sole basis of theory. He should ask, how can I make more general sense of my findings? What does this tell me about people in general? How? Why? Then he will see the relations between his understandings and any previous theories in the true empirical manner, rather than forcing the previous theory upon his findings. No doubt such theoretical de-focusing is always only partial and much more affected by prior theory than one's experience in a new setting need be affected by prior theory. Ideally, perhaps, there is a complex interplay between previous theory and the understanding based on one's findings in the new setting. But the attempt to first deal theoretically with the findings on their own terms has different effects and, I think, is the most valuable device for doing creative, empirically based research.

The most obvious example of this approach is this work itself. Rather than approaching the question of how to do field research in terms of prior theory of methods, we approached it in terms of how we do in fact go about finding out what's true in our social research experience, then we tried to find out what the implications of this were for doing research generally, and then we related this to the ways research was done in the past. Because of the way we read and learn, this consideration of the relations between what we are doing here and what was done by classical field researchers came in Chapter 2, but it actually came after we had done the research projects and thought out our specific ideas of how we do it. This is a crucial reason why John Johnson's work, *Doing Field Research* (1975), is more concrete, less abstract than this work. His work was done before this and formed an important grounded understanding of field research from which this effort partly sprang. His work was a stimulus to thinking about further research projects which have been done since.

Examples are numerous of the interplay between the upgoing theoretical understandings of our works and earlier theoretical ideas. To me one of the most striking examples is that concerning the supposed tendency of people to "normalize troubles," or to see settings as normal, nondeviant (from their own standpoint) when they might otherwise have seen them as deviant.

In our study of the nude beach, we dealt at considerable length with the ways in which people who are not involved in the scene think of it as a scene in which "creeps are everywhere" and "it's perverts watching perverts watching perverts." We also knew that in the beach scene itself there was a general tendency of people to see everyone else as a creep—"they're all creeps except me." At the same time, we had observed many people come into the scene the first time and, with a look of astonishment, say things like, "Hey, this is no orgy scene! Why, these people aren't creeps! They're real human beings doing natural things like playing frisbee and eating lunch." It was always clear that, given the prevalence of both of these contrasting views of the beach, they were important patterns. But as with all the other things, I never worried about them theoretically during the field research.

Nor did I worry about them in doing the depth probe grounded-theory report. I just reported them. Having written the whole thing, I then worried about them. Using my own written evocation of the scene, I would pore long over the scene, thinking about what it meant for sociological theory. As I was reading about a young couple who was explaining how natural and uncreepy

3. Journalists are a good example of this. Their familiarity has bred cynicism and has nursed their development of investigative methods. Social scientists who have observed journalists at work find them to be highly cynical, especially about political officials. This cynicism is not a birthright, nor some quirk of the profession. It is born of their everyday experience with politicians and many other kinds of people often trusted by the public—church leaders, evangelists, gangsters, and the like. They observe the striking contrasts between the public pronouncements and the private behavior; they know the lobbyists and see them plying their trade at parties; they are privy to the secret sex lives and economic dealings of public figures; they know that the public figures themselves sometimes look cynically at their own actions. They know from personal experience that there is much more going on than meets the public eye and by simple extrapolation expect that there is more than they see. They have developed their investigative paradigm of society from these experiences and insights and have devised their investigative methods to get at what goes on behind the public scenes.

4. Fortunately, this man was really a geographer, not a sociologist. But I would have reported on him even if he had been a sociologist. Indeed, I would have considered it far more important to "rat him out."

5. I've always found it strange that people reported it so difficult to think about their natural experience. As far back as I can remember, I've always been overly self-reflective; I had to learn by experience to stop watching myself. I suspect the same is true of most intellectual types. Consequently, the second step is apt to be easier for them than the first step—*living* everyday life. The so-called natural attitude is not all that natural to us (nor all that dominant in the lives of most natural people, since almost everyone is self-reflective at times). It is a curse of extreme consciousness, but of crucial value to sociologists, unless it is carried to the extreme of making them unable to live everyday life or simply too "awkward" to be friendly and trusted.

6. This all may sound simple and obvious to many readers. Yet it is quite the opposite of present practice in sociology. Field research is still regarded as some kind of practical appendage of theorizing. Graduate and undergraduate students are mainly taught theory and abstract ideas of methods (statistics, verification procedures, field research methods, etc.), then they are allowed to go forth to do research to test a theory. It is assumed that anyone can do this—after all, any student can surely interact or he would never have gotten as far as he has. The same people who would laugh uproariously at the idea of sending any ordinary person into the front line of the L.A. Rams, or putting the ordinary student of violin on the stage at Carnegie Hall, or putting a scalpel into the hand of the premed student, will send *all* graduate students out to "get the data" on almost any group or setting, and then analyze the reports entirely on internal evidence—which means primarily on how well they write things down, do theoretical analyses and integrate whatever they report as the facts into the theory. Fortunately, it's possible for field researchers to learn the hard way—by jumping in and doing it—without the drastic consequences of the other acts mentioned. Experience is the best teacher in this, as in all other things, and it's best to start out right away. But treating all people as equal to the task and all reports as somehow equal as far as the observations goes is a ridiculous result of the classical paradigm. In fact, it takes special kinds of people with special skills to penetrate the complex and convoluted layers of mistruths and deceptions in our society. Anyone who doubts this should simply notice all the people who studied organizations without finding the crucial aspects Melville Dalton (1957) did through the use of his investigative methods, including his member status, years of experience, great abilities at interacting with those people, and blackmail.

7. As noted in Chapter 3, I believe this whole argument leads logically to solipsism and makes research merely a dilettantish activity for those who have nothing better to

do in the way of introspective reductions of the world. Nevertheless, it is an idea that has proven appealing to many graduate students who have been carefully nurtured over years on the airy rationalism of academic life, so we are dealing with it in this book.

8. Coming from a lower-class background, where no one in my extended family had ever even attended college, and no one else in my immediate family went beyond the tenth grade, I had a bad case of professional hang-ups in the early years, complete with identity crisis and anxiety neurosis. I could literally *feel* the professorial role weighing upon me like a Durkheimian external object and I could not escape it. When I went to the supermarket I was still a professorial sociologist and could almost feel people looking at me like that. If I ran into a student in the supermarket, or even in the street, I used to feel embarrassed because I was out of proper setting for the Professor. (What a crisis it would have been for a student to see me changing a diaper!) But I learned to separate myself from the roles, to hide from the roles, and eventually not to bother much about them until someone forced them on me.

9. Because of the mass media's tremendous importance in our society today, there are all kinds of pseudo-information, much of it aimed at giving an appearance of direct experience and knowledge. Senators and other politicians make one-day visits, with TV cameramen and dozens of journalists in tow, to carefully chosen (and lighted) front sites, such as a vineyard where the grapepickers are working, "to show you what it's really like down here, folks." A senator from California held a press conference where he raised high a pair of broken-down shoes, read a letter from a man saying he'd recently bought these for his son at some high price, and then the senator told how this showed the evils of inflation, as well as other things.

10. Role play gets at nothing but the public, general cultural presentations. It may be useful for studying some of the most generally shared cultural experience, such as linguistic statements, but not for getting at anything more situated.

11. One might say it is biographically situated or contextualized to distinguish it from more generally shareable experience, which is what we normally mean by saying experience is transsituational.

12. The readers who know me will note that this is not a description of me. I am much more these things in a research setting than in my sociological settings (mainly, no doubt, because I am not in competition with the members and am consciously cultivating these attenuated aspects of my personality). Still, I have never been in danger of being "the best-liked researcher." I prefer to think of this as being due to my inability to hide my superior intelligence, which intimidates people, and my "air of objectivity." But when honesty demands it, as this work does, I am able to admit that it is simply because my biographical context has limited my friendliness and openness. (I was a much friendlier baby than I am an adult.) As we shall see in our discussion of team field research, such failings can be made up by choosing teammates who complement one's self.

13. As we are already aware from our general plan of research, the best way to make up for these lacks is through the communications from friendly and trusted informants, with as much checking out and testing out of these as possible. We shall shortly consider these in detail. But we should note that there is an important form of key informant that does more than anything else to make up for any lack of direct personal experience. This is the direct personal experience of colleagues who are part of one's research team and that of informants who are "turned out" as researchers. We shall return to this in later chapters on team field research.

14. Phenomenological sociologists, following Schutz, have long used what they call a member test of validity. The original meaning of this, the reader will recall, was that of seeing if the members recognize, understand and accept one's description of the setting. But this was later extended to mean also being able to interact effectively with the

members. The two are completely different and should be named differently. This is the reason for the new term introduced here.

15. We could also distinguish a kind of in-between form of passing. This was common in our studies of emergency rooms. In the press of the moment the emergency staff commonly made the researchers into part of the team. Phillip Davis was given specific instructions on how to stay out of the way of the staff and not to get involved; but his first night there the staff was *forcing* him, much to his nausea, to help with drug overdoses, take blood samples, etc. Dennis Stouffer quickly wound up helping to insert chest tubes and other emergency measures. He was even presented by the staff at one point as a doctor to patients to provide them with support in getting the patients to do things. It is common for such staffs to pass the researchers off as one of themselves, if for no other reason than to avoid questions.

16. I have said nothing about how one comes to have the grasp of a situation; it comes from experience. As a researcher, I am interested in having the grasp of the situation, then using this to arrive at an understanding. To arrive at an understanding of how one grasps experience would be an introspective task, rightly left to philosophers and psychologists. In doing research, I don't need to know how I do it any more than I need to know how my eyes see. I suspect it will eventually prove worthwhile to understand how we grasp a research setting, but first things first.

17. The form this takes might be called a literary research report. The goal is similar to the ostensible goal of the new journalism of Tom Wolfe and others (1974). But in many ways it is quite different. The new journalists have almost no ideas of research methods. In fact, they almost never tell the readers anything about how it was done. Because of this, a couple of students and I took advantage of our being in La Jolla, where Wolfe had done his "research" for his famous essay on "The Pump House Gang" (1969). He did it about ten years earlier, but several of the main characters (key informants?) still live in the area and were glad to be interviewed on tape. By all accounts, Wolfe necessarily looked like a "weird" outsider to the kids because he was so much older; spent his time with two older limbo-members; mistook the group for a bigtime surfing group when they were actually a beach crowd in which the few surfers were low on the totem pole of surfdom; mistook them for rich kids when most of them were far from this and a few lived with divorced mothers who supported them by working as waitresses; published one account of surfing as a true account when the girl who wrote it told him it was fictitious and asked him not to publish it; and recounted things supposed to be important to the kids which they found mysterious or strange. While I believe they have at times provided some beautiful satire on our society with its own "moral truth," the new journalists' claims to truth are highly suspect.

18. These comments do not apply to most so-called "investigative reports" by journalists, since these almost always involve a uniperspectival position. Journalists commonly do investigative work only when they are called in by one side to expose the others. They are commonly politically inspired investigations and, in fact, it is common for the report to be followed the next day by announcements that politicians have supported the report, called for further investigations, and so on. These are often "set-ups," but the degree of conscious intent varies greatly. As a rule of thumb, the more multiperspectival one's investigative report, the more attacks there will be from all sides.

Chapter 7

THE GENERAL STRATEGIES OF INVESTIGATIVE FIELD RESEARCH: BUILDING AND USING FRIENDLY RELATIONS AND CHECKING THEM OUT

In spite of the many pervasive forms of falsehood and deception which a field researcher faces, almost all worthwhile social research necessarily involves reliance upon cooperative methods as well as more strictly investigative methods. We should now be able to see that building and using cooperative methods, especially friendly and trusting relations, is a major strategy of the general investigative paradigm. As such, it is always seen in the general context and used in conjunction with the other strategies and tactics of the paradigm. Most important, the things we learn through friendly and trusting relations are always conditioned by, pervaded with, the things we learn through direct experience and they are, whenever possible, checked out; for the investigative researcher likes and trusts informants, but never more than necessary.

The necessity of using friendly and trusting relations should be clear from our argument thus far: It is necessary to get at inner, emotional and symbolically meaningful experience, in order to adequately understand human beings. And it is possible and often necessary to get at such experience from the direct experience of the researcher in the setting. But we also know from our previous discussion that different people have somewhat different experiences in the same setting. Physiological and biographical contexts are different; so are the actual experiences in the setting; and so are the individuals' partially free constructions of the meanings of such experiences. Consequently, a necessary part of one's direct experience of a setting is receiving truthful accounts from others, which come from building friendly and trusting relations and checking out accounts as much as possible. We reduce our dependency upon this trust as far as possible, but there is always a final act of faith—trust of our fellow human beings when we absolutely have to.

Since the investigative paradigm continually emphasizes the necessity of checking out all vital member accounts, I want to point out that, while I strongly believe this is right, I also believe firmly that the right use of friendly and trusting relations is not only a necessity of research, but also a powerful one. Once established and checked out, and tested out by the researcher's own grasp of the setting, they make it possible at times to get vital insider information, sometimes in minutes. Given the great time constraints of our study of drug crisis intervention and its transcontinental spread, we found this to be vital in certain ways, especially when in writing up the report I found that we needed to check out some vital bits of carefully guarded information. Robert Gilmore, one of the team members, had developed friendly and trusting relations with a researcher who was in one of the most vital spots in the nation for observing some of the things we needed to know about drug programs. This person was willing to give him "very secret" information by long-distance telephone when we needed it most.

Indeed, I believe the extensive cultivation of friendly and trusting relations with people in all kinds of settings has been vital in giving us a different perspective of the social world from that developed by the phenomenological sociologists. It was a basic mistake of the phenomenologists (probably born precisely of their lack of extensive friendly and trusting relations with individuals of practical common sense) that they looked at common people as encapsulated by their natural attitude, unable to step outside of it, and that ethnomethodologists believed people continually "normalize troubles."[1] I doubt that this has ever been the case, but it certainly is not so today. Every group of people today of any size (say 20 or more) almost inevitably has some members who have at some time "bracketed" almost any experience one can think of. Today a significant percentage of members of the Western world have even bracketed existence at some time, have "stared into the abyss of nothingness."[2]

A researcher must always keep in mind that a significant percentage of people, possibly a majority, have at times had deep fears that they were going insane because they found themselves thinking and feeling "weird" about everyday, natural things. It is precisely their fears of these experiences that often lead them to insist on the naturalness of the everyday world and to hold tight to their absolute categories. The natural attitude is sometimes a self-deception. If the researchers get to know them intimately enough (and it usually takes real intimacy, not colleagueship) and get them in the right situation, they may even talk about this sort of thing.

I know a young woman researcher, for example, who was studying some legal officials in their everyday, bureaucratic activities. They gave every appearance of taking a natural attitude toward their activities. Then she became intimate with one of these who always looked as if he took his official duties to be absolute. At that point his absolutist bureaucratic attitude fell away and he articulated his doubts, the problematic nature of what he himself was doing, and so on. We should always remember that people are more often frightened than dumb. They may hold fast to an absolutist attitude out of deep anxieties or simply out of fear of what the researcher, or someone the researcher may tell, will think of them if they raise all their questions, doubts and fears about what they are doing. Spies and traitors have played upon those fears for centuries. Field researchers need to find those people who can be reassured enough by friendly trust (not necessarily just a good bedside manner) to talk about their fears and the things they have been hiding.

John Johnson (1976) has shown that establishing trust, maintaining it and using it are highly problematic. The researcher may be trusted and let in, only to be quickly thrown out. He may be mistrusted and later trusted. And trust may hold up for some experiences but not for others. Letting someone in the front door, with a great show of trust and cooperation, is often the best way to make sure he doesn't discover there's a trap door leading to the lower depths. After all, who is more open, heartily aboveboard, real buddy-buddy, than a crooked politician? A key strategy of those who have something to hide is to appear open, never to give people reason to suspect them, such as by refusing entree. Johnson has explored these labyrinthine complexities of trust in detail, so we need not repeat them.

Although trust is vital and is a partially independent variable, it is secondary to friendliness or liking. While no one to my knowledge has carefully explored the complex relations between liking and trusting people, they are closely related to each other. Most often they appear to complement each other in everyday experience. If we have one, we tend to have the other. But we also know there are important exceptions. Most important, we know from our experience that there are people we like, especially people we love, whom we do not trust; and some we trust, but do not like. And we know that this love often leads us to do things that put us way out on a limb, that put us in situations where they can betray us, even destroy us. The complex, interwoven feelings of friendly-liking-loving-wanting-to-be-near-and-to-possess tend to be dominant in our human relations. There are many people one trusts but whom one would never allow around long enough to study him—because he doesn't like them. Perhaps they bore him, or turn him off, or repulse him, make him feel bad, or else he can't stand them.

If one does like someone, he usually gives that person a chance to establish trust and he finds reasons to trust the person, in spite of contrary evidence. Friendly feeling, affection, feeling for, sympathy, intimacy—such are the emotional stuff on which human relations are built.

The field researcher should try to be liked first and on that liking he can build powerful bonds of trust. If he isn't liked, it won't matter much whether he's trusted—he won't penetrate to the inner depts of things. If he is well-liked, he can get away with a lot, and can cover those rough spots of distrust that almost inevitably arise in any close human relationship. Indeed, if he's studying an intensely conflictful situation in which he must eventually play the traitor to all sides, his only hope of being forgiven and riding out the storm will be that people like him; they will be sure that he cannot be trusted. The affection will help them see that he is, hopefully, telling the truth when he says that he has betrayed them in the short run because he wants to help us all in the long run.

Needless to say, the emotions of liking are highly problematic. Liking may occur at first sight, or it may take years to establish; it may be a steady feeling, or wax and wane within a brief situation; it may last all trials in spite of oneself, or be crushed out at the first seeming betrayal. The researcher's best approach is simply to try to build liking, along with trust, over time. While I shall not pretend to tell anyone how to be liked by their subjects, I would mention a few obvious points. One obviously has to be friendly himself; that is, he must be sociable, show he likes being with the other people, be open to them, sharing himself with them, especially the private parts of his life, and doing things for them. In American society it is almost always important to be egalitarian, unthreatening, nonassertive (it's better to be somewhat submissive in most groups, except in tough lower-class groups), easy-going, supportive, possess a sense of humor, and be emotionally labile, even to the point of being hearty and openly emotional, something which seems to help people "get out of themselves." Sharing things with people, doing things for them, being with them, builds up over time. They tend to overcome most other lacks, such as being too quiet or rather unattractive.[3]

As one is trying to be liked, he is also trying to be trusted. For the most part, since they complement each other, when he does one, he does the other as well or makes the other possible. The obvious ways to establish trust are to demonstrate one's honesty and strong commitment to protecting the interests and person of the subject. (In building affection and trust it does not matter whether the researcher is honest or merely doing presentational work. [See

Warren, unpublished MS.] But he must be convincing.) The researcher does
these things in the way one normally does, but there are a few other things he
is careful to do, especially if he is doing overtly defined research. He is careful
not to pass stories about other people in the setting. He has to show that
what they tell him will not be passed on. And he is careful to show his respect
for and commitment to the scene, to what people are doing and what they
are. Also important, the researcher exchanges intimacies with the subject,
especially if he is known to be a scientist or professor and if his subjects are
"disreputable." Simply, he shows them that he's into it too—that he is
human, disreputable, etc. He thereby establishes commonalities, makes himself open to them, makes himself equal to them and, significantly, shows he
trusts them. While it does not always work, friendliness and trust invite and
breed friendliness and trust in return. Several examples of the actual workings
of establishing and using friendliness and trust will help make all of this
clearer.

John Johnson's (1973, 1975) study of welfare caseworkers is an excellent
example of the pervasive importance of friendly feelings in doing field
research. The fact that it was a study of welfare casework, rather than
something else, was itself determined by the prior existence of friendly
feeling. As with a high percentage of other field studies, he was casting about
for a subject to study and naturally thought in terms of personal contacts,
that is, friends who might let him study them.[4] He was interested in riding
the insider's coattails, or getting that person to run interference for him in
negotiating entree to the setting. When he talked with me about the problem
it seemed obvious that this was a chance to use a long-standing friendship
with a social worker who had been a brilliant and dedicated student six or
seven years earlier and with whom I had maintained some contact.[5] We
found she was willing and interested in the whole idea. Her talk with Johnson
went well, which I think was based almost entirely on her liking him. Liking
was always the crucial factor involved. In fact, I cannot remember trust ever
being much of a question, perhaps because she knew all about field research
and knew we weren't going to expose her or anyone else.

There was another instance in which I sent a researcher to talk with this
welfare worker about another subject. She told him what he was interested
in—again there was no question of trust raised. But she didn't like this
researcher at all, said so, and made it clear she wasn't interested in doing any
more research with him. (I think her objective comment was "Yukh-h!")
Many field workers have asked why subjects should help researchers; after all,
social life is based largely on reciprocity, and the question can be asked of
what's in it for a subject of research? Generally, there isn't much more than
friendly feeling and exchange, but that's a lot for most people. People do

things for people they like, and the more they like them the more they do for them. But this does not mean necessarily that the more they like them the more they always "do truth" for them.

Johnson's second stage of research involved moving to a nearby city to study a similar form of casework. In this setting his key contacts were friends of his wife, who was also a welfare worker. These friends proved crucial in his being able to do the study at all, though·this was not a consideration in the beginning. The caseworker who eventually became most helpful distrusted Johnson at first, but they had a lot in common and, for whatever reason, liked each other. This friendly feeling became the basis for building a relation that also involved deep trust. Eventually, the worker even allowed Johnson to see how he did certain illegal things and could obviously get him fired if they became public knowledge.

The primacy of liking over trust was probably most obvious in the nude beach study. No one is a better example of it than the young man we called Jon. Jon distrusted everyone in the setting. (Even his first name was false.) He and I had seen each other going our own ways on the beach for a year or more before I ever spoke to him. He was into the nude scene and I was a "straight," merely running or walking by. Every indication was that he didn't trust or like me, any more than most nudes would trust or like anyone with his suit on.

Once I had decided to join and study the scene, I quickly made my move on Jon, since I had seen that he was one of the ultimate regulars and knew lots of people. My impression was that he still didn't like me, and he certainly wasn't going to trust me with anything. But I kept working on him, talking with him, joking mostly, whenever I got the chance. He was really a friendly person and apparently came to like first me and then Paul Rasmussen, a team resercher. He still didn't trust us, since he would never allow Rasmussen to tape an interview with him and whenever I talked about how he might help Rasmussen, he simply turned the idea aside. (We never told him I was doing a study. I was the insider; Rasmussen the insider-outsider. See the chapter or team field research.) But because he liked us, he let us get close enough to see nearly everything he was doing. Rasmussen was able to go around with him to pick up girls (hunting). I was not only able to see his activities on a day-to-day basis, but he also told me many things about what was going on, and importantly, he introduced me to his girlfriend. His girlfriend was not only friendly, but much more trusting. It was through her that I learned all about his double life, lying about his name, a big blow-up involving his wife and her family, etc. (These life histories are presented briefly in Douglas and Johnson, 1977). As Jon told Rasmussen, he was anxious not to have aspects of his life written down, even under a pseudonym. We liked Jon, regardless of the lack of trust, and always felt badly writing about him, even knowing the chance was slight that he or anyone he knew would read what we wrote. It was our liking for him that made us feel badly, not any betrayal, since he never entrusted us with anything and since field research is inevitably a partly traitorous activity we had accepted as necessary. He, of course, was right not to trust us. His mistake was in liking us.

Another case from the nude beach study, that of Pete, a friend and key informant, reveals the lengthy building of a relationship that is sometimes necessary to establish enough trust to get at basic things. Friendly feelings came long before trust. Indeed, early lies, told in distrust, later became a partial stumbling block to friendly feelings. Even when the distrust was overcome, he hid things, probably because it would reveal he had distrusted us and, thereby, would endanger the friendly feelings. This is a minimal form of the problems of intimacy. Rasmussen has described the way in which Jerry progressively opened up and came clean about himself. (All of these things checked out with other observations.)

Pete and Carol Ann first met while both were taking a dip at the water's edge. Their friendship began with a simple exchange of hellos, then progressed to long discussions while walking the beach, and finally, Pete joined Carol Ann while sitting on the beach. I first met Pete while their friendship was in transition between the discussion and "towel-sitting" stages. He claimed to be an ex-Navy man, here from the South, and while here had decided to finish his education in biology at the local state university. He said that, while he lived with a female roommate, they were only friends, not sexual partners. She did the housework in consideration for a reduction in rent. His interest in the nude beach was limited to "freedom from the tensions of college" and "naturalness of the experience," which he also equated with his interests in biology.

We all became closer friends as the summer wore on. He'd look for us or we'd look for him on first arriving at the beach. His interest in our research became keener, and he actually became an ad hoc member of our team, joining us on our treks up and down the beach, searching for likely subjects to be interviewed. It was during this time that Carol Ann mentioned I was married. Pete was really taken back by this new information. The first time Pete and I were alone he told me he, too, was married. He said he'd done his best to bring his wife to the beach, but she was too prudish to continue after the first try. I was sworn to secrecy, "because Carol Ann might not understand the problems of us married men."

We maintained this understanding until one day when Pete and I were listening to a taped interview Carol Ann had done with three beautiful girls. During the interview, Carol Ann had referred to Pete as a "super good friend, sort of like a big brother." Pete first turned bright red from head to toe, then asked: "She really doesn't think I'm interested in her sexually?" We exchanged strategies about the best way to keep from being seen as either the big brother or the super lech and then ended in a discussion of his marital problems. He had been cut off from any sexual contact with his wife for the past six months and was down at the beach hoping he could find a sex partner, hopefully with Carol Ann. During this same discussion I also learned that he was a zoology major rather than a biology major and he was enrolled at a local junior college rather than at the state university, although he had applied and was expecting to be accepted.

The discovery of these fronts took more than one year. I've known Pete for two years now and continue to find out new things. Just the other day, I was writing him a check for some money I owed him. When I filled in his name, I wrote the one he had always used. When I handed it to him, he kind of blushed and said I'd gotten his name wrong. I apologized and said I had always thought it was [the first one]. He then admitted he sometimes used different names.

Our belief in the predominance of friendly feeling over trust and of the crucial part friendly feeling plays in producing trust is clearly based on the bedrock fact of direct experience. The explanation of this fact is secondary, since we are mainly interested in the results. But it does not seem to be any mystery. We have already noted that friendly feeling provides much of the motivation for the subject and the lack of it commonly makes the interaction with the researcher a minus, a cost, rather than a plus or reward.

It is fortunate for all social research that friendly exchange is its own important reward and that friendly feeling makes people want to open up and talk with the friend, to share with him or her his personal life, including his innermost thoughts and feelings. This basic truth is most obvious at the extreme of love. When we love someone we want to be with that person totally, to share everything, to be open to him, to merge our lives. In moments of intense love, such as that felt by new lovers cut off from the world and totally engrossed in each other, people typically feel the need to tell everything about themselves, even damaging things. Spies have always relied upon in-bed revelations from those who have let down all barriers in the heat of love as their best source of information on national secrets.[6] People obviously are not that unguarded in the friendly revelations of most field research relations, but the friendly feelings lead them in the same direction—openness, sharing one's life, revealing what are otherwise secrets from the world.

Those friendly feelings are precisely the right motive for getting at precisely what the investigative researcher wants to get at, the private realms of life normally kept secret from the public realms. Giving and receiving friendly feelings, then, are the supremely important exchange in field research. They must be cultivated.

There is an immediate and important implication of this basic idea of field research; and one that is in striking contrast to traditional forms of research (mainly interviews), which often involve paying subjects for the time they give. Friends do not pay each other for favors, so friendly researchers must not pay people for their information and other research favors.[7] If one pays a lover for her services, one prostitutes her; and he gets phony love, mere self-presentations, in return. Pay, money or any other *direct* form of payment, is the harsh coin of public exchange that must be avoided.

But this does not mean that the researcher does not do favors for his research friends. Far from it. When we like someone, we do all kinds of things for them. If we love him or her, we might give almost anything we have. The important point is that things are given and favors done as friendly acts, not as payment for something. They are generally indirect, no strings attached. They often consist of things like giving information and advice, helping people find a job, and so on. In studying illegal activities researchers sometimes help as much as they can with friendly advice, support, running around and searching for legal advice when his friends are busted or doing things that might get themselves busted. For example, Rasmussen did a great deal of this when one of his key informants on massage parlors was busted. On his advice she switched to the lawyer whom the research revealed as the ultimate expert on massage parlor law. She was acquitted of all charges. The research helped her and, of course, Rasmussen became involved in all the inside details of her defense, which helped the research even more.

In addition to being natural parts of friendly exchanges, doing favors and making it clear that further favors in the future will be done, and that, of course, the subject will be expected to do favors as well, is all part of the general process of tying or committing the subject to the researcher. For the investigative researcher is a friend, but he is also a hard-headed realist, not a sentimentalist. He does favors out of friendship, but he also does them as a way of building the web of trust.

Trust has two major aspects. Trust is ultimately an act of faith, an assumption that someone is telling the truth about things the researcher is not experiencing directly, and that someone will act in accord with the researcher's best interests in those situations where he is not able to make sure they do. (In St. Paul's definition of faith, it is "a hope after the unseen.") It is built most directly upon demonstrations in actual experience that one does act that way. That is, for example, people learn from others that one has said good things about them when they were not there; and that the things told to them turn out to be true when they have the chance to test them out directly. An obvious instance is the researcher's distinction between trustworthy informants and untrustworthy ones. In the nude beach study one of the most talkative people was a guy named Ben, who would almost invariably run out to me and tell me all kinds of things as I went by. Most of it checked out (see next section), but some accounts of police activities proved to be unreliable. I came to see Ben as not being particularly trustworthy, but probably because of excessive drinking rather than any intention of being untruthful. (As Ben put it, "You know, my mind sometimes plays tricks on me.")

But truth is also dependent on our belief that the other person has clear motivations to tell us the truth and to act in accord with our best interests. We *hope* he has an internalized commitment to tell the truth and feelings of guilt when he doesn't tell the truth. But we have seen in considerable detail how unreliable this is—only innocents and survey researchers "take people on faith" to that degree. The investigative realist demands hostage commitments (or side commitments) to telling him the truth and acting in his best interest. He gives trust to the degree it has been shown to be justified by past experience and to the degree he sees one has hostage commitments to telling him the truth and acting in accord with his interests. The meanings of this are clear when one considers the answer to the question: How do I know I can trust what you tell me (to be true or to be an honest prediction of your future acts)? The first answer might be: You know you can trust *me*! That is, past experience shows it. But the answer to this, especially in situations where we do not have long histories of relationships, as in most research settings, is: *How* do I know? The answers (which can be found in any detective story) consist of enumerating the hostage commitments of the individual to oneself. First, there is friendship. Since friendly feelings are valued in themselves by most people, a friend can be counted on to some degree to want to keep a person's friendship, so he doesn't want to lie or act against that person. But all sorts of other hostage commitments exist as well, which will count for more in those settings where someone is not a close friend. These are things like his fear that the researcher will find out he's lying and he'll suffer for it (as the gangsters in movies always say menacingly, "You better not lie to me, baby!"); his hope that you can help him in the future, such as by getting him a job; and so on. The researcher builds a web of these commitments in order to build a web of trust. He ties the subject to him by them. (We shall see in the next chapter some further ways this is done.)

At this point I fear that some readers might now extrapolate our discussions of friendly and trusting relations to conclude that the researcher need only spend a lot of time with the subjects, become well-liked, then trusted, and thereby get them to tell the truth about the setting. That, of course, would precipitate one right into the (classical) cooperative model. To forestall that possibility, and to expunge once and for all any lingering belief in the it was, unlike what they had thought before they came, I thought about the obvious way they were normalizing the scene, seeing it as undeviant.

But that same normalizing tendency was embedded in all the material about the outsiders categorizing it as "super-creepy." Some people obviously normalized; some did the opposite, abnormalizing. And there were different degrees. Was it something about the people? No, it seemed to be too consistent. It had to do with their relations to the scene. It was then easy to work out what seemed to be the conditions under which the opposite cognitive tendencies tended to prevail. I then worked back toward the phenomena by thinking further about this in the scene. And I worked in the other direction as well, considering the relations of these to consonance-dissonance theories, the implications for moral and political conflicts in general, and so on.

Conclusion

Direct, in-depth experience of the researchers is the crucial beginning and foundation of most investigative field research. At times it is impossible, and other methods must be used. At times it does not seem necessary because the general cultural experience and understanding of the researchers makes it superfluous. But it is the foundation and when it cannot be provided in some way the research data must be discounted accordingly.

However, it is not the whole structure of investigative field research. The other major strategies are building and using friendly and trusting relations and then checking out the people and the information. In addition, there are some important investigative tactics we shall consider in Chapter 8.

NOTES

1. We argued in Chapter 1 that our basic common-sense feelings and ideas of truth lead us to rely subconsciously upon certain basic tests of truth and a great many more specific, less reliable ideas. These general tests of truth correspond closely to the general strategy of investigative field research we shall propose here, and the more specific ones are used in conjunction with this more general strategy.

2. Introspection and the closely related empathetic understanding have their own uses. Introspection, as I have argued in *Existential Sociology*, 1977, is vital in getting at basic, general properties of the human mind; this is a philosophical task that impinges upon and adds to sociology, but is certainly different. Empathetic understanding is certainly useful in testing out the plausibility of an idea when we have no direct experience. Empathy is valuable to the extent we have personal experience that bears on the experience being empathized.

essential goodness and trustworthiness of people, let us look closely at one of our memorable experiences with friendliness and trust.

Rasmussen and I decided to study massage parlors, partly because we'd been following the growing controversy in the local mass media and it seemed like it would be fascinating to find out what the truth was about parlors; and partly because we had a hunch that parlors were an important part of the basic changes taking place in the whole realm of body feelings and sex. We could have begun with the direct personal experience of setting up a massage parlor or becoming customers. We rejected these two approaches for various personal and public reasons. (Even had we tried these approaches, we would probably have been fronted out initially.) At the time we had not developed any good insider contacts. So we had to fall back on a more classic approach of overt entree, hanging out, building friendly and trusting relations, etc. He made the direct assault upon a parlor that happened to be near his home. (I was working on the beach report and, besides, personal reasons, such as my wife, relegated me to the more august status of "team director" in this study.) He told the owner he was a student working on a term paper for his course and would appreciate being allowed to study the parlor.[8] The owner wasn't very happy about it and never did get to like Rasmussen. But he didn't throw him out, and Rasmussen soon learned he could drop by when the owner was out. The girls were quite friendly. Within a few months he'd gotten well-acquainted with each of the day-shift girls and particularly friendly with one of them, Ursula. They all consistently told the same story. And Ursula was the best and most insistent teller. When she told her story she was sincere, open, intimate, confident, friendly, warm, and firm. All the girls said parlors had a reputation for being sex-for-money shops. Some probably were, but that general reputation made it possible for them to get customers without really doing sex. Yes, they suspected some of the night girls did sex at times. But not them. "Straight massage. Honest, honey." And they were firmly against the night-time shenanigans, if it was going on, because it could bring the police down on them all. The boss himself was most upset about this prospect and, if he caught any of the night girls messing around, he would fire them.

Moreover, when Rasmussen talked with people who were customers of the parlors they told him the same sort of thing or else confirmed the masseuses' accounts down the line. A barber whom he had known and patronized for years admitted he was a customer and even told him in detail how important it was for his health. He got bad pains in the lower part of his back from leaning over the customers all day and it helped him tremendously to be able to get a professional massage. Sex in parlors? Lord no, never heard of it. A sociology graduate student went to a few parlors, put on the heavy make, and got nothing but health. The member documentation of their accounts was depressingly consistent for anyone who hoped to find basic changes in American sex practices.

It all sounded sweetly reasonable and sincere, especially to the person, Rasmussen, who was given the face-to-face presentations. Being more of a hard-hearted cynic, with a pervasive sense of suspicion, and not being directly subjected to such friendly, trusting and inveigling accounts of virtue, I didn't find it very plausible; I thought we had to check them out. Rasmussen returned to the parlor with a more probing and suspicious attitude.

One day when business was slow he was sitting around the parlor talking with Ursula and Kim. It was friendly and relaxed, so he went down to the local liquor store for a fifth of vodka to help them through the afternoon of research accounts. After they'd been drinking their vodka and orange juice for some time, one of the local health fanatics came by and chose Ursula for a massage. While Ursula was in the back room, Kim started reminiscing and philosophizing about the job. She said that when she had started the job she really never meant to get into sex at all. But her first in-training client was an older guy who'd just gotten out of the hospital and even had scars to prove it. He told her what a long time it had been since he'd gotten off and how he'd really appreciate her help. She felt sorry for him and made her first exception to her not-yet-used rule. Then she said, rather whimsically, "My one exception has become pretty much my rule." But she only did hand jobs! Nothing more. Never. Later that day, in private, Rasmussen casually told Ursula of Kim's admission. She now reluctantly said that once in a while, though only with very good customers, she too would do a hand job. But never anything more. Never.

One day about three weeks later he was sitting around the parlor talking with Ursula and another day girl, Bonnie. A customer came in and chose Bonnie. The customer left a half hour later. Bonnie came in smiling, waving a crisp new $50 bill, and said, "Look what I've got. . . ." Ursula, knowing that Rasmussen knew no one would pay $50 for a sympathetic hand job, quickly said, "Wow, I really get jealous when *you* get all those fifty dollar tips." But Bonnie wasn't playing hide-and-go-seek and replied, "But, Ursula, you get just as many $50 tips as I do." Then Bonnie tried to pull the cover of respectability back over them both by insisting, "Well, they're really all such old guys they can't even get it up, but they sure enjoy getting nude with a young chick, and being massaged. . . ."

Shortly after this, Rasmussen discovered that a close friend of his was visiting the parlor as a customer; they had a casual talk about it. The friend insisted that he always tipped the girls for a blow job; and they all did it with no hesitation, as long as the tip was right.

About the same time, a friend from the nude beach decided to become a masseuse. She did her on-job training briefly at another parlor and interviewed at several others where the bosses insisted on "trying her out." She was giving us concrete, taped and written details on the whole scene. It was clear that in all those parlors sex, including "balling," was always negotiable. She was now looking for a new job, largely because she had gotten too emotionally involved with some customers at her first regular job and wanted to start anew where she could be more impersonal. Having heard about Ursula's parlor, she chose to go there. She continued to provide us with detailed descriptions of the whole scene, including each of the girls' sexual activities. Shortly after this, the other girls falsely accused her of theft (probably because she was a rate buster) and she moved to another parlor.

Once she was gone, Rasmussen confronted Ursula with what he now knew reliably that she did in the parlor, but never telling her how he knew. She now admitted it, including details on "balling" in the parlor, how she lied to her boyfriend, and why they had lied to him. By this time we already knew why she had lied. To the girls there are two kinds of men in their lives— potential customers who have to be let in on the truth of sex in the parlor; and actual or potential boyfriends who must be fronted out about most of the sex,[9] for fear they will not stand for the whole sex-for-money game. It was precisely because Rasmussen was so friendly and invited such trust that she had "put the make on him" and she and all the others had fronted him out. Once we knew this, it made sense. After all, it is nothing new to discover that the intimate one is sometimes the last to learn of one's betrayal or that friends have hidden things from one to avoid hurt all around. (But it would also be no discovery to learn that intimates also sometimes tell one the worst things about themselves because they cannot stand to be traitors.) Intimacy and trust count, but not for everything.

Rasmussen was now able to confront outer people with the detailed facts of what goes on in the parlors. He went back to the barber and told him what went on in the parlors, how to play the word-games to negotiate sex (see Rasmussen and Kuhn, in Douglas, 1977c), how much it costs, and so on. The barber chuckled and said simply, "Oh, yeah, well you know how it is, old buddy. I mean, a guy's gotta be real careful about something like that. Ha-ha. Just think what would happen if my wife found out what really goes on in those 'health spas.' Besides, I wasn't lying to you. I mean, it's just like I said: It's really great for my health. Nothing in the world makes me feel better than a good blow job. Ha-ha." He did know what it was like, now. But almost everyone went to a lot of trouble to try to make sure he wouldn't know what it was like, until he already knew. Once the researcher has already drawn them out, blown open the setting (see the next chapter), checked them out and confronted them with concrete details about how it's done, then they often help him to see in greater detail what he already knows in general. But until then they have all the wily methods of eons of human dishonesty to use in fronting him out.

One wonders how many social researchers of all kinds have been successfully fronted out by the wily members because they put too much trust in trust *and* in friendly feeling. Since most field research, and almost all other social research, has involved deep reliance upon trust and, to a lesser extent, friendly feeling, I suspect that most have been fronted out of the deeper secrets of our social lives. Friendly and trusting relations are vital to social research, but they are commonly reliable only when they have been systematically and thoroughly checked out and/or tested against one's own member experience.

Testing Out and Checking Out

Testing out consists of

(1) Comparing a supposed fact, member account, etc., with the most reliable ideas and generally patterned facts the researcher has from his prior experience, and
(2) Comparing one's own ideas and inferences with the observed facts in a setting.

We have already talked about the second kind in our discussion of analyzing research findings. What concerns us here, though only briefly, is the testing out of supposed facts in a setting. Testing out is an initial step in checking out. It involves estimating the plausibility or likely truth of the supposed fact in terms of one's prior experience and understandings. It may be based on one's general cultural experience or with the particular setting involved. It is a less reliable check than checking out (and, obviously, the less direct it is, the less reliable it is). At one extreme we have hunches or guesses based on general cultural experience. It's the sort of idea people have in mind when they say, "Well, it's just my feeling that she's lying. I mean, a woman like that doesn't do that kind of thing." At the other extreme, we have the feeling of *lack of fit* received when we have a thorough grasp of a setting. When Rasmussen told me that the masseuses all reported no sex at the parlor, it was my hunch that they were lying. When one of the old-timers on the nude beach told me the police were arresting people for nudity in an area I knew had long been safe, I didn't believe him. It could have been true, but it didn't fit my grasp of the scene and I would have to be shown first. They weren't.

Testing out is a creative enterprise and cannot be detailed as well as checking out can. But there are a number of important points to be made about it.

First, we have insisted that the proper investigative research attitude is that of tough-minded suspicion. Always expect there is more going on than meets the eye, etc. The obvious complement to this is expecting to find more in early stages of research. "Okay, we find x and y easily. It's all clear. Now what else is there? This isn't all. Let's find the trapdoor. The trapdoor will lead to z." The ideas that there is a trapdoor, that it is of a certain kind, and that it can be found in some ways, are all hunches. But they must be pursued. They are the suggestions, the hints, of the most important discoveries in the research.

Second, always think about the practical context of the supposed activity or event. Where does the money come from? How can they make a living if they stay at home all day? What's that van for? (That sort of thinking also led to the discovery that "Doc," dealt with by Rasmussen (discussed later), had made a lot of money by getting people involved with him in speculations, then declaring bankruptcy.) This is one reason for believing that a straight massage parlor is unlikely—there aren't that many health fans and a clip-joint living off the sexy reps of other parlors won't last long. So my hunch was that the only semi-straight massage parlors are found in real health spas.

Third, always think about it from all angles. Look at it legally, economically, in terms of the personal pleasures and risks, etc.

Fourth, always think of anything that's relevant. The search through one's mind for similarities can often unearth all kinds of things.

Fifth, listen to what others have to say about similar events, about their hunches, and so on. And get them to explain as much as they can about their hunches.

Checking out consists essentially of comparing what one is told by others against what can be experienced or observed more directly, and therefore more reliably, or against more trustworthy accounts. Checking out against more direct experience or observation is done so that things are not taken simply on trust; it becomes as well a basis for building trust, for discovering from reliable experience who is trustworthy and who is not, and to what degree. Checking out against other accounts by other people consists of checking out the less trustworthy against the more trustworthy. Checking out is a vital and pervasive part of all investigative research and is important in direct proportion to the amount of indirect evidence we are using—that is, the more we are using evidence that does not consist of our own direct experience and observations, the more we must check out the evidence.

There are at least three major, well-recognized forms of checking out:

(1) Checking out against direct observations of "hard facts;"

(2) Checking out against direct experience acquired for that purpose, which we can call recycling to direct experience; and

(3) Checking out against alternative accounts.

When the systematic and multiperspectival checking out confirms the evidence, we let it pass. When it fails, we may write it off if it seems unimportant, but if it is important, either for other reasons or in itself (because bad evidence is often an important discovery about the setting), then we use the disconfirmation to explore further or to confront and open up the subject. These warrant some examination.

If one uses only his general cultural experience and understanding, or that gained in a specific kind of situation, to evaluate the truth of a statement, he is simply testing out the truth of it, estimating its plausibility in terms of similar events and situations. But as soon as he moves to making direct observations of the concrete events or situations about which the members' accounts are purported to be factual descriptions, or about which he has hunches, he is checking out the account or hunch. The distinction is not always clear-cut for a number of basic reasons.

First, the relation between the account and the events or situations to which it supposedly is directed tends to be problematic, though to varying degrees. As we have seen in detail in our discussions of falsehood, members commonly manipulate these uncertainties of relations between concrete events and accounts precisely so they cannot be pinned down and found to be wrong or dishonest; they can then try to wriggle out of it by claiming, "I didn't say that exactly," "Yes, but that's not what I was talking about," "You're putting words in my mouth," etc.

Second, of course, the common conception of facts as being "hard" (unproblematic) is both a misconception and a rhetorical device for asserting the absolute truth of one's position and the falsehood of one's opponent's position. We shall shortly see that what are taken as "hard facts" of legal and journalistic evidence are commonly dependent upon complex forms of general cultural experience and understanding. Nevertheless, while all such complexities must be kept in mind and used continually by investigative social researchers in evaluating their checking out procedures, the distinctions between directly observed facts and mere accounts is vitally important. The distinction is actually a difference in degree of reliability, but the differences can be immense and everyone knows they are vital in our worldly and scientific affairs.

Let us consider briefly a few sharp contrasts between unchecked-out accounts and those that have been checked out. A well-known example of traditional interview methods, involving the use of almost entirely unchecked-out accounts, is found in Garfinkel's (1967) analysis of the case of "Agnes."

"Agnes" is used as a case of sex-role change, of a male passing as or becoming female, and his/her accounts of sex and sex behavior are used to analyze sex-role accounts and behavior in our society. The crucial point is that the accounts used in the lengthy analysis of the case are taken from accounts given by Agnes and probably a few others (Agnes' mother) to doctors. They are office accounts. They purport to be accounts of how Agnes has lived and how Agnes has actually felt, looked at, thought of, and linguistically described his/her sexual life in society. There is no attempt made by the sociologist to directly observe Agnes in everyday life beyond the office. That is, there is no attempt made to check out the accounts against what they purport to be accounts of, nor against similar accounts that Agnes might give in his/her everyday settings. Almost anyone with much knowledge of relations between patients and doctors, especially psychiatrists, can immediately suspect that Agnes is simply doing a classic form of patient manipulation of the psychiatrist by using accounts rhetorically. This suspicion is based on the massive evidence showing that psychiatric patients, like human beings in general, create and learn complex ways of using falsehoods to manipulate the psychiatrists.

A crucial aspect of this manipulation is telling the psychiatrist what he wants to hear, just as people generally learn to do when they want to manipulate those who have more power than they do.[10] (Students commonly learn to "regurgitate" the professor's talk in order to get good grades, even when they don't for one minute agree with him, or even understand what he is saying.) In psychiatric settings this consists in part of learning to tell him what he wants to hear—in his own words. Now, anyone knowing these things should take one look at the Agnes accounts and conclude, "Wow, did she (he) put that guy on." Indeed, part of the Agnes account consists of the argument by the doctors that Agnes did put them on for a long time and only later told them the truth. How do they know the second form of Agnes accounts is the true one and the first the false? (There was some attempt to use alternative accounts, but this was apparently only from his/her mother, which fails as an independent account.) They used almost nothing but testing out, including such tests of "reason or logic" as the internal-consistency checks. It is, therefore, entirely possible that Agnes was not giving truthful accounts of how he/she lived, nor was he/she giving truthful accounts of how he/she would normally even talk about himself-herself in everday life. Indeed, I expect this is the most plausible interpretation because it tests out against our experience with this kind of setting and it would agree with Agnes' attempt to convince the psychiatrist to give him/her a sex change. The failure to test out adequately and the absence of any significant checking out of this case would lead the investigative social researcher to look at it as disconfirmed and reject it immediately—rejected until further checking out.[11]

An investigative social researcher would have approached this case differently. Indeed, it is so complex and problematic that I would have insisted all the major forms of checking out be carried out. First direct observations, then combine this with recycling to direct experience, then independent accounts. In fact, when anything is this complex and problematic, it should probably be studied only if one already has the in-depth, direct experience and this case is a part of that setting one is studying. Otherwise, one will generally find that an individual such as Agnes is now living in a nonnatural setting (determined in part by the researcher) and has already adopted psychiatry-talk. Checking out is immensely difficult and time-consuming in such cases and probably not worthwhile for scientific purposes. Let us keep this case in mind as we go through the ways in which we do in fact check out accounts members have given us in research settings.

Checking out against direct observations ("hard facts") is the one most people have in mind when they think of "seeing if it's true or not." This is the form one is aware of from detective stories.[12]

In most instances we look for direct, natural observations, rather than such supposed "hard facts." These direct observations are the most reliable, whereas the supposedly "hard facts" commonly have to be pinned down to our own direct observations before they can be relied on. The reason for this is that supposed "hard facts" commonly depend on the accounts of other people (independent accounts), which are inherently less reliable than direct experience. For example, legal investigators commonly take "hard numbers" and "hard official data" as hard facts, whereas sociologists have consistently found these forms of official numbers to be among the least reliable forms of information.

This does not mean we reject all forms of numerical data by any means. There are times when our own checking out through direct observations leads us to see even some forms of official data as useful. For example, in *Drug Crisis Intervention* there are several forms we used, such as blood-analysis data on drugs ingested. But the crucial point is that we accepted and used these only because they checked out against our own direct observations and we always viewed them and reported them as problematic. (Carefully controlled observations have shown that even simple and legally important blood-sample tests, such as those for drugs in urine, have been systematically wrong by as much as 75 percent. The tests in hospitals are far more rushed, complex and problematic. Moreover, they are not used nor sanctioned legally.)

A further example will show the contrast. In our study of massage parlors we found an intermediary who was able to set up a friendly contact with an accountant who handled the books and general business affairs of a successful massage parlor owner. This accountant was willing to talk with us informally about how much the owner made and how. While this would have been interesting, I decided it wasn't worth the time required. The reasons were simple. We knew by systematic observations of masseuses and customers in many different parlors how much was taken in. This was highly reliable evidence. I was more interested in the accountant to see if I could detect forms of diverting or skimming money from official books, but even that wasn't important to us. Knowing the often complex forms of "ownership" of the parlors and the kinds of people involved, I didn't doubt that there were complex ways of diverting the funds. (We already knew the schemes of the girls to avoid any official reporting for income tax purposes.) And the accountant would have almost certainly been too untrusting to tell anything like that, if he knew it. We wrote it off. A journalist or legal investigator, being concerned with legal forms of documenting a case against someone, would have gone for that rather than the epistemologically more reliable forms of direct observations, experience and independent accounts.

Let us consider a reasonably simple form of direct observation and then a more complex form to see how we do our direct observations. In the discussion of the case of Phil in Chapter 5, I mentioned that another regular had strongly asserted to us that he had recently seen some people doing sex on the beach and "couldn't understand why they didn't see that it would ruin the beach for everyone." My immediate thought about Ralph's assertion was simply, "Woweee . . . haven't I been casually observing Ralph doing casual exhibitionism on the beach for months?" I was already reasonably sure from previous observations that his whole thing on the beach was exhibiting his sex organs to women. But it was certainly possible I had assumed too much or that he was so subtle at it that he and others might interpret it differently. I decided to check him out more carefully, which consisted of simply watching for him and carefully, systematically observing and analyzing what he was into. In the next several days I did observe him doing what I had thought. He would seek out women, especially pretty young girls, walk up close to them, watching their eyes. This wasn't so unusual. This was the standard form of moderate exhibitionism, quite acceptable on the beach. He went a bit beyond by standing around the women, even circling them at times, and by swaying his hips to provide a genital swing which would also produce slight tumescence; but all of this was acceptable on the beach, not to the point of "doing sex" that people thought might lead to repression. Check and confirmation of my thought, but not to the point of disconfirming his implied assertion that he opposed and rejected heavier forms of "doing sex on the beach." I started watching for him at greater distances, since he might be avoiding anything more if he knew I might spot him. A few days later I spotted him from several hundred yards away. He was at the water's edge, standing about 20 yards from three teenage girls near the water. He had a complete erection and slowly moved around. Check and disconfirmation of his account. But only partially. Anyone can have a physiological accident with the autonomic nervous system (a basic fact of body language). The standard practice on the beach was to sit down or go in the water to cool it off. He did not, but still. . . .

In the days following I spotted him from greater distances doing the same things. One day I spotted him a few hundred yards ahead and down-sun (which meant I could see him much better than he could see me). He had a complete erection and was circling three teenage girls who were about ten yards away from him in the water. He would approach them, then draw back, never saying anything to them. After about ten minutes of this, I continued along the water. He could now see me. He turned and jogged down the beach. I retreated out of sight. While I was talking with another regular about 15 minutes later, out of sight, Ralph returned to the three girls, erect again, and continued circling around for at least 15 minutes.

The girls eventually left and he walked down the beach to where I was talking with the other regular. As Ralph walked by, he simply said "Oh, hi there." Check, double check and total disconfirmation. I did want Ralph to eventually talk about this whole exhibitionist trip, but not for any form of checking out, member validation, or documentation of my conclusion. The checking out was total. I wanted him to talk about the internal experiences I could not directly infer. (It was obviously exciting to him, but it was not obvious what he thought of it, how it fit into his life pattern, and so on.) I could not confront him about it, for that would have produced total denial, been a violation of the standard beach practice of inattention to other people's sex trips as long as they didn't get superheavy, and it would have broken off the relationship between us. I started further exploration, which consisted largely of trying to draw him out (see next chapter) by talking about how much women liked to voyeurize the guys, etc., how normal this was, etc. But two years later he still had not opened up.

Sometimes a simple direct observation can provide the crucial bits of information that help unravel complex situations. Such a critical direct observation itself is almost always embedded in extensive previous direct experience which has produced a real grasp of the situation and generally extensive understanding, allowing the formulation of specific questions; and it must generally be followed by further checking out and exploration. But the critical observation crystalizes things, makes the pieces fall together in what the observer generally senses immediately to be an adequate understanding of the setting. (These are "Well I'll be damned" observations.) He then knows what further information to seek out and how to formulate questions and get answers to fill in the rest of the pieces. All of this was strikingly clear in a critical observation made by Phillip and Sharon Davis in our study of drug crisis intervention. We had been trying for weeks to find out just what police could and did do about heroin cases in emergency rooms, how they were contacted, who called them (doctors vs. nurses), whether they arrested the people and so on.

Then one day while observing and interviewing the staff in a large emergency room they directly observed a concrete case which immediately led them to explore further its implications in the setting. The observation and subsequent exploration almost immediately crystalized the situation for us:

A patient had been brought in by County Rescue earlier that morning. He was unconscious and barely breathing when they were called to his home by a relative, and they could give no background or history on the patient to the emergency room staff.

The staff gave the patient a "finger-stick" test which is a quick way to ascertain the possibility of diabetic-insulin shock. This test proved positive so blood was drawn for more extensive lab tests. These tests showed the patient to be diabetic. At the same time they noticed needle marks on the patient's forearm, prompting one nurse to call the police, who arrived within minutes. The officers were shown the needle tracks and they then questioned the patient about his habit. The patient denied being a drug addict. One nurse described the situation thusly: "The doctor felt that they should not give him Narcon since if it was heroin the drug might throw him into withdrawal. . . . When he [the patient] found out the police were going to arrest him, he just told them, you know, that he had just shot up, and admitted to it; that he was a heroin addict. . . . He had denied everything until he found out that they did not believe him and were going to take him for questioning."

After the patient had been taken from the emergency room by the police, the staff individually reported different "understandings" of when the police were to be notified. One nurse indicated that the policy was different now that the State Hospital Group had announced a new bill which frees the emergency room staff of the *obligation* to notify the authorities of overdose patients. According to her, it was now a matter of how each emergency room interprets the statement that they are no longer required to call. She would call the police only under certain conditions, for example, if the patient was threatening the staff. The nurses are to call when the doctor tells them to do so. She was asked if she would be more likely to notify the police with a heroin OD (overdose). She said, "I think at that point is when the doctor would request it."

The second nurse, when questioned alone, indicated that they notify the police when the doctor tells them to. She said that he feels, however, that they should always be called with overdose patients. It was learned later in the day that this nurse had called the police. She said in a later conversation that she personally felt that the police should be notified because "If there is anything that can be done that might help other kids, then it should be done."

The doctor was interviewed regarding his policy of notifying the police. He said that he now operates under a recent statement by the hospital attorney that the rights of the patient must be protected and they should not be forced to incriminate themselves. "We haven't been calling for every overdose, the reason being that we want them to come in and get treatment, whereas before they wouldn't do it. But if we felt there may be criminal intent in there someplace, if there's even a suggestion of it, then we call the police. But there's still a little hangover of the old ways, of calling routinely and we probably call them a lot more often than we absolutely would have to. Such as this guy with the heroin. We didn't have to call the police on him, actually . . . he was no public threat, he was only killing himself. I didn't call the police and I didn't ask them to call the police, but then the old routine went through, you see, and they didn't even ask me, and the police came. And almost arrested him. They would have too if I hadn't insisted that he needed treatment for his diabetes. I did insist on that so they wouldn't arrest him. 'Cause I think these guys need help."

A phone check with the arresting division showed that the patient was booked at Central Hospital for the (internal) possession of narcotics and for being under the influence.

All further checking out showed that the patterns revealed in this case were a consistent pattern. It was a real breakthrough in understanding the whole complex setup for handling ODs.

While direct observations of concrete events like this are sometimes crucial, we often find it necessary to get in-depth direct experience in a setting to check out some important statements or hunches. The obvious thing is simply to recycle one's study at this point and use the various entree and in-depth methods we have already discussed. But this is often not possible in those situations in which one wishes to check out, or else one would probably have started with in-depth experience. If this is the situation and if the checking out is important, the researcher may now consider infiltration techniques. (See Chapter 8.)

Let us consider a detailed case in which we thoroughly checked out a taped interview by recycling to direct experience. This instance shows all of the dangers of classical cooperative methods, especially of those using interviews not checked out as a basic source of information. It shows the power of checking out and how difficult it often is. This case arose as part of another study, as is often the case.[13] That was a study of a nudist camp. I had known two independent contacts (potential coattails) for several years who were members of the nudist camp. Both had approached me to tell me that their experience over years in this one camp indicated it was not like the nudist camps on which Weinberg (1969) had reported in his fine study. They found that sex was much more open. I tried for several years to get someone else to pick up these fine research contacts. All turned it down (generally in mild panic). I finally got Robert Gilmore to sacrifice himself to the cause.

Soon after managing the ordeal of entree to the camp, he learned from one of the contacts and others about "Doc." Doc was well-known and central in the life of part of the camp. Our main contact hated and distrusted him, but he seemed to have many friends and acquaintances in the camp. He'd been a member for about 20 years (and was now about 50). He sounded like a good inside-informant. Then Gilmore met him while helping at a "Nudist Booth" at a state fair. They hit it off well and Doc readily agreed to do a taped interview at his house. He seemed open and willing to talk. Gilmore and his wife went to do the interview one night, found Doc alone because, he said, his wife had a cold. They set up the recorder and talked for two hours about nudism, the nude beach (which Doc said he was now going to steadily), and swinging. Doc proved to be an intelligent and articulate interviewee. He did most of the talking and told his story well. His delivery was warm, consistent and sincere. The tape sounds like a man who is committed to what he is saying, to the cause of nudism and swinging. For our purposes here, let us focus on his account of swinging. The following is an excerpt of his major statements about swinging.[14]

Doc: My first wife and I slowly grew apart. One day, after we had been married 14 years, she told them [our nudist camp] she was resigning her membership and, consequently, as a result of doing this, that I would not be allowed to come, nor would the children be allowed to come anymore. And I went out and filed for a divorce the next day . . .

And I'm that serious about nudism. I have allowed my membership to expire last March and haven't renewed it. I don't know whether I will or not because I'm very, very much involved in the nude beaches. I love the beaches far more than the camp . . .

My present wife and I lived together for about a year and have now been married about seven years. And we've been avid nudists before and since our marriage. I think truthfully that probably there are two things, and I'll put them in order, that my wife and I share in common that keeps our marriage together: (1) Sex, we are very compatible and (2) our love for nudism . . .

I think that swinging will destroy a weak relationship, whether it be marriage or whatever. I think that it will strengthen a strong relationship. I think that swinging in many cases will revitalize the marriage as far as your sexual interests and desire (goes). I think that everything is comparative. I think that in order to know how much you enjoy each other physically or sexually that it is absolutely necessary sometimes to compare. I think that variety truly is the spice of life. And I think we accept this in everything other than sex . . .

I've been discussing with you where as I was taught that sex was a "no, no," that it was bad and it was wrong and it was sinful and all these things. I raised my son and my daughter 360° or 180°, if you should choose, in the opposite direction. My son has brought girls home, takes them in his bedroom and does his thing, since he was 14. And my daughter, I guess I must have started her at 13 with birth control pills. She and her boyfriend are all living here with us for quite some time. Both have been around when things were going on but they do not participate. They go into their own bedrooms and do their own thing. I am very much aware of contributing to (the delinquency of) minors . . .

When I was a young boy I had established sex as a goal in life and that I wanted to sleep with as many women as Solomon had wives. . . . I kept a diary until I passed 15,000 and then I figured it was kind of foolish and I threw it away. . . .

Truthfully, I think almost all people would like to be involved. I think that they are prevented from getting involved for a number of reasons: Inhibitions, background, brainwashing, not being able to handle it. Usually, people, as is the custom in society, when they go together, when they fall in love, they do it on a very monogamous basis. They convince each other that you're for me and I'm for you and Holy bonds of matrimony shall never. . . . Then they go out and cheat on each other. . . .

I don't know why it is but—to tell you that I think I'm a special person, but I'm sure that because of my attitude that's what it boils down to. But I have known a lot of people that are members of the Sexual Liberty League, for example, and uh, I feel about, truthfully, the Sexual Liberty League the same way that I feel about the Singles Set of Apartments over on Greer Avenue. I don't know if you're familiar with what I'm talking about. But I think that they're basically a bunch of rejects who have banded together searching for something and they have found a bunch of other rejects. Now the parties I go to and have myself have a lot of young people. We sometimes have girls that work at the Hot Spot and other girls that work in parlors. Age isn't all that important, but what is are that the people think highly of themselves and take good care of their bodies . . .

When Gilmore and I listened to the tape a few days later we were struck by a number of things. First, while there was some obvious bravado (e.g., the Solomon bit), there were a number of things about the tape that checked out well. Most importantly, the things he had said about the nude beach checked with what I, Rasmussen and Flanagan had found. Unknown to Doc, I knew who he was from Gilmore's earlier descriptions, and what he said checked out with my outsider observations of him and his group, and with my insider understanding of the general setting.

Second, what he told Gilmore about the nudist camp checked out with what Gilmore had observed directly and with what others told him.

Third, this was not a completely de-contextualized account. Gilmore knew him a bit and knew others who knew him well.

Fourth, his accounts of the swinging scene and his part in it checked out against what social scientists and others had been reporting in various publications for some time.

In spite of all this, Gilmore and I had a hunch that all was not what it seemed from the interview.

First, our best contact, someone we trusted pretty well, did not trust him.

Second, and more important, we discounted the other social science reports because in general we believed they fail to get at the inner truth of things.

Third, Doc had obviously put a heavy make on Gilmore and his wife at the end of the interview to get them to join the swinging scene. Gilmore's wife had felt this strongly and freaked out over it. They taped their discussion about the whole thing while driving home—part of our standard debriefing procedure—and the tape made that point stunningly clear.

Fourth, we tested out our hunch with others who had considerable general cultural experience with such things. Looking at the whole thing, they too felt doubts. All things considered, we didn't know what to think. (Gilmore did know that he and his wife were not going to the party!) We decided to check it out in depth, primarily because the whole subject of swinging was potentially of basic importance in understanding changes in sex in our society today.

The checking out took a lot of time and effort, but it was greatly facilitated by the fact that the setting was squeezed between our nude beach study and Gilmore's nudism study. (When the researcher can catch the members in a research pincer's movement they're pretty helpless—they almost have to surrender the truth to him.) We decided to do it independently. Rasmussen and Flanagan would pick up on Doc and his swinging crew at the nude beach, making no mention of Gilmore (beyond the fact he too was a graduate student) and not telling him about their knowledge of the tape. (This is important to prevent a subject from hiding or from trying to make his future activities fit his past statements.) As far as we could ever tell, Doc had no suspicions of being checked out this way. Rasmussen and Flanagan checked him out from every angle and Rasmussen did the following analysis of Doc's major statements about swinging.

Doc: My first wife and I slowly grew apart. One day, after we had been married 14 years, she told them (our nudist camp) she was resigning her membership and, consequently, as a result of doing this, that I would not be allowed to come, nor would the children be allowed to come anymore. And I went out and filed for a divorce the next day . . .

Researchers' Comments: Actually what happened was that Doc and Denise (his second and present wife) got caught having an affair by Doc's first wife. Both Denise and Lola (a close friend of both) saw Doc's present actions, playing around and all, as a repeat of the same thing. First, he would start playing around and then he would leave her.

Doc: And I'm that serious about nudism. I have allowed my membership to expire last March and haven't renewed it. I don't know whether I will or not because I'm very, very much involved in the nude beaches. I love the beaches far more than the camp . . .

Researchers' Comments: According to Doc's later statements, he got into some kind of political feud at the camp and was asked not to return. According to Denise and Lola, he was asked to leave the camp because he had become too aggressive sexually and the members got together and asked him to leave.

Doc: My present wife and I lived together for about a year and have now been married about seven years. And we've been avid nudists before and since our marriage. I think truthfully that probably there are two things, and I'll put them in order, that my wife and I share in common that keeps our marriage together: (1) Sex, we are very compatible, and (2) our love for nudism . . .

Researchers' Comments: At this point in time, Doc's and Denise's marriage was anything but together. She had just returned from a six-month vacation with her boyfriend and there had been doubt that she would ever return. In fact, Doc was so certain that she would not return that he had given some of her clothes to Lola, which was a source of conflict between them when Denise returned.

Doc: I think that swinging will destroy a weak relationship, whether it be marriage or whatever. I think that it will strengthen a strong relationship. I think that swinging in many cases will revitalize the marriage as far as your sexual interests and desire [goes]. I think that everything is comparative. I think that in order to know how much you enjoy each other physically or sexually that it is absolutely necessary sometimes to compare. I think that variety truly is the spice of life. And I think we accept this in everything other than sex . . .

Researchers' Comments: Doc may or may not have believed this at the time, but in later private statements to me Doc explained that Denise had failed to keep up with other people and had let herself go. That he looked at swinging as a way to get rid of her without telling her flat out to leave. Further, after we'd been studying him for about eight months, Doc fell in love with a beautiful 19-year-old, Darlene. He was terribly possessive of her and jealously guarded his "rights." He would hardly even share her conversation with the young men; he most definitely had no intention of "sharing" her so they could "compare." Doc also gave up his free sex life and played it 100 percent straight. No parties and no cheating.

Doc: I've been discussing with you where as I was taught that sex was a "no, no," that it was bad and it was wrong and it was sinful and all these things. I raised my son and my daughter 360°, or 180°, if you should choose, in the opposite direction. My son has brought girls home, takes them in his bedroom and does his thing, since he was 14. And my daughter, I guess I must have started her at 13 with birth control pills. She and her boyfriend are all living here with us for quite some time. Both have been around when things were going on but they do not participate. They go into their own bedrooms and do their own thing. I am very much aware of contributing to [the delinquency of] minors . . .

Researchers' Comments: Several things here were simply not true. While Doc's son was a free-wheeling sex participant, his daughter was not. She was very much opposed to their parties and their friends and always made it a point to be absent when the orgies were taking place. The son on the other hand was very supportive and on occasions actually took part in the parties. These facts came to light when Denise and Doc were discussing just how two people brought up in the same environment could be so different.

Doc: When I was a young boy I had established sex as a goal in life and that I wanted to sleep with as many women as Solomon had wives. . . . I kept a diary until I passed 15,000 and then I figured it was kind of foolish and I threw it away . . .

Researchers' Comments: While Doc was anything but celibate, and he did spend a great deal of time trying to recruit new girls, it is clear that he could not have had that much sex. With all of his recruiting, it's safe to say that he was doing well if he could average one different girl a week. While he may have had sex with as many women as Solomon, he would have also had to have been as old as Methesula to have reached 15,000 . . .

Doc: Truthfully, I think almost all people would like to be involved. I think that they are prevented from getting involved for a number of reasons: Inhibitions, background, brainwashing, not being able to handle it. Usually, people, as is the custom in society, when they go together, when they fall in love, they do it on a very monogamous basis. They convince each other that you're for me and I'm for you and Holy bonds of matrimony shall never—. Then they go out and cheat on each other . . .

Researchers' Comments: As with most swingers, Doc is attacking the traditional form of extramarital sex, cheating. While Doc also attacked cheating in private talks, it was clear that he also took part in it. On one occasion he showed up at my house with two 17-year-olds, whom he had promised to get high-paying jobs in the massage parlors via contacts he knew. It was clear that Denise didn't know about this and he asked me not to tell anyone. On another occasion, I actually took part in a coverup for Doc. He and I were supposed to have gone up to Oceanside to draw some money out of his bank account, while we really had arranged to meet two 21-year-olds down at the nude beach. As with the 17-year-olds, he had promised them a job working in a massage parlor, using the contacts he had made. While the 17-year-olds bought the story and became involved with him doing sex, the 21-year-olds flipped out and demanded to be taken home immediately. They couldn't imagine getting it on with someone the same age as their father.

Doc: I'm 43 now, and I started my practice as a chiropractor here in the Orange City area in 1958. I believe I heard from one of my patients that there was a nudist camp out in Box Canyon. I was very intrigued by this and I wanted very much to find out about it. [Once I got into the camp I also got involved with the swingers and now both are a way of life. I made enough money as a chiropractor to retire comfortably and that's all I do now . . .]

Researchers' Comments: Within one year of my knowing Doc, he had aged to 49. But even that changed from time to time, so it's anyone's guess. I think the 49 is most accurate because one of his girlfriends had checked it out on his driver's license. Doc's retirement plan was a little inaccurate. He had worked as a chiropractor, but he left that to become a salesman for cemetery plots for a local cemetery. He made a fortune "selling" the plots by getting bank mortgages to himself and then paying the installments with the money from his commissions. The idea was that land prices were increasing and that eventually he would be able to sell them at a higher profit. He got caught by the company and had his license suspended. He also had floated personal loans from friends for well over $100,000. Lola's ex-husband was one of *them. He got soaked for $60,000—which was part of the reason Lola told all of Doc's secrets. But his feast was almost over. He was in the process of filing for bankruptcy and his only valuables were his house, which he had homesteaded, and his car. Denise was to get anything that was left in settlement for the divorce.*

Doc: You get involved in a lot of things in swinging, you get exposed to a lot of things in swinging as individuals, that you might not be exposed to if you never got involved. Uh—example—you will find that probably better than 95 percent of men like to see women participate in homosexual relationships. Uh, you'll find that probably 94-1/2 percent of those same men cannot bring themselves to participate in homosexual relationships, because they feel that it makes them less manly. Uh, I am of the opinion, and always have been, that there's no such thing as heterosexuality or homosexuality. I strongly believe that people are just plain and simply sexed . . . [Although, I personally have no interest in sex with other men nor have I taken part in any . . .]

Researchers' Comments: Doc's preference was obviously female, but on several occasions he became involved in homosexual acts. In one case, he was complaining to a friend that he did not appreciate his having "piled on" in a group sex scene. "Nothing could be more disgusting than making it with a girl and some guy comes up behind and slips it to you!" When asked about this, Doc claimed that having been in swinging for so long there wasn't anything that he hadn't done and enjoyed. "You simply enjoy some things more than others."

Doc: I don't know why it is but—to tell you that I think I'm a special person, but I'm sure that because of my attitude that's what it boils down to. But I have known a lot of people that are members of the Sexual Liberty League; for example, and uh, I feel about, truthfully, the Sexual Liberty League the same way that I feel about the singles set of apartments over on Greer Avenue. I don't know if you're familiar with what I'm talking about. But I think that they're basically a bunch of rejects who have banded together searching for something and they have found a bunch of other rejects. (Now the parties I go to and have myself have a lot of young people. We sometimes have girls that work at the Hot Spot and other girls that work in parlors. Age isn't all that important, but what is are that the people think highly of themselves and take good care of their bodies . . .)

Researchers' Comments: Doc did in fact have a large number of girls at his parties who worked at the Hot Spot and different massage parlors—all of which were owned by the Jones family. An arrangement had been made that the Hot Spot could send over customers to Doc's parties in return for a supply of young women. The couples that arrived from the Hot Spot were for the most part rejects. But this didn't bother Doc, because he thereby had all these young masseuses. Doc's obvious concern with age was most evident in his concern with the young ladies. Doc's wife had commented on this and she had hypothesized it was because he was getting older and feared aging. He realized that in a few years or so he wouldn't even be able to get it up. For whatever reason, Doc ran off with the beautiful young 19-year-old and, at last sighting, was on his way to Hawaii, supposedly to set up a health studio. His wife had filed for divorce and she and Lola were throwing swinging parties at which there were no masseuses and a great over supply of young men.

The researchers observed many other things not directly relevant to this tape that showed how dedicated and effective Doc was at using every form of dishonesty to achieve his goals. We have presented many of them, without analyzing them, in *Nude Beaches*. For example, he carefully controlled the interviews of one of the network TV crews that did a study on the nude beach. He set up the people they were to interview, including making sure he was not one of the people (because Doc knew his demonic appearance would "queer" the cause with most middle-class people). He carefully chose people who would give talks about how "I've been coming to this beach for 25 years and I've never seen any sex down here at all." After the TV crew had packed up their cans of filmed truth and departed, Doc turned to Rasmussen and, with a smile of pride in a job well done, said, "Well-l-l, we sure fed 'em a line of shit that time."

Doc not only illustrates the vital importance for the researcher of the techniques of checking out what people tell him, even super friendly people, he also illustrates the general point that in most settings, especially those straight ones controlled by highly successful entrepreneurs, organizers, politicians and so on, there are generally some crucial gatekeepers who are tremendously astute everyday life politicians; that is, experts in the creation and manipulation of falsehoods intended to front out the dangerous outsiders. His accounts about swinging were merely one form of his many rhetorical accounts. (It was a seduction rhetoric.) It might be reassuring to one's sense of normalcy and an inspiration to one's trust in human nature to believe that "Doc is just one of those pathological liars found in deviant activities." There are indeed pathological liars, but they are not difficult for experienced people to spot. Doc did delight in putting one over on people. (As Lola said, he would rather steal a dollar than make a thousand.)

But Doc was no pathological liar. He was a tremendously astute everyday politician who played for big stakes (other people's lives, integrity, honor and money) and he generally won. His enemies were legion, but many of them decided to join his schemes because they could profit from his abilities at seducing people. They became supporters of his fronts, helping to deceive new victims. Most people were taken in until it was too late. He could easily take in any researchers who did not thoroughly check out the accounts he gave them.

The crucial, most reliable part of this checking out was, of course, direct experience and direct observation. They are, in that order, the most reliable forms of evidence in general and in this case they were vital. As the reader probably noted in reading the researcher's commentaries, they did make extensive use of accounts provided by other people and even by Doc in assessing the truth and falsehood of his taped interview accounts. But all of those accounts were provided by people in the natural setting, after they had in-depth experience and knew the people well. The same people, such as his wife, would commonly support his lies with strangers, because they were part of his schemes and benefited from many of his seductions. They would provide supporting evidence as seemingly "independent sources" to an outsider. But once the researchers were inside and were friends with Doc, Denise, Lola and many others, they were able to see that they too commonly delighted in the dishonesty of the accounts. The insiders talked to insiders like that, but all of them had a standard line or front for outsiders, such as researchers.

Conclusion

The combined and integrated use of the three major strategies of investigative field research constitutes the most powerful attack in solving the problems of field research. But they are made even more powerful by combining them with the major investigative tactics.

NOTES

1. People also "create troubles" and "abnormalize settings," as I pointed out in the last chapters.

2. I experienced this at the age of 17, at the beginning of my self-education in philosophy. It was a shattering experience, involving simple anxieties like fearing to look into mirrors because this raised questions such as "How can I *possibly* exist at all?" Yet my anxieties and bracketings were small compared to those of some friends of mine.

3. Need I point out that an attractive woman or man is often the best-liked researcher? (We shall talk about this a bit later when we discuss setting the members up and drawing them out.) But an attractive researcher might also be threatening, which can hamper research efforts.

4. It was natural because that's what members do common-sensically all the time. Everyone knows that personal contacts are the vital cement and lubricant of our social life. Contacts involve two crucial ingredients. They obviously involve personal knowledge of someone—someone known through face-to-face contact. But, less obviously, they involve *friendly* contact or liking, for an unfriendly contact would never do any good. Generally when someone offers a personal contact for use, he gives some estimate of the degree of intimacy involved in order to estimate how useful the contact will be—"life-long friends" to "we only met once, but. . . ." Everyone assumes that personal contacts go beyond values and laws and all the paraphernalia of our seemingly absolutist public life. Personal contacts, because of the friendly and trusting relation, do things for one, give one wholesale prices, go out of their way for one, and in general circumvent public rules. They are the bedrock, the foundation, of life and everyone tries to get to bedrock when he wants to build a firm relation or to launch an important enterprise in life.

5. This is actually a deliberate strategy of mine and one I suspect many other social researchers use as well. I collect insider coattails; that is, when I have friendly relations with someone who is inside something interesting, I categorize that person as a potential research subject who can get us in. I also purposely develop close relations with people who are inside such interesting things and then put them in the mental file of insiders with good coattails. Given this collection of inside contacts, I then solicit people to do the studies, unless it is one I want to do myself. And I purposely match up individual researchers with insider coattails before soliciting them. Mainly, I try to see who will be liked, will be fit, able to penetrate deep into the setting. And, of course, we also search out contacts; that is, when we want to study something where we do not already have a good contact, we search for intermediary contacts who can set us up with insiders who are friends of theirs. We shall discuss the web of contacts in discussing team field research.

6. While remaining true to my intention of not imposing my own moral standards on others, I am not proposing that researchers use in-bed interview techniques. While I am sure that this happens, and has in fact been referred to in certain recent research confessions, relations of great intimacy have so many problems that I doubt their usefulness in most research settings. I have already mentioned how important liking was in getting Johnson's study of welfare caseworkers started. But in the initial stage the liking also eventually became too intense. Key informants made emotional demands upon us that we were not willing to meet. This led to bad relations which were an important reason for shifting the research to a new setting. (There were also some excellent positive reasons, like getting comparative information and getting closer to home.) We shall shortly see another instance in which intimacy became a reason for trying to front out a researcher. We must also remember that the investigative researcher will eventually do a public report which may seem like a betrayal to an intimate. He should avoid becoming overcommitted to the private lives he is studying or he will suffer—or choose dishonesty.

7. Since no rules are absolute, there may be situational exceptions to this one. Offhand, I can't think of any we have encountered, though I know of at least one situation where we considered it.

8. We had long since learned that most people in any slightly disreputable position like students a lot more than they like professors. Professors are seen as being "pompous asses" and "know-it-alls" with moralistic attitudes—repressors. Moreover, professors are part of the establishment and thus may blow the whistle—and the media and control agents listen more to their whistle. Students are "innocent victims of the systems," young, fresh, cool, hip, and don't blow whistles—or, if they do, nobody listens. Consequently, in studying such activities we almost always hid the professor behind

some innocent-looking student. But the students were Trojan-students. We shall see more evidence that people will tell students all kinds of things they wouldn't think of telling professors.

9. The girls commonly tell their boyfriends about part of the sex. Generally, they admit they do hand jobs and blow jobs, but deny all else emphatically. There appear to be two reasons for this. First, the greatest proportion of sex in parlors consists of blow jobs, simply because that's where the market is, the demand by the customers. The boyfriends are worldly-wise enough to know this, so once they know the girlfriend is working in a parlor, they figure that's what's happening. (A few girls go to great lengths, including espionage techniques, like hiding their cars far from the parlor, to prevent the boyfriend from knowing they work in the parlor. But most get caught, probably because the boyfriends get suspicious when she suddenly loses much of her interest in sex with him.) They accept that as not involving much intimacy, whereas "balling" is looked at as intimate. Second, the girls are commonly willing to feed the boyfriend data about these lesser sex acts as evidence that they tell him the whole truth, so that he will not probe deeper to find the whole truth. This is a very important common-sense tactic for hiding things and one all researchers must remember. It involves giving half the truth (or less) to hide the whole truth. (People assume that where there's smoke there's fire. When you can see they see the smoke, you show them half the fire with anguished proclamations about how terrible it is they now see the whole fire.) The researcher must expect that where there's some truth there is more to come. (Where there's some fire, there's bound to be more fire.) Keep looking.

10. Field researchers do precisely the same things when they are trying to talk their way into a closed research setting. Field researchers even adopt cowardly, and servile stances in which they literally agree with and support the attacks made on their attempts to gain entree. The purpose is simply to mislead the powerful gatekeeper in the setting into thinking the field researcher is not a threat and that he is a "company man." The ploy is used when there is no further hope of getting one's entree request accepted and he simply wants to build the base for getting in somewhere else. I myself have done this a number of times, even though I am combative by nature. The pretense of submission and identifying with the repressor is widespread. It has long been recognized as a basic strategy of lower-caste people, such as American blacks in the South. It works, as every student who has "regurgitated an exam" knows.

11. Ethnomethodologists, of course, will object that Garfinkel, in accord with his definition of ethnomethodology as the study of accounts in themselves, was simply doing a study of linguistic accounts and, therefore, the situations and so on were irrelevant. This, however, is patently false. Most of the book in which that case appears (1967) implicitly and explicitly sees the situation of an account as a necessary basis for a sociologist's or anyone's interpretation of the meaning of the account. The best that one could argue is that he was doing a study of psychiatric talk about sex roles in American society. But if that is all he intended to do, why did he not simply use the hundreds of thousands of pages of previously published psychiatric talk about such things? It would be more representative. Failing that, why not just use the masses of tapes of talks on it? No, the ethnomethodologists have consistently reverted to an absolutist cooperative model of field research that is close to survey research and fails even by the tests of the Chicago school.

12. Since most people are aware of the checking-out procedures done in detective stories, I might make a comment about their general lack of relevance for social research. There are really three different forms of detective story checking out. The first is the classical arm-chair method of Sherlock Holmes and Hercule Poirot. This involves an overwhelming dependence upon "reason and logic" which actually comes down to

complex forms of testing out in which reason and logic play minor parts compared to a massive knowledge of tobacco leaves, dental practices, etc. The testing out allows the master detective to then set up a minimal but crucial form of controlled observations, even natural experiments in some cases, which provide the hard facts upon which the conviction is based.

The second form, which is the dominant form in the hard-boiled tradition of American detective stories, is the Lew Archer method. (Perry Mason is an earlier generation of more genteel European methods. He uses mainly the classical method.) This method uses a massive amount of "shoe leather" to run around making direct observations, getting the feel for the characters, and once in a while diverging into the brutal methods of police torture. (Generally, however, the detective is the one tortured.)

The third form is the police torture and subversion method, which combines some checking out of the second kind with a lot of more direct torture methods. It is found especially in modern espionage fiction, but is also common in the Mickey Spillane and Norman Chandler types. The classical method is most like the classical positivist and cooperative models of social research. The second is most like the investigative methods. The third is most like actual police methods, though police work is moving more toward the investigative model proposed here, especially because of the highly complex and problematic forms of modern crime.

I would emphasize, however, that while there are these similarities, I have never found any detective stories to be very realistic about how such things are done. Obviously, I think of the Lew Archer method as the most relevant to investigative social research as practiced by sociologists, detectives, and investigative journalists. But even that is generally far from the truth and of no significant help to any social researcher. Most detective work, for example, is really an immense amount of shoe-leather searching for simple and very hard facts, such as finding a "missing person" who has purposefully hidden. (The laundered memoires by Bernstein and Woodward, 1974, of how they helped to "crack" the Watergate caper is a good account of the massive amount of shoe leather, tire rubber and telephone juice involved in modern forms of "getting one's man.") This work is mainly a matter of massive checking of official records (telephone books, social security, etc.) and talking to people who might know something. Journalistic and sociological investigative work is almost always concerned with something far more complex and problematic than the detectives ever think of. I've read a lot of detective fiction, but only as diversion. It is diverting precisely because it is not real to me.

13. Almost any good field research opens up on many other excellent research possibilities because of all the in-depth contacts one makes and the involvement of those contacts in other settings. If a researcher ties his subjects to him properly, he could wind up spending his life going from one setting to another that the first opened onto. One has to make careful estimates of priorities in research, since the world is full of so many things worth studying and so many excellent opportunities.

14. The transcription is verbatim, but excerpted and rearranged somewhat for the convenience of the analysis that will follow. These do not affect the meanings. The few bracketed statements are standard statements Doc made to people and which were implied in the context of the tape, but not actually on the tape.

Chapter 8

MAJOR TACTICS OF INVESTIGATIVE RESEARCH

Strategies are concerned with the more general aspects of research, the research tactics with the more specific aspects, especially those in face-to-face, short-run encounters. There are, of course, an immense number of tactics used by people in their everyday lives to get at the truth. We cannot deal with more than a tiny fraction of such tactics. We will assume that people know how to use such tactics effectively. (John Johnson, 1976, has dealt with a number of these and we shall not duplicate his efforts.) Instead, we shall be concerned with a few that have proven to be the most important and powerful methods of getting at the truth when people have proven relatively unwilling to let the truth be known.

Infiltrating the Setting

The cooperative model of field research assumed the researcher could walk into the scene and do overt research without much problem. John Johnson (1977) has shown in detail how mistaken this is and has described numerous tactics used in complex organizations to penetrate these organizations. In his research, however, he was dealing primarily with situations in which the researcher did come in the front door because it was a closed setting, and he chose to do so. We have found it necessary to develop more devious tactics for many settings. Rather than seeking entree, we infiltrate the setting.

The simplest form of infiltration is worming one's way in (also see Johnson, 1976), which sometimes consists of nothing more than coming in the back door. Though we did it only to a small extent, because we decided our evidence was checking out and we did not need more, we used this in studying some emergency rooms, especially the giant one to which we were denied direct access. We found that the drug overdose cases were supposed to be shipped directly from the emergency room up to the psychiatric ward. The only serious question we had was whether this was what happened. We already had wide-open access and cooperation from that ward, so we could see all the overdoses they got. It was possible to enter the emergency room with the psychiatric staff (the head gave me a guided tour the first day) and with the ambulance staffs that brought in cases. These back-door infiltrations made it clear we did not want to spend more time infiltrating or in making a more direct assault on the setting.

In this setting, as in many others, it was entirely within our range of alternatives to make a brutal direct assault, which we called using the crowbar. In fact, we had partially prepared the way for this once we had discovered their resistance to being studied, both because their resistance made us suspicious and because we were not yet sure that we could get all we needed from the psychiatric ward. In this case we had the official aegis of the National Commission on Marihuana and Drug Abuse, which gave us a great deal of help from local and national medical officials and made it easier to get publicity for our efforts, if we needed it at any stage. Preparatory to the direct assault, we sent our foremost expert on medical officials, Dennis Stouffer, to talk with the head of the hospital. Wrapped in the mantle of his official letter from the National Commission, and using his best deskside manner, his earlier successful contacts with medical officials in other parts of the city, and his successful in-depth research in the emergency room at the second largest county hospital, he was able to get complete and friendly cooperation from the head of the hospital and his subordinates. He explicitly approved our study of the emergency room, not knowing we'd already been barred. We could almost certainly have used this and publicity about their secretiveness (which would have had some impact because they were being investigated by the county grand jury) as a crowbar to pry them open for our observations.

There are times when a researcher may find this useful, but I suspect the only times would be when he is reasonably sure there are some "hard facts" or immediate observations he needs in the setting and when he no longer needs anybody's cooperation in that or related settings. The crowbar is the nuclear weapon of field research and is only used on Doom's Day. For the crowbar—any forced entree—will produce bitterness and a desire for revenge. Since revenge is one of the most powerful of human motives, and since it will lead some members to spend all their time trying to "get" the researcher, it has all the opposite effects from those of friendly and trusting relations. Worse, as with all those pursuing revenge, the members will pursue the researcher from their setting to others, so the contamination effects (spillover from one research setting to another) can be terrifying.[1] The crowbar will also obviously lead to an immediate hiding of all potentially damaging information and no one would dare be friendly and trusting. In this particular case, we had quietly prepared the crowbar in case we wanted to use it, but decided it was not necessary. We gladly let it pass. Realizing we now had no reason to try further to get into the emergency room, we decided to neutralize as much as possible any spillover effects of our rejections. We tried to be friendly, appear trusting, and even agreeable with their decision. As a general rule, once the researcher realizes he isn't going to get into a setting or that it doesn't matter, it is best to commend and support those who have rejected him. That may help to neutralize future adverse spillovers.

This, for example, is what Dennis Lum and I did when we were firmly rejected by two lieutenants of a mayor's office we were trying to study (as part of our team field research on a political convention). These two lieutenants (henchmen) had insulted us. They told us that only journalists had the right and duty to impose themselves on public officials for studies, had lied to us blatantly, and had put our proposal in the same category as the request of elementary school kids wanting to study the convention. Nevertheless, we were understanding and supportive of their insulting response because we already hoped to use our initial foray as an aid in achieving our lesser goal of studying the planning department, something the lieutenants could prevent if they wanted to.

That was our fall-back goal, something a researcher should think out before making his approach for entree. It's hard for them to reject a researcher twice, especially if he can set them up in the first rejection so that they open the other research possibility as part of the way of letting him down easy. One of the favorite ways of cooling the researcher out is to send him to something else to study—"Anything, but get rid of him." Knowing this, the researcher pretends he wants to study something they'll never let him study, in order to get into the place he really wanted to study all along.

As soon as we left their office, we spent some time venting our anger, but our servile and cowardly attitude did pay off. They later let Lum into the planning department.

If the researcher can show enough saintly submissiveness, the members may even feel guilty enough to help him—or they may decide he's such a spineless boob he could never possibly hurt them. Playing the boob is sometimes the best ploy for infiltrating an organization where they are afraid of researchers because they have something to hide, but where it is hard for them to reject. One can play the boob to look like he's no threat and to flatter their pretensions to intelligence.[2] This misperception is enhanced by using the hair-brained academic ploy, which consists of the researcher telling them he's doing a theoretical study that is so abstract it could never hurt or help anyone—and couldn't even be understood by anyone except hair-brained academics.[3] It is especially effective to tell them in some detail how, "We're doing a phenomenological-ethmethodological reduction of your natural attitude in order to display and document the invariant interpretative procedures which are constitutive of the transcendental-ego and hence of inter-subjective cognition." If that isn't good enough, the researcher can tell them that he will, of course, submit all of his tentative findings to the members for "triangulated member-validations" and that the conclusions, once cleared by them, will have no sustantive or practical relevance to anyone.

However, we have found that probably the most effective way of convincing the members that one is not a major risk to them is to use the various ploys of indirection. The best way for a researcher to gain entree when they are afraid of research is to convince them that he is not really studying them, even though he is seeking permission to do just that. He tries to show them that he is studying them only because he is really studying something else with which they are slightly involved.

For example, in our initial approaches to the TV news people and many other settings we told them what was true—that is, we were studying the planning for the national political convention from all angles and they were one of the angles. The point was that we were really studying the convention and were only studying them incidentally, so how could we be a threat to them (the latter implication being left unsaid). What we did not say was that we were also getting our foot in the door to entree so that we could then go on to study them in depth. This was part of our way of worming our way in, as well as quite truthfully a part of a bigger study. Once the researcher gets in, it is hard for them to throw him out without being boorish. Moreover, if he can make enough friends, it is costly to throw him out because his friends will be unhappy.

He can also hope that the members will forget how he ever got in or why. They will thus forget the rationale for throwing him out. The political convention never even really happened, but Altheide and Rasmussen were already in the TV newsrooms. The station Rasmussen was studying was not scared, so they never asked why he was still around—they probably also forgot. But even in Altheide's station, where the director was unfriendly, it was months before the director remembered to challenge him with "Hey! What are you still doing here?"

After our official study of drug crisis intervention was completed, we went on studying drug overdoses, never mentioning that the National Commission had died of natural causes months before. (Our official letters had no termination date and most people would not read the newspapers closely enough to note the death notices. Besides, we saw no reason to bother renegotiating the rationale for doing our study.) Stouffer had almost become a taken-for-granted intern at one of the giant emergency rooms before anyone thought to ask why he was still there. (As usual, the challenge came from an enemy he had unintentionally made. A nurse got mad at him for taking the side of a patient and started a campaign to get rid of him. It was she who unearthed the fact of the Commission's unfortunate demise and challenged his reason for being there, screaming that he must really be a journalist bent on exposing them. That really scared the administrators. Someone quickly expropriated his notebooks and I was soon getting urgent calls from the director wanting to know who he was and what he was up to. Little did they know that Stouffer always contended that this hospital was the best of them all and that they treated overdoses splendidly.)[4]

There are many situations in which infiltration is obviously possible (it almost always is, if one just tries hard enough[5]), but in which it is too costly to make it worthwhile.

Another good worming tactic uses a variant of the phased-entree tactic. If the researcher wants to study a group he cannot get into, he studies one he can get into and which he knows has entree to the other one. This proved effective in several instances in our study of the national political convention. Altheide used this phased-entree tactic successfully in penetrating both national political conventions, especially the inner recesses of the massive TV news setups. That became a major part of his whole theory of "The Social Organization of Security" (1975). (This was no minor undertaking, since security measures at the national conventions were massive and serious. That one study made Altheide one of the foremost practitioners of assault tactics in investigative field research.) This method of infiltrating complex organizations tends to be relatively easy and powerful for three reasons: (1) Once the researcher is into one part of the organization, they rarely tell others with whom they deal that the researcher is merely a researcher; (2) They are relatively amorphous and most insiders are relatively anonymous; and (3) Anyone with presumptive insider credentials (which, as Altheide found, often means little more than that one is in fact inside) is difficult to challenge without raising serious issues.

Building Friendly Trust and Opening Them Up

We have dealt at considerable length in the last chapter with the strategies of building friendly and trusting relations. All of these are relevant to building friendly and trusting relations in face-to-face, short-run encounters, such as in-depth interview situations. One must obviously always be using charm, seductiveness, humor, and openness.

But there is a special tactic of great importance in investigative research, especially in short-run, in-depth interviews. This is the tactic of opening the members up. It begins with one's being open with the members, but goes beyond this to sharing intimacies with them and, if possible, making oneself vulnerable in the same way they are in the interview, making oneself a hostage to their friendly trustworthiness, often by implicating oneself in the same things for which they are being studied. (This shares some important aspects of the phased assertion tactic, discussed later, but involves revealing oneself.)

This tactic, like any others, obviously depends on the people one is dealing with. Some people cannot be opened up, regardless of how hard the researcher tries—they are the proverbial clams. Some people don't need to be opened up because they just ooze personal revelations from every pore. (This, for example, was the case with Jon's girlfriend on the nude beach, whom we have mentioned before. She was explicit about it: "I don't know why, but I'm really just trusting. I know I get stepped on by people for being that way, but I just can't see being any other way. I mean, why should I hide from people? I just want to be honest and open and get them to be honest and open too." Everyone went around saying how much she was letting herself in for trouble, because everyone knows how dangerous it is to be open and honest. But it was good for researchers, especially when her open statements checked out consistently.) And, of course, some people may be open initially but clam up if the researcher gets too intimate with them because they begin to feel threatened. Just as with the phased-assertion tactic discussed later, he has to move in phases, watching closely to see if his tactic is opening them up. If not, he probably has to switch tactics.

The simplest forms of opening up are those in which people respond almost immediately. As the researcher starts telling them incriminating things or intimate things, they may look a bit surprised and smile, or even chuckle, and then begin to open up. (Often they initiate the opening up and the researcher just follows.) I had two standard opening up ploys in the beach study. The first was my obstruction of justice ploy. I'd spot someone who looked interesting doing something illegal, such as being nude out of the legal area, or smoking pot, or drinking (apparently under age). I'd approach and hail the person, "Hey, don't you know it's a capital crime to go nude beyond that sign?" (I was already making fun of the law, showing whose side I was on.) The person generally didn't know, so then I'd tell him the dirty politics of the law, tell him to watch for the white police van, especially at 11:30 a.m., 3 p.m., and 5 p.m. Then I'd tell him how people lied about their identities, that the heavy-set and balding cop was the one to watch out for, and so on. It was like giving him a free lawyer's services and at the same time showing him that I was one of them, all in the same boat against "the pigs." (I have to admit that, try as I might, I could never bring myself to call the cops "pigs." Sometimes I'd get mad and mutter it to myself, but the term just had too much disrespect for people who weren't generally even in favor of what they were doing. I would have lost my inhibitions if they had been really aggressive, but only one of them was. My inhibition in using this term no doubt queered my relations with a few people—I could feel myself being immediately shut out. The field researcher must be cruel to some people, if he is to fit into most social settings in this conflictful world.)

This obstructing justice ploy would often lead not only to the person's opening up, but would make him friendly forever. There were instances in which people given this treatment would later shout out as I went by, "Hey Jack! Over here, man." Then I'd have to search through my memory to try to remember the person, while acting as if I remembered well. (This ploy also marked me as one of the ultimate insiders, which made people want to be more friendly—hobnobbing with the insiders is always valued.)

One day I came across three hip types and gave them this legal spiel. I also began telling them about the sex on the beach. Pretty soon they were opening up in every direction, so much so that I began to get embarrassed. For example, I started out by saying things about sex, such as that a guy lying nearby was going to get sunburned genitals because he was lying straight up. Then they began to open up, one of the women talking about why her husband wouldn't come down to the nude beach; before long this woman was doing things like running over to tell the guy he was going to get sunburned and ought to roll over. (He thanked her and rolled over. Obviously a clam.) I started the rarely used retraction gambit, acting less open to calm them down and close them up before we got arrested for indecent exposure.

The importance of revealing guilty facts about oneself, even when not true, was revealed in a classic opening-up operation by Rasmussen and Flanagan. They had been watching a gay guy on one of the nude beaches in Santa Barbara, then went up to him with their recorder and asked if he'd talk with them about the beach scene for a student paper. He started out reluctantly. Then they started telling him about themselves, intimating some things that were not quite so, but which made them look like they might be part of his world. He started opening up. During two hours he got more and more detailed. He went all the way from vaguely agreeing to talk about the beach to giving them detailed instructions on where to park to go to some gay nude clubs (illegal) in Hollywood.

Rasmussen and I had a similar experience with Whitey, one of the ultimate insiders in the gay scene. We'd been able to see much of what was going on at the gay beach simply by walking past, but we had only a few informants in the gay scene at that time. It was proving to be a tough problem. We had seen Whitey over the years, but never spoke with him. Then we had to hunt him down at a new beach he'd moved to in order to see if he would talk. He recognized us as someone from his old beach and we started talking. He wasn't saying much. Then we started using the language of the gay community and facts about the local community (which I knew primarily because Carol Warren had done a study of them). He started talking about his lover problems at the old beach, about how upset he was over the screamers who had invaded it, and so on. He gave us specific instances of sex on the gay beach, etc. Opening up is a powerful tactic. It is even more effective if the researcher first sets the members up for the opening up.

Setting Them Up

The researcher sets someone up by deliberately and unobtrusively putting him in a situation that encourages him to be friendly and trusting toward the researcher and thence to open up about himself. When a girl invites her boyfriend over for dinner and gives him the wine-roses-and-candlelight treatment, she's setting him up. Researchers do the same kind of setting up by prearranging the situation, but it's harder for people to notice and discount it or to protect themselves from it because it's not a standardized thing in our society. It's possible to arrange in-depth interviews in informal settings, with beer or wine, and lots of personal friendly atmosphere to encourage exchange of confidences. It's also possible to arrange the cast who are there so that it does the same thing. Arranging the cast is the vital part of interviews in settings where one does not control the physical props.

A couple of beautiful examples of this are found in the study of massage parlors. We had long known that the ultimate insider in the massage parlors was a local lawyer who represented the massage parlor association and about 80 percent of the cases. We wanted to open him up, so we tried to set him up for it. We began by casting a wide net for inside contacts with him, and we found a good one. Rasmussen discovered that a good friend of his who was a lawyer had worked on the draft resistance movement with this lawyer. It proved to be a good contact, but we wanted much more. We wanted to make it manifest to the lawyer that we were on the inside and could thus be trusted. We knew it wouldn't do any good to give him verbal commitments— "Hey, man, we're on your side, you can trust us." He was used to every possible deception and double cross from all angles. It would have to be made manifest, physically real. We could have gotten ourselves arrested by starting a massage parlor, and then hired him for our defense, but that did not appeal to our sense of propriety—or practicality. We did the next best thing. We got two young masseuses to go with him for the interview, showing by their presence and trust in him what angle he was coming from. (We were using the Trojan student ploy here; that is, Rasmussen led the lawyer to believe he was just a student writing a term paper.) As they were ushered into the lawyer's office, two employees at the parlor where one of the girls with Rasmussen worked came out and they had a grand reunion right there. (Researchers need luck as much as anyone else.) As the interview progressed, the two girls talked of their work. One of them, as we knew well, was under indictment for her work in a parlor. They talked about that. She was impressed by the lawyer and shifted her case to him. At the end of the interview, the lawyer told Rasmussen he could use all his files, make xerox copies of them, use his name in doing his research, accompany him on cases, etc. We felt sure there were some things he wasn't telling us (and one of the girls later started working with him to get at more and check it out), but that seemed okay for the first hour.

The masseuse-on-each-arm ploy went so well that we used it for other things after that. One striking use was Rasmussen's interview with a local TV news reporter who had done some carefully laundered stories on parlors. (We knew how he was laundering because of the studies of the TV newsrooms. One of the insiders had told us that this reporter was a customer. He gave us all the details.) Rasmussen arrived at his office with the two girls, but did not introduce them as masseuses. The reporter started out slowly, hanging out the laundry, as we call this laundering work people offer for naive researchers to swallow whole. After about a third of the taped interview, one of the girls started telling how she did it in the parlor. The reporter apparently had an attack of apoplexy. On the tape (which is all a hidden professor gets to hear), he suddenly ejaculates in a squeaky, unbelieving voice, "You're a masseuse!??" They then told him the other girl was too. About all the reporter could do was chuckle for a while. They told him where they worked, what they did, and so on. Then he started taking in the laundry: He opened up, slowly but steadily. By the end of the tape he was telling about his visits to some orgies, how he used his TV-celebrity status to get the best girls at the orgies, and how he hid it all from his wife. It pays to set people up. At the least, it can save a lot on the laundry bill.

Adversary and Discombobulating Tactics

The most simple-minded investigative research tactic is that of taking the adversary or oppositional method. Just as some "fringe sociologists" have adopted a method of criticizing everything before studying it, so some journalists have done the same in what they commonly call adversary or oppositional journalism. For the journalists, as for other social thinkers, there are two different levels of the adversary perspective. The extreme form is the ideological-adversary perspective. This perspective involves the assumption of an ideology, defined as any set of systematically related and closed assumptions about what is true in concrete reality. The ideology assumes, or takes for granted before any investigation is made of the natural social world, that certain things are true and others wrong or evil about that social world.

There are many different, complex forms of the ideological-adversary perspective in social thought today, but most of them are directly derived from the assumption that "Marx was right and it is our job to show people precisely how his preconceived ideology fits the present state of the world." Most of these works, such as the central works of Marcuse and members of the so-called Frankfurt School, are intentionally unempirical. They are absolutist theodicies, explaining for simpler minds the absolute truths propounded by Marx, in precisely the same way Augustine explained for simple Roman minds the absolute truths of the Bible. Indeed, Augustine was far more empirical than most of these modern ideological adversaries of our worldly society, as anyone knows who has read *The City of God* and compared it to *One Dimensional Man.* These works do not really involve research methods, since they have already presumed to know what is true about the social world. Any "data" they may contain are merely examples, illustrations, displays, reductions, etc., of preconceived truths. Data or research findings are rhetorical devices meant to teach the truths to those who suffer from false consciousness (i.e., those who have not received grace and embraced the revelations). Consequently, they do not really concern us here.

The adversary perspective in interviewing uses an adversary approach or manner to wrench the truth from interviewees assumed to be trying to manipulate the interviewers and, thence, the public. This is common today in journalism and police work. For example, in his aptly named book, *The Information War,* Dale Minor (1970) argues that about 90 percent of journalistic information comes necessarily (given time constraints and so on) from interviews and that these are generally with adversaries who want to manipulate the journalists and their public. His book is intended to show journalists and other social researchers how they can win this information war. How? Primarily by being aware of the war and devising interaction strategies that will make the interviewees "give off" (as Goffman would put it) the true information which they don't want to give. There are a number of specific strategies used, all known to the reader because they are all developed from common-sense methods.

A major one is hitting them between the eyes when they least expect it to throw them off guard, thus revealing what they don't want to reveal. This is the discombobulation tactic. It was used in the famous Kissinger vs. Journalists War. When Henry Kissinger returned triumphantly from five weeks of whirlwind negotiations in the Middle East he held a press conference to discuss the negotiations. The first journalist to ask a question asked him if he was going to get a lawyer to defend himself against felonious perjury charges. As Kissinger himself expressed it a few days later in his famous Salzburg counterattack: "Last Thursday (when hit by the adversary questioning him about perjury), a number of you commented on the fact that I seemed irritated, angered, flustered, discombobulated. All these words are correct. After five weeks in the Middle East I was not thinking about the various investigations going on in the United States. I did not prepare myself for the press conference by reading the records of investigations that I believed had been completed." They hit him when he least expected it, right between the eyes, and he acted as if he had been hit right between the eyes when he least expected it. But many journalists assumed that a discombobulated interviewee meant there really was something to the hypothesis inspiring the adversary question. In the next few days several major newspapers, especially *The New York Times* and the *Washington Post,* drew precisely those inferences from Kissinger's discombobulation and went on to question his integrity in general on that basis.

This approach and the closely related adversary tactics may be useful in doing someone in, but it has several major problems with it as a social research tactic.

First, it pretty much assures the interviewer of no more interviews and certainly of no closer contact that would allow him to directly experience and observe things. The adversary approach, at least when done in this way, involves a declaration of war and not many interviewees are apt to put up with being observed by self-proclaimed enemies. This kind of adversary journalism almost forces journalism into an even more extreme position of opposition, probably into an ideological-adversary position.

Second, once stung, ever after on guard. The adversary approach tends to turn all future research into a war and no one is going to want the enemy in his presence. Social research is already largely eliminated from the back regions of most of the vital and powerful settings in our society, such as business and the mass media, because these people know that researchers are often de-maskers and that some of them are really ideological adversaries disguised as researchers merely seeking rhetorical data to better convince the masses they were right about what they believed before they ever did the research.

Third, it certainly does happen that discombobulated interviewees unintentionally spill the beans, but how will one even know he is now telling the truth except by using the more fundamental methods of establishing the truth, that of checking out what he says by direct experience, observation and other means. Indeed, there are many instances in which subsequent checking out reveals that people will even confess to terrible crimes under the discombobulating pressures of police interrogation. For example, one of the best investigative reports done by reporters for the *Los Angeles Times* involved checking out the story of the young man who confessed under the pressure of police interrogation to setting a fire that killed several people. The police had lied to him, kept him off balance, and continually asserted his guilt. He told them his story many times, got thoroughly discombobulated, signed a confession, then later insisted that his original story was true. After his conviction, reporters went back and checked out his story, confirming it on each major point. In the end, the prosecutor sought to throw out the conviction and the police adversary approach was once again called into question.

Situations do occur in which the sociologist will want to use the discombobulating adversary methods of the journalistic information war. These are the same situations in which he would be willing to use obtrusive methods in general, discussed in Chapter 2. Specifically, they may be useful when for some reason an informant is suspected of not telling the whole truth, or when he might be stimulated into some interesting insights by being forcefully confronted; when the research is short-run and self-contained, so that there is little chance that the discombobulated subject will become a research fury forever seeking revenge; and when a research project is all but done, so that any fallout won't be disasterous.

In general, though, I have almost never used this discombobulating confrontation method. This is no doubt partly a personal thing: My natural inclination is to seek cooperation and trust by being friendly, at least until the other party clearly shows himself to be an enemy. But it is also based on the presumption that truth is best gotten by a combination of trust and cooperation with the other, direct experience, checking out, and other face-to-face tactics that do not involve such brutal confrontations. It is also based on the utilitarian presumption that every cooperative informant is a potential future contact. Anyone who has been willing to help by being interviewed for free is probably interested and friendly enough to be willing to help in the future. (Even in short-run interviews I generally open the door to future contacts at the end by asking the person to be on the lookout for other informants and to keep in touch if anything really interesting comes up.) In general then, when a research subject lies we write him off for then, let it pass, and try to win him over for the future. As we saw earlier, putting up with lies has proven helpful in a number of instances in getting them to let us do the research. Taking an adversary stance might have revealed a small truth, but lost us some much bigger ones. The good field researcher must often be a humble person, even at times playing the dolt, but biding his time, accepting the day-to-day losses that may prepare the way for winning the war.

Drawing Out and the Phased-Assertion Tactic

Rather than taking an adversary stance, or using discombobulating confrontation tactics, the sociologist is more likely to find the related assertive stance useful in drawing out an informant. The assertive stance involves acting as if one already knows what is going on behind the deceptions and fronts, saying something to the informant which either involves a direct statement of his guess about what is going on or, more likely, which is based in part on assuming the truth of his guess about what is going on. The basic purpose is to make it look as if he is already in-the-know and see if the informant buys his interpretation. If he does, and if the researcher has successfully avoided the dangers we shall discuss, then he has gotten confirmation of his guess and established himself as more of an insider than he is, which he then uses to further draw out and open up the informant by more guessing about the truth, going out in steps.

There are all degrees of guesswork involved in this tactic. At one extreme we have what is popularly called simple drawing out. This involves little more than trying to get people to talk, possibly by allowing it to look as if one knows more than one does, but not doing much asserting of the truth. At the other extreme we have fishing, where one guesses blindly with the hope of hitting the mark. Going on a fishing expedition is where one just starts thrashing around with many guesses. (John Johnson, 1976, has already dealt with these forms.) Drawing out is standard and fishing is dangerous, since it is easy to be shown as ignorant. It can be useful, but is not as powerful or reliable as the phased-assertion tactic.

This, the phased-assertion tactic, is the most powerful of the short-cut, semi-cooperative, investigative research tactics. It is powerful in penetrating deceptions, lies and fronts because it does a number of things at once.

First, it causes the researcher to appear to be in-the-know, an insider—so why not talk with him about the whole thing? If the researcher is really successful, the informant doesn't think about it as a question. The researcher is an inside member, so the informant talks to him like he does to anyone else.

Second, if he does think about it and consider whether he should talk openly, then he faces the danger of looking like a liar if he lies to the researcher. That is, since the researcher seems to know about it, if the informant denies it or says something different, then he's a proven liar in the researcher's eyes, or so he thinks. Few people want to be caught lying, so this is a real motive to buy it, if it's true. Obviously, the more the person can be led to believe the researcher has independent sources telling him that what he's said is true, the more danger the informant runs of being seen as a liar, so the more powerful the assertion of the truth method.

Third, the method allows the researcher to assert what he thinks is true by stages and in veiled terms, so that he doesn't run as much risk of being revealed as ignorant or a liar himself (which he is). Though the specific strategy obviously depends on the situation, the researcher commonly begins with hints and with the things he knows most about, throwing out bait for the informant to snap at, hoping he'll bite and run with it so that the researcher won't have to risk important mistakes.

People use the assertive strategy all the time in everyday life. Most of the time it's in simple form, like "All right, Johnny, I know what you're doing." Sometimes, at least in the Byzantine world of modern bureaucracies, it gets more complex, as we can see in the method of "playing both ends against the middle," a nice strategy for getting both information and commitments that John Johnson (1976) used all the time in his welfare agencies. Journalists and field researchers can go further by more carefully constructing both their phased strategies and the appearances of having independent evidence.

A classic example of the journalists' use of the method, which reveals only the strengths of the method, is found in Bernstein and Woodward's (1974) interviews with an accountant who worked for the committee to reelect the president. They were faced with a situation in which they suspected, on the basis of references by earlier informants, which were so indirect they had to guess the woman's identity, the accountant was unhappy about what was going on and wanted it revealed, but without playing the traitor to her friends and political party. Having guessed who she was and that she might talk if given the encouragement of knowing that others had already ratted, they lied to her about what others had told them and proceeded to work out a complex interactional strategy with her by which she would evasively confirm or deny their guesses about what was going on, but would not directly tell them anything. This complex guessing game allowed her to evade responsibility for her treason (how could it even be labelled treason when she merely said yes or no to things they already "knew"), while allowing them to get information.

A few examples from our own research will help to make clearer the strengths and weaknesses of this method. I became very aware of how useful the method is and, indeed, how necessary it can be in getting at the truth when members are being evasive or hiding behind fronts in trying to get at the sexual feelings, motives, thoughts and actions on the nude beach. It was clear that people did not want to talk about their own sex on the beach, even when their bodies made it obvious to me what they were into. (But, of course, talk is a partly separate reality, as we have continually emphasized.) I knew most reliably what the regulars were into by watching their bodies. Of course, it was interesting in a way to get at their talk as well, since the talk could be a partly confirming form of evidence and, more importantly, because it is of value in itself as a subject of study.

But it was the people who came briefly, tourists and others, who posed the real problem. Some of them made their internal states obvious; but not many.[6] It seemed like a good idea to have some way of talking with some of them about such things. It was clear from our study that we could not talk about how they as individuals felt. We would have to support their evasiveness and lying about the self by never bringing it up. We would have to talk about people in general, "what people are doing down here," and hope that some might provide subtle indications that they were people like others. But with most of these people with whom we did not have close relations of trust, this protection was not enough. When we would start them talking about "people on the beach" they would generally talk about the naturalness of it all, which was a standard, nonconspiratorial front, a cover for their nude bodies, used in the very act of denouncing covers. This we believed from all our observations and experience. How could we get any more direct, verbal confirmation from these visitors? It proved easy enough when we used the phased-assertion strategy.

An example illustrates the use of it. Walking along the water's edge one day, I came across a student I know vaguely who was nearly nude (wearing his shorts low-rider with his fly open). He was half into the scene, half out. He was uncomfortable. We walked along and talked about the scene. He admitted he'd been getting into the scene and started talking about what it was like. He started saying how people felt so natural without their clothes on, etc. I immediately recognized the beginning of a production of the Naturalist Ethos, accepted it with "Oh, yeah" (don't challenge the member), and then opened the door onto the likely truth. "But people who come here have to have a strong motivation to see others' bodies and that sort of thing or they wouldn't go to all the trouble to come down the hill and climb back up . . ." He then did an almost immediate switch, declaring "Yeah, you know it's really strange how almost everyone tries to avoid talking about the sexual motives for coming and all, even when it's obvious . . ." This was almost a standard scenario: The person would open the curtain on act one of the Naturalist Ethos; we would accept it, but indicate we know what "those people" were into; the screen of the front would come down and behind the first stage would lie another one, but one talked about *in abstracto*, except in a few instances.

At first, I thought this was a simple matter of a consciously contrived front which we had penetrated. But I came to believe, on the basis of all our experience, that it was much more complex, with different people involved in different kinds of self-deception and deception of others, involving situational views of the truth, so that at some times they felt and believed the naturalistic ethos, while at others they accepted it as a front.

The same strategy proved to be even more useful in dealing with the police patrols on the nude beach. The police had followed a policy on the nude beaches of active enforcement of state and local laws against drugs, drinking under 21, and having dogs on the beach, whereas everyone knew that they were passive on the clothed beaches. All of this had made them quite unpopular on the nude beaches, especially since most people there didn't like the police to begin with. But two earlier covert observations by colleagues studying and teaching the police had indicated that in general the police had mixed feelings about the nude beaches. On the one hand, they commonly looked at all the people there as "pukes" (a technical police term used all over California to refer to young, hip types), but, on the other hand, they generally didn't feel they had the manpower or interest to bother doing more than active patrol. When the nearby property owners went behind the scene to put political pressure on the city council to pass a new municipal ordinance restricting nudity to one area of one beach, police department representatives publicly stated their misgivings about the possibilities and costs of enforcing such a law. We had reason, then, to believe that the police might not be active supporters of the law and that this might affect their discretionary enforcement on the beaches. As soon as the law became effective, the police patrols spent a week intensively warning people to get up to the new designated nude area. They acted in their usual authoritative manner: "All right, don't you know you can only go nude in the officially designated area? All violators are subject to arrest." They threw in extra patrols and kept cruising the beach almost all day for the first day or so. The massive presence (contrasted to no patrols at all during the off-season nine months and one or two a day during the summer season for the past two years) and their manner led everyone I talked to on the beach to believe "The goddamned pigs are at it again. Man, they're really out to get the nudes." Even the few people who knew the police department had been less than lukewarm at the official hearings took this view.

After following the patrols around for a day and talking with people just after they'd been dealt with by the police, I approached two motorcycle patrolmen (who I knew were on special duty, since they rarely came down) and asked them about the new ordinance, whether it was going to be enforced, what the penalties were, etc. They gave me the straight-line, authoritative perspective: "Nudity out of the area will be a muni-code violation like any violation of the municipal code; it will be enforced and violators face up to six months in prison and a $500 fine." They stonewalled me (though I was respectfully garbed in swimming trunks), giving every impression, as they stood there on the nude beach in their hardhats, with guns strapped to their sides and dark glasses screening out all human contact, of being ready to cart off all offenders and maybe even gun down every "puke" who got in the way of law and order. In fact, I first started to explain the legal details to them and raise the question of the legality of such a law. They seemed to become more alert and to be ready to oppose any such objections: "Yeah, well that's the law and we're going to enforce it."

Then I completely switched my strategy. Using my prior information and observations, I asserted, with a bit of a question in my voice, "Well, from all I've heard, even the police aren't much in favor of this law and don't feel they have the manpower to enforce it effectively." One of the patrolmen immediately said, "Oh, *yeah!* Why'd they ever pass this law? We can't see what it's all about. I don't see how they're going to enforce it in some places. But why do they need it anyhow?" I explained the politics of the thing to them and at the end of the pleasant discussion, while one patrolman turned aside to get a nearby dog-walker, the friendlier one leaned over to me and said, "Man, I like to go skinny-dipping myself and the last thing I want to do is be the first guy to bust someone for nude bathing."

In the next few weeks I tried this approach on the other two sets of regular patrolmen, now implying that I knew some patrolmen who weren't happy with the whole situation, and found the same about-face each time I'd start talking about the police not really wanting this law. I found that in my second talk with the sergeant, who came down once in a while to see how the whole thing was going, he got to the point of asserting that, while they would enforce the law, it had taken a lot of manpower for something they didn't find very significant, that he couldn't see why they didn't make the whole beach nude, and that it must be just "a lot of politics." At the same time, it was clear that they looked like dedicated enforcers of that law whenever anyone challenged their authority. While I was talking to the sergeant once, I had just mentioned that most of the people on the beach were mad at the police for the whole thing and felt the police should be doing more important things when a guy came up and said aggressively, "Hey, what are you police coming down here for to hassle people for nudity when there are so many more important things they should be doing!?" The sergeant almost arrested him a few minutes later for being nude out of the designated area and threatened him in no uncertain terms. All of the indications were that the police in this instance were unwillingly "caught in the middle," that the people blamed them and wanted to demonstrate their dislike, that the police would get mad in response to attacks on their authority, and that they well might decide in time to *want* to enforce the law as a way of expressing their counteranger.

These instances, and many more that I could draw from field research, show the value of the phased-assertion technique when it is used correctly, including considerable caution to avoid determining the data rather than merely uncovering it.[7] The crucial ingredients and steps are revealed in these examples.

First, in each instance we had already made a great deal of direct observation of what people did with their bodies (showing obvious physical signs, etc.) and of what the police did (warning people, etc.). Because of the nature of this scene, we were able to observe a lot of what would normally be back-region behavior.

Second, we had developed close, trusting relations with people who were deeply involved with many other members of the scene and could tell us what they experienced and observed independently of sociological research. Carol Ann Flanagan had been a member of the scene before becoming a trusted researcher of the scene. Some colleagues were able to tell us from their personal contacts with the police who came down to patrol it that the police had mixed views and that some of the administrators were especially aware of the problems involved in putting manpower into such enforcement. We were, then, able to use extensive knowledge of both the people into the scene and the police in making our estimates of what people were really experiencing, thinking, and doing. This was crucial in doing our assertive work.

Third, we proceeded with caution in most cases (though in some we could afford to jump to conclusions just to see what would happen), asserting by steps. We did not hit people with the assertion that, "Hell, man, you're lying. You're here on a sex trip," or "Yeah, I know you cops aren't really in favor of this law." We prodded them cautiously, in steps, drawing them out, as people commonly refer to this kind of communicative technique, rather than confronting them, affronting them, threatening them. In these cases a direct, extreme assertion tended to produce highly defensive denials. "A sex trip— me!? Hell! It's you whose got the dirty mind. I'm just doing the natural thing since my bathing suit wore out." In many situations a direct assertion may also lead people to agree with one either because they really don't know or because they just want to get along. The researcher must have good reason to expect they have a certain feeling or view and then must proceed cautiously in drawing it out. If he merely suspects it from some preliminary observations, then their confirmation and additional information or their denial and defense will remain much less reliable.

NOTES

1. Just as good relations and contacts in one setting can be vital in opening up other settings, bad ones can do just the opposite. The researcher always inadvertently makes

enemies, like anyone else, so he must be adept at hiding his enemies from new subjects. Sometimes he must hide his past research altogether because of the danger that his enemies will be contacted for references, but more commonly he can simply set it up so his friends will be contacted rather than his enemies. Fortunately, we academics are already experienced at this because we are taught how to do it for "professional recommendations" from the time we are undergraduates. As in most other things, it takes years to learn how to be dishonest effectively, and this long training in academic dishonesty is invaluable.

Sometimes a researcher can learn who his real enemies are in one setting by learning they've knifed him in another setting. For example, when Phillip and Sharon Davis tried to ride one city's ambulance they were denied permission. Their investigation of this revealed that the emergency services director of a university hospital had put out the "bad word" (contract) on them. This shocked us all, since that director had been publicly cordial to our study of his emergency room. In rethinking our relations with him, we came to believe that he was mainly upset about recent disclosures made to the mass media (definitely not by us) about an overdose case delivered by ambulance to them, but that he might also have felt some pique at our presence because in getting into his realm we had relied a bit too much on the help of a prestigious national commissioner, so we may have been feeling a bit of the crowbar backlash. (As they say in the trade, when you put the arm on a guy, you've got to expect him to come hot.) We immediately put him in our Suspicious Character category and started hiding our relations with him, while trying to mend our fences with him.

2. Carol Warren has reported an instance of unintentionally benefitting from the boob ploy. She and a team of researchers wanted to do in-depth studies of drug rehabilitation centers. Her government support and their dependence on the same agencies for support made it hard for them to say no. But they certainly would not normally want such studies. She decided that they let her in largely because they felt a woman sociologist wouldn't be effective enough to be harmful. They were wrong.

3. I dislike using this ploy for personal reasons, but have no doubt at times been the unintentional recipient of its help. When Altheide and I were negotiating entree to a TV newsroom our inside contact told the director we were doing "a phenomenological study of the construction of the news," then turned to me and asked me to explain what phenomenology was. Overcoming my sense of faintness, I did so in a few sentences. I think this helped convince him we were no threat to anyone.

4. Our society is so complex and problematic these days that it's often hard to tell the difference between a traitorous enemy and one's own public relations person.

5. Field researchers often come to take pride in being able to penetrate any setting—and scoring on a previously impregnable setting is a major aspect of researcher bravado. A research team with real researcher *esprit des corps* often comes to feel confident they can blow open any setting. Sitting around planning and then executing one's assault strategy can be tremendously exciting. In some settings there are really great risks and those who crave excitement can find them a happy hunting ground. Besides the excitement of taking great risks, penetrating a setting has all the thrill of trying to outwit one's enemies. It's a modern form of big game hunting. Some field researchers demand physical excitement. Jack Haas, for example, soared "the high steels" to do his thesis on the construction workers who build skyscrapers in New York. Most of us prefer lower physical risks and settle for moral or professional risks.

6. Some people will talk much more than others, sometimes even inadvertently revealing what their friends don't want to have known. Sociologists have long emphasized the importance to research of inside-dopesters, those who delight in showing how

important they are by telling the secrets they know. But rarely have they noted the importance of this general difference between people in their degree of secretiveness and openness. Some people literally have a compulsion to be open, to spill the beans to almost anyone, to the point of being verbal exhibitionists. These people often delight in shocking others by telling them the most intimate and secret things about themselves. (Such people are often said to "be all out front," "let it all hang out," and "have lots of nerve," "are full of gall," etc.) This was strikingly clear on the nude beach. For example, one of the super regulars who was unwilling to talk about what he was obviously into had a girlfriend who would tell me almost everything about the two of them (but only when he wasn't around; she never said much when he was) and I learned it was even possible to indirectly check what she said with him by using my information in talking with him. Everything she said checked out with what could be seen and with what he and others confirmed in various ways. Again, one day as I came down one of the canyons onto the beach I found I was walking behind Bob, who could not see me. He was a dedicated, old-line nudist from L. A. with whom I'd talked several times. He always looked and talked like the old-line—naturalistic ethos, etc., so I wondered if he was one of the few people who might not be into a sex thing on the beach. As I walked behind him, I realized he was jockeying into position to pass near an approaching young woman, a common form of exhibitionistic confrontation, but this could also just be a coincidence unless accompanied by other forms of body language or noted as a pattern of behavior. I speeded up and passed him, not looking at him (inattention to acquaint-ances' sex things was *de riguer* on the beach), then a bit further on turned to walk back. He had returned to his gear and was talking with another old-liner who'd come down with him. I greeted them, demonstrating my surprise at suddenly coming upon them ("See, I didn't even recognize you as I walked past you a minute ago"). As we talked, they drifted back down to the water's edge, and drifted south. Then I noticed two girls drifting north along the water. The newcomer said, "Hey, Bob, here they come again—only this time without the boys . . ." As they approached us, the newcomer took another sip of his beer and said, "Hey, man, I wish they'd just come right up here and suck us . . ." One more naturalist exposed by body-language and a secret sex trip confirmed by a talky friend.

7. One of the claims of some ethnomethodologists has been that, because sociologists are inevitably involved in the interaction that produces the activities they then observe and use as data, their data is necessarily self-determined data, so *all* data is merely a display or index of preconceived ideas of the sociologist himself. I should imagine this idea would be most strongly applied to the assertive technique, since it obviously involves action by the sociologist to observe what he suspects exists in the minds of the people he is studying. But this ethnomethodological idea, like so many of their other ideas, suffers from a failure to distinguish degrees of involvement and determination. It is simply not the case that one is either totally involved in determining the data or not involved at all. The world, as all common-sense actors assume, is not an either-or phenomenon. All of our experience is made up of more-or-lesses, of degrees, generally small degrees; and anyone who loses a sense of degree, of balance, of measure in his everyday life winds up appearing to be eccentric, mad or downright dangerous. When a man says, "Well, it sounds like an interesting investment, but it's too risky for me," or "I suppose he's intelligent all right, but not intelligent enough for this job," or a woman says, "Sure, I like the guy, I guess, but I don't like him *that* much," or a child says, "It's okay to go swimming when there are only a few jellyfish, but today there are just too many," they all know perfectly well what they mean and so does everyone else—degree counts! One doesn't love or hate, any more than there are either an infinite number of jellyfish or none at all. In the same way, a sociologist doesn't either completely

determine what he observes or have nothing to do with its production, nor are things either totally indexical or else absolutely unindexical. Absolutist thinking is as much a curse of ethnomethodological theories as of structural theories. We can and do use varying degrees of direction in our dealings with members of society to get them to say what they think is true, to do what they naturally (without our sociological intervention) do. Structuralists and some earlier field researchers were wrong, to varying degrees, in seeing the world as relatively unproblematic; the ethnomethodologists are wrong, also to varying degrees, in seeing the world as so much the product of uncertainty effects that we should deny all difference between social research and the most passionate commitments of madmen.

Chapter 9

TEAM FIELD RESEARCH

Almost all social research has been aimed at four general goals, either singly or, more commonly, in some combination:

(1) Providing us with knowledge of the members' situated experience— that is, social meanings, the way it looks to the members of society, and so on;

(2) Providing us with knowledge of how the different experiences of different individuals and groups are related to each other in concrete settings—that is, the interaction of multiperspectival experience;

(3) Providing us with knowledge of the extensiveness or representativeness of members' experience, with special emphasis on providing knowledge of the universally shared experience of the world—that is, the representativeness of findings about social meanings, the structure of meanings, and so on; and

(4) Providing us with knowledge that can be used in practical efforts to solve social problems—that is, policy-oriented knowledge, relevant knowledge, and so on.

As we have seen, the first goal, that of getting at the members' experience in natural settings, has been the traditional goal of field research studies. Almost all justifications of field research methods have emphasized their superiority (or, at least, equality) in providing us with knowledge of the members' experience in their natural settings. The best of these have contended that the prolonged and close participation of field research is essential for getting the members' experience in a manner that retains the integrity of that experience—that is, field research has much less uncertainty-effect determination of the observation made by the researcher. Almost all field research studies have pursued this goal by going in-depth, which has almost always involved choosing a limited setting and spending full time studying and reporting on it in detail. The greatest of these *(Street Corner Society, Men Who Manage, Outsiders, Urban Villagers, The Racing Game,* and so on) have almost always been studies of small groups. The best ones have always had the immediate implication that their findings were far more representative of the social world, but they have almost never tried to show this, largely for the practical reason that it took a long time to study even the limited group.

The second goal, that of providing knowledge about the ways in which different groups are related to each other in concrete settings, has sometimes been a shadowy ideal of both field research and controlled research proponents, but has almost never been attempted. In almost all instances of stating the abstract ideal, and certainly in almost all instances of actual attempts to carry out the ideal in research, the absolutist or cooperative model of society and of methods has led to an attempt simply to show how the groups studied fits into the web or structure of society. This, for example, is the approach of the social anthropologists, the survey field researchers, like the Lynds, in the 1920s and 1930s, and of Whyte in trying to show how the corner boys in *Street Corner Society* relate to politics, education, jobs, and family. Dalton's great work, *Men Who Manage,* is a rare but only partial attempt to see how the experiences of different groups in a concrete setting are related to each other. In this case, he shows how different cliques within industrial chemical plants compete with each other to capture power. Gerald Suttles' recent work, *The Moral Order of the Slum,* (1968) is a rarer attempt to use field research to study how partially conflicting groups manage to live together peacefully. Even those recent works that attempt to get at multiple realities in a concrete setting generally show merely how multiple realities co-exist—one is here and the other there. There is a web or structure of multiple realities. (This is not surprising, since the Schutzian model of society, from which the idea of multiple realities is taken, assumes the universally shared meanings of the natural attitude and so on. See Altheide, in Douglas and Johnson, 1977.) In general, the field research studies that manage to get at the experience of several different groups in a setting almost always do so uniperspectively; they almost never consider the multi-perspectival nature of the members' social reality. They do not show how the different groups are in conflict and cooperation with each other, how the experience of each is partially determined by its interactions with the others, and how this experience changes over time as a result. This is due both to the cooperative, absolutist model of society they have inherited from classical sociology and to the practical problems of not being able to simultaneously go in-depth in different, often conflicting groups in one setting. One can almost never run with a street gang and ride around with the police at the same time.

The third goal of getting representative findings, of determining the extent and distribution of any social phenomena (values, attitudes, behavior, etc.), has been the primary focus of the quantitative methods in sociology, especially of the well-known survey methods. Whereas the field researchers went in-depth, the researchers using the various controlled methods of this quantitative approach went extensively. They gave up the depths of society to go across the top of society. These methods were adopted almost entirely for preconceived reasons, mainly their assumption that the positivistic theory of knowledge and science is right, but when they did consider the questions they thought their methods were justified by the cooperative model of research and by the structural model of society. The structural model assumed that there exists a structure of society, which was almost always thought to be values, and that this structure was the basic determinant of social action universally. Therefore, one's methods were aimed at getting those things shared by everyone (structure) and one would be able to use highly cooperative methods, like asking strangers questions, with the expectation that one would generally get the truth. (Errors, such as lying, would necessarily be randomized.) This was fortunate, since it allowed one to use the highly controlled and quantitative methods demanded by classical, absolutist science.

The fourth goal of providing policy-oriented information of value in practical attempts to solve social problems has always been a basic goal of sociology as a whole. There are no doubt many reasons, but the most basic seems to be the fact that societies would probably not be willing to support, or possibly even put up with, the social sciences in general, except for the expectations that they will contribute practical information. This goal has strongly complemented the goal of achieving representative findings because in our mass democracies information must generally be representative of the whole society or some large part of it to be of practical value.

This is most obvious in the case of public opinion polls, which are probably the most massive and famous form of survey research. These polls have literally become quasi-votes or elections. When it is found that 56 percent of the people believe this, that or the other (such as that a president should be impeached), this is taken as strong indication that this course should be seriously considered; and a growing percentage of people seem to feel that the polls should determine the actions, rather than merely have government consider them as one input. This demand for representative findings has been a major reason why almost all government and public-agency support for social research has gone to the quantitative, controlled, across-the-top forms. These were the forms that promised representative findings which would hold good for the society as a whole; so they were the ones that would be of practical value to the government agencies making public policies, so they should be supported. If one looks at it from the standpoint of government officials, such as congressmen who ultimately appropriate all such funds, one can easily see the rationale for this. Consider, for example, an agency making policy to deal with gangs in the large cities. Field researchers could propose that the few in-depth studies of gangs be used as the basis for policy. But the officials' immediate objection would be that a gang in Boston or one in San Francisco tells us nothing about gangs in Dallas or Chicago. How do we know they are the same? How do we know that even the gangs in Boston are generally like this one? What are we going to tell the congressman from Dallas when he objects that we don't need such a national policy because there are no gangs like that in Dallas? The policy-maker immediately demands the big picture. It is vital to his practical concerns.

In general, then, the field research sociologists have concentrated on going in-depth, in trying to get really reliable information on small parts of society. When they have moved toward getting a more representative view of society, they have generally moved quickly toward the use of more formal, con-trolled, and quantitative methods. For example, the studies of gangs through-out Boston by Walter Miller (1958) were begun as field research studies and they retained the participation aspect; but to get a representative view they used formal categories of analysis and quantitative methods of analyzing them. On the other hand, the formal, controlled, quantitative methods have generally failed to get at the in-depth truths about society. They have not tried. Rather, they have sacrificed any in-depth knowledge for the big picture. The quantitative methods have then captured the policy-oriented research and almost all government and private organization support. Because of sharing the cooperative and absolutist models of methods and society, both have failed to deal with the multiperspectivai nature of our complex, plural-istic and conflictive society. Even when the field researchers were dealing with something that demanded a multiperspectival approach, they could hardly do so because of the reliance upon a single researcher, who, as we argued in Chapter 6, is almost inevitably stigmatized as a member of one group by those in the conflicting groups.[1] (This was clear to researchers like Becker, 1970. Also see Habenstein, 1970.)

For many reasons, classical field research has almost always used the Lone Ranger approach. That is, they have gone out single-handedly into the bitterly conflictful social world to bring the data back alive. This approach has demanded considerable strength and courage much of the time and almost always an ability to operate alone, with little or no support and inspiration from colleagues.[2] It has also demanded total honesty of its practitioners, since there was no one else around to help "keep them honest."[3] And it demanded that he be a jack-of-all-interactional-skills, since he had to be all things to all people in his research setting.[4] As long as field research was restricted to the Lone Ranger approach, it was restricted to going in-depth in relatively small groups, or small parts of large groups; it operated largely *in vacuo* or at least unseen; and its results, the research reports, depended overwhelmingly on our faith in the honesty of the researcher and in his supposed ability to be all things to all people and to solve even the most difficult problems of field research. The fact that so much really good field research was accomplished with this Lone Ranger approach is testimony to the skills, courage, audacity, integrity and ability to accept suffering of so many young sociologists. (Anyone who doubts that all of these are demanded, or that they have been forthcoming, need only read the honest and representative account of real field research given by John Johnson, 1976. And see Roy in Habenstein, 1970.) But, of course, these abilities and the willingness to suffer only go so far. The willingness to suffer is especially short in supply and this probably accounts for the fact that most field researchers only do one study, their doctoral dissertation, and then retire to the study to do theory and send forth unsuspecting graduate students to do battle. It is probably an even more important factor in the decision of so many graduate students and professionals to dedicate themselves to office interviews and, wherever possible, mail-order research. Putting a questionnaire in the mailbox may demand some faith in the postal department and the unseen subject, but it requires no suffering or courage of the academic. He can remain safely in his office and avoid all those vulgar conflicts.

There have, of course, been a number of important field research studies done by a cohort of researchers. (See especially Hughes, 1971.) But these have almost always involved a simple sharing of the same tasks, a pooling of efforts to report on a scene thought to be too large for one person. They were rarely aimed at getting multiperspectival views of society or any of the other important things we shall shortly consider. In fact, almost all of these cohort field studies followed the pattern set at Chicago in the 1920s and 1930s. (See Chapter 3.)

Team field research offers the only alternative to the Lone Ranger approach in field research. It involves the careful, systematic integration of the investigative field research efforts of a number of people in one setting as well as interacting settings. Investigative team field research allows us to do what classical field research has tried to do—go in-depth—and what the controlled, quantitative research has tried to do—get the extensive, representative, structured information on the settings. It also allows us to get the multiperspectival view of society that neither of these even aimed at doing. It offers us the best hope of combining reliable in-depth knowledge with the overall picture, and the multiperspectival understanding with both. Our experience with investigative team field research in a number of major and different settings has proven this method to be powerful.

Team field research involves a number of people working together in a flexibly planned and coordinated manner to get at the multiperspectival realities of a group, constructing the team to achieve the research goals of the project in the concrete setting, utilizing the specialized abilities and opportunities of the various team members, providing both support and cross-checks on the work of each member by the other members, and all members (ideally) providing creative inputs to the research, the grasping, the understanding and the final report.

The team is always constructed provisionally and flexibly because of the situational and changing demands of concrete settings. It is constructed in accord with the demands of the concrete setting and the research goals we have in that setting, such as whether we are aiming at the practical goals of policy-oriented or basic-science data. It is also constructed in accord with the different abilities, such as sociability and specialized knowledge, and special opportunities, such as contacts, of the team members. However it is constructed, the members work creatively to support and help each other in their tasks and to cross-check on each other's work, to provide retest (objectivity), emotional support, stimulation, help with contacts, and so on.

Given the kind of research setting, the research goals, and the kind of people involved, some teams are so loosely organized that they run into or overlap with what we called a field research cohort. But the crucial point is that this particular construction should be chosen in the light of the setting, the goals and the people. At the other extreme, some teams, especially large ones, are highly structured and overlap with what we might call field research organizations. Even in these, however, it is vital to have all the members of the team making their creative contributions to the research, the understanding and the report that the team produces, in order to achieve the internal retesting the team form makes possible. (Obviously, I am providing an ostensive definition of team field research, that is, a description of a natural type as we have found it in our work and that of others.) The meaning of team work, its values and problems, can only be determined by looking at each of its major aspects in detail. Hopefully, further experience with the method will reveal other, possibly more important, aspects.

Team Field Research Design

Traditional research designs are constructed and used as a way of making sure that the research is based on an abstractly preconceived, controlled—scientific—plan. A team field research design is, of course, constructed in accord with the basic ideas of reason and so on. And it is provisionally constructed in accord with what has previously been found to be effective team work. But it is constructed primarily in accord with the demands of the situation and for the purpose of coordinating the work of the whole team to achieve the research goals. The design is not "laid on" the setting; it is used as a guide for the whole team to approach the setting flexibly in such a way as to avoid determining what will be observed as much as possible (that is, to minimize the uncertainty effects).

The first thing, as usual, is to determine what one's research goal is and to consider how this is to be achieved within the practical constraints. Also, as usual, it makes a great difference whether one is doing pure science or practical research. If one is doing pure science in which the practical constraints of time are small, as they almost always are or else one would not attempt it, then the design can be minimal and flexible. If one is doing policy research and the practical constraints are great, then design becomes much more important. And the greater the number of team members involved, the more important design becomes. Let us consider the pure science form first.

Any research begins with some kind of overview of previous studies, literature, insider reports, and so on concerning the setting. In a pure science team project, prior sources are consulted cautiously. Its crucial goal is to provide new information and insights. One does not want to get committed to looking at the setting in the ways those doing earlier work have done. One tries to use the earlier sources as a source of hints about the structure and extent of the setting to be studied. Even this is done primarily for those settings where it is difficult to know where to begin, which are generally tightly closed settings. These are settings where one must get some kind of formal entree, and to do so he must go to the right people and know from the beginning how to deal with them effectively—which is a pretty tall order. The literature may sometimes help. But getting too deeply into the literature can make it all the more difficult to de-focus in doing the research. It's better to leave the more extensive literature search until the stage of understanding, especially the later stages of seeking retest information.

Most of the time we have relied simply on throwing a wide net to find contacts with insiders. We talk with all kinds of people, especially those who are apt to have contacts in the kind of setting we want to study, telling them about the desire to do the research and the need to find contacts. If one has successfully built a web of contacts before, it's generally easy to find some specific contacts for almost any setting one wants to study. In doing this, one makes contact through the mutual friend and talks with him about the whole setting, but especially trying to find out the extent and structure of the setting and the best ways to get into it to do research that is as free as possible of constraints. If the researcher cannot make such contacts, he has to walk in cold (go in blind), which can make it harder. If he walks into a tightly closed setting cold, he should try above all to use a phased-entree strategy. That is, he should try to get into a setting that is not crucial to him and get as much as possible from the gatekeeper about the setting, the nature of the language, any good sources he's missed, and the nature of the crucial setting. Going in blind gives him a low life expectancy, so he wants to get as much as possible out of this phase to help him get into the next phase. It is precisely because he can expect to fail in getting into the cold settings that he goes to the most dispensable first. He should leave the core setting (the most important) until he has learned enough about such settings to be reasonably sure of success and until, hopefully, he has made some good contacts who can help him to get into the core setting. (I always like to say that one should "weave a circle thrice" around the core setting before launching his attack on this research citadel. We shall see below how we did this in the drug crisis intervention study, in which the citadels were important, the settings quite closed, and we quite cold.)

If the setting is not centrally organized, the researcher can go in cold at any point and start learning the hard way. This, for example, was the case with the massage-parlor study. From anything we knew, massage parlors had no central authority, ownership or web of communication that would "queer us" throughout the universe of parlors if we loused up the first ones—or any number of them. Rasmussen simply chose the one closest to his home because it looked like any others and was easy to get to. Then he walked in and started talking.

In any kind of setting it is important to choose the point man carefully, that is, the person who will enter the setting first to scout it or case it, to make contacts and determine the structure and extent of the setting. One might assume off-hand that the head of the team, if there is one, is the obvious person to send in. But this is far from true. The head needs always to know more about research and, of secondary importance, about the whole setting than any other member, or else he shouldn't be the head. But it may be obvious that he's the wrong kind of person for the setting, at least as point man. It is even possible that for some settings it may be useful to use a phased-researcher strategy, that is, send in someone intended to be expendable, a "suicide squad" that doesn't intend to become a real insider in the setting. (In that case the researcher would obviously keep this person's relation to him secret.) Whoever the point man is, he runs all the risks of being stigmatized by the members. The main reason for this is that he does not know the structure of the setting (assuming he is going in reasonably cold), so he is apt to come in with one clique or one point of view and be stigmatized by the others. It is precisely because of this that most team members do not enter at once. He will provide the information on the structure that will allow the others to decide how other members should approach the setting, what entree strategy to use, what groups to align with, which to shun, what perspectives have to be studied and so on. This information provides the basis for the minimal design needed in a study where the researcher has plenty of time and can keep going until he's satisfied he has the important truths about the setting.

When his goal is to provide policy-oriented information, the design becomes more important and so do the problems of starting the right way. It is essential to be able to get at all of the important parts of the setting with reliable results and the practical constraints of time are great. These were true of our team field research study of drug crisis intervention. Our attempts to deal with them are well-illustrated by this study.

The time constraints of the study were intense. We had two months to get at the major aspects of drug crisis intervention throughout the nation. The total budget of the study was slightly less than $25,000, which is small by ordinary research standards. That meant we could hire ten to 12 researchers at most.[5] We would have to make some big compromises in our study, but we equally wanted to make the best bargains we could in our compromises.

We began with a rough formulation of the problem and goal; we wanted a representative and reliable picture of the way the nation dealt with drug crises, which we thought of primarily in terms of overdoses and psychiatric panics—bad trips or freak-outs. We talked with members of the National Commission on Marihuana and Drug Abuse and other possible contacts about the whole thing. They had a few more direct contacts, but very few. In formulating the problems, they could only confirm what we more or less thought: we should study hospital emergency rooms, hot lines, free clinics, and anything else that proved important. We made a search of previous literature, which was easy to do because of the centralized resources of the National Commission and the National Institutes of Health. We got huge, well-annotated bibliographies on all kinds of categories that might have bearings on drug crisis intervention. (As anyone who has done it knows, even a literature search involves considerable creativity simply deciding the categories to use in the search.) But extensive searches of all the literature quickly revealed what experts in the drug field already believed to be the case: There were almost no previous studies of any kind directly concerned with drug crisis intervention. This meant we would be going in pretty cold, with tight

time constraints, and the need to provide roughly representative and reliable information on the complex realm of drug crises and their treatment. Fortunately, we had already used team field research techniques in attempting to study a national political convention. We were able to adopt them in the study of drug crisis intervention. We could never have done the study in depth without them. They proved more powerful than we had dared to hope and helped develop the methods further.

We were forced to begin with little more than knowledge about drugs and a general knowledge of the problems associated with them, such as our knowledge of many cases of drug overdoses and deaths and some cases of bad trips or psychotic breaks, and a vague focus on finding out what happens in concrete cases when someone needs help for a serious drug problem, a drug crisis. This meant concretely that we would begin our study by finding out all we could about emergency-room treatment of drug cases, about hot lines, free clinics, and so on.

Given this initial formulation of the problem, we could have tried to get a general picture of what is done by emergency rooms, hot lines and free clinics about drug cases around the country by sending out questionnaires to a representative, national sample. This approach appeared doomed to failure for four basic reasons.

First, so little was known about the field to begin with that there was little of the pretest knowledge used by survey researchers to determine how to formulate their questions, to whom to send them, how to code the answers, and how to make any sense out of the answers returned. Indeed, what little we did know made it clear that there was no adequate national registry of hot lines and free clinics. (We later discovered that it is often not even clear when a "hot line" actually exists or when an "emergency room" is in fact an emergency room, since registered "hot line" services often consist of nothing more than answering telephone calls during the regular business day and telling people whatever the answering person happens to know, and registered "emergency rooms" are sometimes unequipped and unstaffed to deal with most emergencies.)

Second, anyone who has dealt with doctors knows that they have little time during working hours to devote to answering questions, so questionnaires would either be thrown in the trash or hastily filled in—probably by a harried nurse.

Third, our knowledge of the controversial nature of drugs and of the services dealing with drug problems led us to expect that any respondent to a questionnaire about drugs or the services would be faced with a real temptation to tell the researchers "what they ought to know," that is, the public fronts or ideals of organizations (P.R. work).

Fourth, questionnaire studies can only get at those things the respondents have already conceptualized clearly enough to put into words and cannot reveal new dimensions of meaning to us, whereas we wanted as much as possible to come up with new ideas about drug problems and their treatment.

It was clear that, rather than trying to get a superficial picture of services for dealing with drug problems around the country, we wanted to get an in-depth view of drug problems and services and we wanted to be able to check out any information by making our own observations of the services. This meant that we would do field research on the problems and services. At the same time, however, we were much more concerned with getting a view of these which would be far more representative for the whole nation than most field studies are, since we were ultimately concerned with developing nationwide policy proposals to help improve the social services for drug problems. We decided to choose two large metropolitan areas for intensive study to give us a broadly representative view of the whole nation and then get a better idea of the representativeness of these cities by checking other areas that seem different. We wanted two very large standard metropolitan statistical areas because 80 percent or more of Americans live in metropolitan areas and the vast majority of drug problems are located there. We wanted one city in the West and one in the East because the evidence indicates they are the areas of greatest drug use. Two different regions could also reveal possible differences in drug problems.

We built the initial structure of the overall team on the basis of what we had learned from our earlier team study. We knew that with a team of 12 or more people, centered in two cities at opposite ends of the country, and studying diverse subjects, we would have problems of coordination. This was eased somewhat by the fact that the team was skewed to the West, because the Western city was many times the size of the Eastern city. Most of the team would be in the West and I would be able to spend most of my time working with them. As director (see the section on role specialization), I would be the primary coordinator. I would shuttle between the two cities. But Eastern City would have a separate quarterback, who would be directly in contact with and responsible to me. Moreover, we tried to increase coordination at all levels by getting members to communicate with each other at all levels and between cities. The two most important people in the East first had direct experience in the West and got to know that part of the team. The most important point here is that the team and the research design were constructed together and changed together.

We now had the overall design, but we still had to construct the specific designs. We developed a distinctive kind of design, which is specifically what we called the team field research design.[6] It consists of four major steps:

(1) Determining the rough dimensions of the universe to be studied;
(2) Selecting from this a concentric zone set of subuniverses consisting of a core-subuniverse, a secondary subuniverse, and residual subuniverses;
(3) Selecting samples from each subuniverse; and
(4) Searching for negative instances and continually revising our natural categories, samples and ideas in accord with the findings about these.

The specific steps we followed in doing this for Western City illustrate well the general method.

Let us consider first how we dealt with the emergency rooms, though this was only one part. Defining the dimensions of the universe of emergency rooms was no easy task. We knew we needed to find all of the emergency rooms, hot lines and free clinics in the city (actually a metropolitan area which included the city and the county).[7] We started with this task. It may sound like an easy task to someone who has never tried to find some central source of information about social services in a major metropolitan area in America; it wasn't. In fact, at first we got the horrified impression that finding the total dimensions of our universe was like looking for all the hotels and motels that might have a vacancy in an American city with a lot of conventions going on. We feared we would have to go to each one. (This is different from a city like London, which has a centralized booking agency which can be called from anywhere in the United Kingdom.) We could see ourselves running around from one hospital to another trying to find out which ones had emergency rooms.

One of the first things we did was adopt a strategy for finding the people who might know the things we needed to know. We canvassed our key contacts in the medical world for information on centralized sources of such information and for further contacts who might know about this. They did not know how we would get information on all those hospitals with emergency rooms. But they sent us to others, who in turn sent us to others who might know. We finally did get this information from a county agency. Most of the key contacts we had had did not know about the agency, the lines of authority, and so on. (I now have specific strategies for searching for municipal agencies in such situations, but then I did not.) Indeed, we eventually discovered that there was a small but highly effective research organization working for the county government studying emergency medical services throughout the county. But it wasn't until the study was half over that we discovered this group! (The search for sources of information was, of course, a continual part of the study. It was part of the continual search for new contacts.)[8]

What we found, as shown in Figure 2, was the following distribution of hospitals and emergency rooms. There were three general county hospitals which had massive emergency rooms, one of which handled several times the case load of the others (this was Central County Hospital). There were 75 hospitals throughout the county with contracts with the county to provide emergency medical services, with the county guaranteeing payment for these. There were 50 private hospital emergency rooms, with no county contracts and limited emergency services. There were, then, 127 emergency rooms, out of a total hospital population of about 200. As we were talking with our many informants in the early stages, we were continually picking up all the reliable information we could on the different hospitals. We had learned the overall structure of their operations. Drug emergencies, like emergencies generally, seemed to go to the nearest contract hospital, if picked up by the ambulances and they could not prove ability to pay, but they were then often shipped to one of the three large county hospitals. (It was actually much more complex, but this was the legally prescribed structure, except in some serious cases.) Nearly half of drug crises that came in to the emergency rooms would probably wind up at the three general hospitals, with the vast majority of these going to Central Hospital. Almost no drug crises were apt to go to private emergency rooms and the contract emergency rooms received cases in rough proportion to their staff size, hospital size, etc. From all of this we were able to construct our team sample and set to work with our initial design.

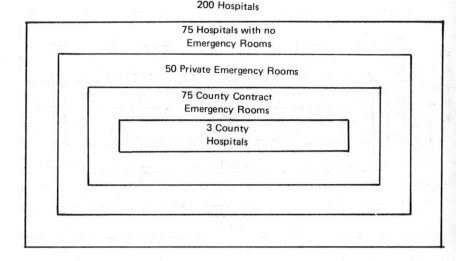

Figure 2: The Structure of Emergency Medical Services
           in Western Metropolitan Area

The samples corresponded closely to the subuniverse structure. As depicted in Figure 3, we see that there was a core sample made up of a set of emergency rooms to be studied. They had top priority—they were the research citadel to which we referred earlier. It consisted of the three general county hospitals. The secondary sample consisted of a choice of what appeared to be a representative sample of the different-sized hospitals in the other categories—those with county contracts, those without county contracts, but with emergency rooms, and those with neither. The sample was already heavily weighted toward the larger county contract hospitals because of everything we had heard. In addition, our secondary core sample was chosen in the light of the existing opportunities of good entree. By now we knew a lot about the different major hospitals. Since we needed in-depth studies we wanted to study those where we had a good chance of getting in-depth.' The residual sample consisted of all those we did not plan specifically to study in-depth, but we had important plans to study them in certain ways.

The first-stage design of the study was now reasonably clear. We had to study the core sample, the citadel. We would, therefore, approach them as cautiously as possible. Fortunately, the contacts of the National Commission and a contact of one of the researchers made it easy to walk into the two smaller emergency rooms of the core sample. But we had no direct contact to

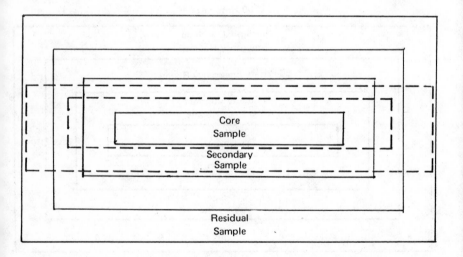

Figure 3: The Samples of the Initial Design

Central; and it handled by far the largest number, maybe as many as all the rest combined. We would hold off on that to try to develop contacts. (We never did find a good contact. From all our contacts we could not even find out who was the director of the emergency room or the structure of things. I had to telephone around to find out whom I should talk to. We were going in cold and it was as bad as we feared. The emergency room shut us out, but we were fortunate to get complete access to the psychiatric services which handled all cases after shipping through the emergency room.)

We would study the secondary sample as manpower allowed. We would move into the secondary sample with two weightings in mind—go from those where we had good contacts to those where we had less good contacts (one should always try to build more as he goes along, leapfrogging from one good contact to another), that is, go from the more important emergency room to the less important.

The residual sample is the group in which negative instances would be sought in two general ways. First, as we pursued our study we would get as much reliable talk as we could about all hospitals. If we heard of any that we thought had a significant chance of being different in relevant ways from those we were studying, we would try to study them, going in-depth as long as we were finding something interestingly different. Second, we would try to do a random sampling of those in the residual category by various methods, going from in-depth interviewing to random telephoning to talk with whoever would talk. If we struck paydirt (something different) we would mine it until the vein ran out.

In the first-stage design we did this same kind of thing for hot lines and free clinics. But there were relatively few of these. We devised methods to study all of the bigger free clinics and hot lines and to do some natural experiment checking of a random sample of the more numerous hot lines. (This is the one in which the researchers would call, say they had a friend with a drug problem, and ask urgently what should be done about it.[9] In this way we could quickly find out who knew what about drug problems and what they did about them.)

An important part of the first-stage design was the study of a general residual sample for negative instances. We threw a broad net of casual (random) field studies and interviews to find out if our focus on emergency medical services, hot lines and free clinics was justified. We studied various drug rehabilitation programs, and so on. Most of these proved to be dead ends, but they were important in our next step.

The first-stage design was quickly transformed into a second-stage design. As we got into depth in our study of emergency services we soon discovered two major things.

First, we discovered that there was good reason to believe that a high percentage of serious drug problems never appear in any system of emergency medical care. This was strongly supported by what we were learning in general from our study of the broad residual sample of the first stage, that is, drug rehabilitation programs, and the like. We realized we would have to know what the problems were in the streets and homes, how they were defined, and how people decided what to do if we were to determine what the problems were, why people did or did not get medical care, hot line advice, or other help. We redirected a special part of our study to the study of street drugs and some feelers toward the study of home prescription drug problems. (These were just feelers because the problem of access was terrible. We got good impressionistic information, largely by drawing on personal experiences of researchers' families.)

Second, we soon realized in the emergency rooms that a crucial aspect of emergency medicine is the ambulances and we were picking up evidence of the "ambulance scandal." We also realized that the ambulances would give us quick entree to certain emergency rooms, a way of becoming an overtly defined researcher in one setting (ambulances) that would literally allow us to ride into another setting as if we were members. Fortunately, we had at least one ambulance chaser on the team and we put him to riding the ambulances, screaming wildly through the night in hot pursuit of the ever elusive data.

All research designs in field research must be flexible and will generally change to meet the evolving realities of the situations at hand. They are guides, not sets of iron rules. They are a wedding of reason with concrete experience in the situation, not the word of God.

Using Team Field Research to Study Multiperspectival Realities in a Conflictful Society

I have argued that team field research is especially vital in studying situations in which conflicting groups come together, that is, in which there are multiple, conflicting perspectives involved in the setting. The study of drug crisis intervention involved relatively little of this because, while it was very multiperspectival, there were relatively few situations in which the conflicting groups, such as drug users and police, came into direct contact in the study. When they did, such as in the hospitals, the team members were clearly aligned with the hospital staffs. We considered ways of trying to get someone to talk with the people who brought patients in, but could not think of a way to disassociate them from the staffs. We knew they and the patients were hiding all kinds of things from the medical staffs. (It was not uncommon for people to be dropped at the door or for people to be almost dying from overdoses, with ice in their pants or other signs of common-sense forms of overdose remedies, but deny having taken any drugs. They were scared of the police.) We simply could not devise any way of studying it from that perspective. We were using a few team specialists to study the street drug scene and one of these was so clearly identifiable as a street type by the medical people that we would not want him studying both. But he was mainly an instance of specializing.

Our first attempt at a team field project, the study of a national political convention, was more thoroughly multiperspectival from the beginning. This convention was to be held in 1972, a period of great conflict. It was well-known that demonstrators were planning a massive protest at the convention. Meanwhile, the police were planning their methods of controlling the demonstrators. Here were two major forces planning to come together in conflict. But there were many other sides as well—the national committee, the mayor's office (which had somewhat different views from the police), the political host committee which worked with the national committee but was independent, and the media coverage of all of this, as well as smaller groups such as the American Civil Liberties Union. We were interested in studying all of the social planning that these groups did, watching to see how plans were related to what actually happened, and then seeing how the events unfolded at the convention. (In general, we were studying the interdependent constructions of social events and their relations to evolving events.) That was the general rubric. It fell pretty much in the middle of immersion techniques aimed at pure science data and more designed techniques aimed at policy-oriented data.

It was clear from the beginning that we were dealing with conflicting perspectives and groups which demanded different kinds of people to study each perspective if we were going to get inside of the conflicting groups. This was so because it took people with special and conflicting perspectives to go in-depth with the demonstrators on one side and the police on the other. But it was also clear that it was unlikely, even if we had someone who could manage to get along with both, that such a person could avoid having his covers blown. The groups were going to come together and they each had undercover agents. Anyone who tried to be deeply involved with both would literally be in danger, because he would probably be spotted and labelled a traitor by each. (I don't remember anyone even wanting to try to join both sides.) We would have to use different people in the conflicting groups and bring their perspectives together in the team study. We shall see later that the method involved certain problems of its own, but it also proved to be the only effective way to do such a study. This particular study was aborted by the abrupt movement of the convention to less conflictful environs.

However, one small team effort, the study of the mass media coverage, continued. Manpower problems prevented our using any full-blown team methods to do this study. But we were able to use two aspects well. Our original intention had been to study all of the mass media in the city to get a comparative view of their coverage of the convention. We were denied access to the two newspapers and constricted our efforts to a comparative study of the two network-affiliated TV newsrooms, studied by Altheide and Rasmussen, with my intermittent participation and coordination. (In addition, a third sociology student, Kerry Teeple, had been an insider at one of the stations for many years and was the crucial part of an insider-outsider team relation.) While it may not be impossible, it seems unlikely that such a comparative study of organizations in direct and intense competition with each other could be done by the same person. It could probably not be kept secret that one was playing the role of double agent, as they would probably see it. The team effort worked excellently.

In this study we also developed further the basic idea we had started with in the study of the convention, looking at how two different sides construct their realities when interacting and how things actually evolved in the situation. The team was helpful in doing this, but not necessary, because the perspectives were not necessarily exclusive.

We took several media events planned by people we knew would be newsmakers. We watched how they planned the events to get good media coverage—that is, to get it told the way they wanted it told by carefully building fronts. Then we watched what happened, even interviewing news people at the scene, and then watched what they put on the air. We did this successfully for a Chicano demonstration planned by a friend of ours[10] and most successfully for the TV coverage of the nude beach. In these cases we had the insider views from each angle of the conflicting perspective and were able to get valuable information in understanding how the media operate.

The study of nude beaches was aimed at providing a multiperspectival view of a conflictful and changing situation. Unlike any other studies of deviance, we were trying to see how the conflicting sides saw the whole thing, how they went about trying to enforce their definitions through political and legal action and how all of this changed over time. We made use of every chance we had of coming at events from different angles, though as usual these were continually constrained by manpower problems. We've already seen some instances of our use of different people in studying different angles on the realities, such as in our discussion of the checking out of Doc's interview statements to Gilmore by Rasmussen and Flanagan. But there were other ways we did this. We used two sociologists who were not involved in the beach scene to get at the police views of the beach. One of these, Altheide, interacted with the police informally in a teaching relation and drew them out on the beach. Another, Phillips, who had been studying the police for some time, did some formal interviews with contacts among police officials. I also got a couple of undergraduate students to study the property owners independently. Perhaps most importantly, and certainly most systematically, we got Carol Ann Flanagan to get at the women's perspectives on the beach, while we concentrated on the men's perspectives. (Cross-sexual communications tended to be heavily determined by sexual concerns—and tended not to be very honest. We found the same thing to be true in important ways in the study of massage parlors and had to use women for the real inside work.) Even women who had just met Carol Ann would sit around telling her how they liked to "size up the men"—and they did it for the tape recorder! But they *never* said those things to us men. There were a few instances in which we thought we'd be safe in doing double-agent observations because we thought we could keep the groups independent; but this generally failed and there were always more personal strains involved. Rasmussen and I studied both property owners and nude beachers. The property owners slowly caught on to me and just didn't say much. Rasmussen was spotted by the head of the property owners' group while he was being friendly with the leaders of the nude beachers' political action group. After that he was stigmatized with a big red N on his forehead. We simply sent him back to the beach in disgrace.

Spies who play both sides of the street often pay severe consequences. For every reason, it is better to use multiple researchers (agents) to study multiple perspectives in conflictful situations whenever practical concerns allow.

Building and Using the Web of Research Contacts: The Multiplier Effect of Team Work

We have continually emphasized the importance of building and using friendly and trusting contacts in doing field research. We have seen repeatedly that they are vital for getting entree, that they should be sought out, collected, nurtured. We have seen repeatedly that having good contacts typically makes all the difference between getting into a setting and being shut out, between getting the truth and being fronted out. This argument has been made concerning all field research, not just team field research. But there are certain aspects of team work that make building and using the web of contacts distinctive and more productive.

Team field research allows one to make extensive use of the multiplier effect in research contacts. Anyone who has successfully built and used a web of contacts in sociable relations, politics or sales work knows that contacts, both good and bad, have a multiplier effect. That is, each time an individual makes a good contact, he does not merely add that person to his list, but he also adds those with whom that person is on good terms, if he has made an effort to do so. This is commonly done by talking with the contact about his possible contacts in some field, sometimes specifically mentioning one's need of a good contact in some field and asking if he has any suggestions—"Hey, who do you know who can help me do. . . .?" The more friendly and trusting people are toward one, and the more they think they might eventually gain from helping that person, the more willing they are to share contacts.

But, fortunately for researchers, people also commonly like to share contacts because it makes them look like a big-time social operator, a big man around town, an inside-dopester. (Naturally, because of these incentives to pass on contacts, some people talk big—that is, they pass one on to someone who is supposed to be a good contact but isn't. Everyone has to watch out for the big talker.) As everyone knows from personal experience, contacts cannot commonly be passed on beyond someone known directly. That is, one's contact can pass on his contacts, though with considerably diminished commitment, but he cannot pass on the contacts of his contact. He can try and sometimes does, but it doesn't generally have much effect, unless he is an important or very well-liked and trusted person. The degree of contact charisma obviously varies considerably and the researcher seeks above all to cultivate those with a great deal.

Team field research can use the web of contacts with even greater effect if it is done systematically. It is done systematically by making every team member an active contributor to the web of contacts. Each person should seek out contacts by making his own, then querying them about other contacts. I have always found it a useful tactic to continually talk-it-up in seeking research contacts. That is, I try to tell almost anyone about the research, as a simple matter of sociability, and invite him to return the sociability by talking about it in turn, especially about any personal experience and any contacts he has that might help. If the researcher hits it off well with a garage attendant, a bartender, a salesman, he tells that person about his work and sees if he knows any contacts he's willing to share. I've seen some extremely useful contacts made that way, but let me consider a more obvious one for social researchers.

Almost any field researcher who is also a teacher or student has discovered at some time that his students are a great source of contacts and are often the people directly involved. For example, if a sociology professor has established friendly and trusting relations with his class on deviance or criminology, he can generally count on having at least 5-10 percent of them into something of immediate interest to his work on deviance. It's a simple matter of self-selection. If he has established the right relations, then makes his research clear, letting them know what it is and arousing interest, and then invites help, he can usually get people to help after class.

In one small class of 30 students, with whom I'd established close relations because of its smallness, I talked up various research projects we were doing on things like drug dealers, the nude beach, the mass media, and so on. I came up with four drug dealers (one direct and three through contacts), three inside informants on the nude beach, one excellent participant-observer study of a swinging party, and an inside account of one of the newspaper decisions to publish the Ellsberg papers. These all proved out as reliable contacts and information (except the news decision, which I had no way of checking out). The drug dealer proved especially helpful and is instructive as an example of the importance of talking up one's research to find contacts.

I had been doing a two-man team study with a graduate student of a big drug dealer and his girlfriend, who had also been a dealer briefly and been busted by federal agents on a large cocaine deal. We spent many hours in in-depth discussions for this study. It sounded beautiful. The internal checks worked. They had also been close friends of his for years. Moreover, we had other forms of direct observation to confirm some of their story, such as her legal problems and some exciting tapes they had already made secretly of their dealings with the federal agents and prosecutors.[11] (Those tapes gave the real inside look at "plea bargaining" in the raw. They were used in a fine thesis on plea bargaining by Gerald Cloyd.)[12] Still, we had little other evidence to check them out. In addition, they were running scared and I had to deal with them through the student. My inherent suspicions are vastly multiplied when I have little or no direct contact with informants. (I generally look at such data as limbo data unless we have excellent ways of checking it out.) Then one day in my deviance class I was talking about some details of this case and, though I was being careful to launder the data, I happened to mention a detail of the man's earlier life in a border town where he first got involved in using marihuana and running it for personal use. A short-haired, clean-cut student in the front row, whom I knew only vaguely, raised his hand and said, "Hey, I know that guy. We grew up in the same crowd back in Texas." I was surprised and dubious. I stepped up to him and asked in whispered tones what the dealer's name was. He immediately gave me the dealer's real name. Later that day he let me tape 2½ hours of talk about the dealer's background, his friends, their activities, etc. It provided a partial check on at least his earlier life (it checked out) and added some new dimensions to his career. My informant told me about his own dealing, which we later taped in detail. He also did an intensive interview for us with a big dealer who was a friend of his but unwilling to talk with researchers. This was the beginning of a much larger team study of high-level dealers (see Adler, Adler, Douglas with Rasmussen, 1977) which provided remarkable checking out of these early dealers, including evidence from a dealer who put out a contract on our first informant.

In the early stages of a team project all of the researchers should build up a web of contacts and pass these on to each other. It is often necessary to keep index cards on potential contacts, what they do, who knows them. It is common to need someone later who is doing something the researcher never imagined he'd need to know about. Soon the structure of the web will become apparent, so that when he doesn't have a direct contact he can find someone who is likely to know the right kind of person for his purposes. Moreover, he not only uses the web of names to make specific contacts, but also for namedropping. All good field researchers are good namedroppers. When the researcher has to go in cold, namedropping can be his research saver. Using what he knows and suspects about his cold informant, he casually mentions in the right context the charismatic and influential people' who have helped him in his research. If he's built his web carefully and learned the art of namedropping, he'll generally hit pay dirt quickly: "Oh, you know Joe, huh? I didn't know he'd helped you with your research . . . He's a damned good man."

Having all the contacts of a team allows one to see the structure of the web more quickly and completely than generally happens in individual research. But there is more to the team effort than this. The team is also building its own personal relations with these many contacts. They are building a web of friendly and trusting commitments of their own with precisely those people of most value in doing the research. And they are able to pass these contacts on to other team members by introducing them personally. Importantly, as in anything else, the team deliberately sets out to build good relations with those people who seem most important in the area. They often get those team members who seem most able to get along with a given person to establish good relations with them so that they can help anyone on the team who needs it. At the extreme, of course, this becomes a form of setting people up. Also important, a team can provide support for each other. The simplest way this is done is by telling informants that a team member is good and can be counted on.

Using Role Specialization and Complementarity of Team Members

One of the greatest advantages of team work is that it allows us to use the specialized characteristics, interests, talents, and specialized knowledge of the members for the multiplied benefit of the whole project. We've seen before that traditional field research tends to assume that all field researchers are alike and that, indeed, most individuals are personally fitted for any kind of field research. Considering what everyone knows about people from his everyday experience, this is ridiculous. People differ greatly, vastly, in their individual characteristics, interests and so on. In the academic world, because of the self-selection of those who are most interested in doing library and book work, there are high percentages of people who are quiet, reclusive, and generally inexperienced and inept at dealing with most kinds of people in our society.[13] They are different from the glad-handing sociable type of person, so prevalent and successful in our society. Regardless of the researcher's personal preferences, he must recognize that they are entirely different types of people, with different effects on other people, and that they must be used differently in dealing with people in research settings.

The most important form of team specialization involves precisely this difference in social abilities. As we have seen continually, one of the most important things in field research is friendliness, being liked. And closely related to this and dependent on it are the vital aspects of building and using good contacts and gaining entree. One of the most vital specialists in team research, then, is the sociability specialist, who is also generally an entree specialist. The sociability specialist is sent around wherever he is needed. (Women researchers seem generally to be better at this than men, both with men and women. We shall deal with this further in the next section.) (Also see Warren, unpublished manuscript.) She is an excellent person to make most of the initial contacts and then pass them on to the other researchers who are planning to work with them more closely. She is often useful just as a social lubricant, that is, as someone who goes along to make a meeting more friendly.

The sociability specialist is often vital in a form of vertical specialization within a team. Some forms of research can only be done this way. The sociability specialist is the one who interacts directly with the other team members or with some of the people being more directly researched, while the quarterback or manager stays out of the way, but makes many of the vital decisions on the basis of what he is fed by the front man.[14] This vertical specialization is especially important in those areas where the quarterback is known as a professor and the people being studied are casual or hip types who don't like "straight professors."

This was especially important in our study of massage parlors and drug dealers. In those studies we even had a well-established practice of my turning over any contacts I made to them, for we knew well that the contacts would be able to get along with them much better. We found this sort of thing useful in such ploys as the Trojan-students, in which students would act on their own, as if there were no professor hiding behind them, because we thought a professor would freak out the people. Being a professor of sociology is one of the worst stigmas one can carry around on one's back in American society, almost as bad as being a "shrink."

The leader role is equally specialized. Rather, it should be very specialized in research, but rarely is in academic types of research. Normally, the bag man (grantsman) is the leader by reason of money, and he spends most of his time misleading. My own experience has always led me to conclude that research projects in which leadership is given mainly by money are like monarchies: Once in a while there is a great leader, but whole families have to be killed off to do it. Almost all money given for social research is given for reasons having nothing to do with truth or research abilities. (This could easily be proven by using unpaid team field research methods.) The only team project I've been involved in that had much support was the drug crisis study. I tried doing this with great emphasis on personal loyalties and so on, but even there the payment had bad effects on people. The finest research has generally *cost* us money.[15] When there is no money the team relations are much more egalitarian, with multiperspectival forms of leadership, each person leading at what he does best. The leader is not a manager, or director, but a quarterback—and there may be a number of different quarterbacks in different realms. The quarterback has to be as involved as possible. He has to inspire by his own work. And his calls have to be right or he gets sent to the bench.

There are many other useful forms of specialization in team research, but most of them are not so striking. We have found that some people are tremendously good as observers and recounters of their observations. These are often the quiet, more reclusive types. They find social relations more problematic, so they are more careful at observing it and putting it into words. (The old Shavian cliche holds true here much of the time, "Those who can do and those who can't teach" us about it.) There are also some people who are extremely good at finding people and organizations. They can find their way through labyrinthine complexities while others are getting lost. I suppose they simply have more initiative, more gall, and a better set of established strategies for negotiating the complexities of our society. And, of course, any team is apt to wind up with the misfits, those at first expected to take to the field research but who turn out to prefer reading the final report on the whole thing. They always have reasons why they could not make contact, find the organization, or get along with the receptionist. They should be made the literary experts. Worse, there are sometimes those who specialize only in "throwing the monkey wrench."

Turning Out Key Informants

However carefully chosen, talented, and variegated a team of researchers might be, there will be some important ways in which a few of those who are already members of the setting being studied are more able to deal with the people and get at the vital truths of the setting. These people have commonly been used as key informants by researchers, though it is apparent that in some cases they have become so integral to the research that they could better be seen as team members. (This was true of "Doc" in *Street Corner Society*.) But almost never have researchers actually made these members full-fledged researchers, probably partly because they did not think in terms of team work, but primarily because they saw a gulf between research and membership. Given our argument about the vital importance of direct experience to everything else in research, and the resulting preference for becoming a member when possible, this gulf is now seen to be a mud puddle that is easily bridged. We have made that bridge with increasing frequency because we have found that members who are turned out into full-fledged team researchers can be invaluable and because we have found that this ties them to us better than anything else can.

We turn members into researchers for the same reasons we turn researchers into members: It proves in the circumstances to be the best way of achieving the goals of the project. Consequently, we turn out members only when we find specific people who look as if they will thereby make a great contribution to the research. It is a big step and our standards have been much higher than those used to hire graduate students as researchers. We have only made a few members into full-fledged team members, by which we mean they come even to share in the rewards (but rarely the costs) of the work. Since there have been a few rewards, this has not been much of an inducement. The primary inducement is generally the interest the people have in better understanding what they themselves are involved in. Moreover, there are now so many Americans involve in everything who have studied the social sciences at college that it is often easy to find people who understand pretty well what the researcher is up to. (This can be a problem if they only understand traditional forms of survey research or other controlled forms.) These people often have a real interest in the subject and enjoy studying it. But when they are not people the researcher wants to make into full team members, he can far more commonly make them into friendly helpers. We've had more of these than the few who have become full members.

Any group generally has at least four special types of members who can help the researcher in vital ways:

(1) Sociability gadflies;
(2) Constant observers or everyday life historians;
(3) Everyday life philosophers; and
(4) Marginal people and enemies.

Let us examine each of these in some detail.

Just as with more professional team members, the member who is a sociability specialist is apt to be of greatest help to a researcher, especially in the early stages when he knows few people and it will take a while to build close friendships himself in the setting. These people are generally easy to spot and to get to know, simply because they talk to almost anyone and are generally lively, but low-key. (In most groups in our society today the well-liked people are generally low-key, or cool, rather than loud back-slappers, though there are also those more relaxed moments when they let their hair down.) In some settings the sociable ones are the key people a researcher must get to know, because they are the ones who know what really counts. But in most settings, the ultimate sociability specialists are women. These low-key women do not threaten either the women or the men. They are liked by and commonly share intimacies with both sexes. Men are simply more threatening to both sexes, even when they are the most sociable.

Carol Ann Flanagan was a classic example of this kind of sociability specialist. I was doing the nude beach study with Rasmussen at the time I first saw her walking along the water's edge. She looked friendly and open. I said, "Hi, there." That was the entree. Within a minute I had said she looked like a student, she said she had graduated from the University of California in anthropology, I said I was a sociologist, she asked if I was studying the beach, and I had admitted I was. (Whenever anyone asked, I admitted it. But that was rare.) We then spent several hours walking along the beach talking about the whole scene. She was really open about it and when she said something with reservation it was said in such a way that, if you knew what it was about, you could infer the whole thing. As we walked along, people would run up to her or shout out, "Hey, Carol Ann! Over here!" She'd go over, talk a while, laughing quietly, share a smoke, promise to see them some other time, then resume our walk and talk. Here was a sociability expert in the grand tradition, no doubt about it. We had long been aware of our need for a woman's work to complement our own, so we moved to interview her more in depth, on tape. We were carefully considering what she was like, whether she trusted us, whether we could trust her, and so on. She was highly articulate, extremely interested in what people were doing and why, had tremendous gall (research courage), and even liked to go up to strangers at times to ask them things for the simple purpose of shocking them. She joined the team and was of great value in that and later research.

The constant observers or historians of settings are more common than sociability specialists but harder to spot. They're more apt to be the everyday life scholars, and a bit quieter. But they are also generally talkers, or they don't have any way to find out everything. They are the people who go around collecting the details on the setting. They know all kinds of things and are constantly learning more and telling it too. In some settings they are older people who spend all their time doing this. Once the researcher determines who is reliable, these people can be great helpers. On the nude beach I had several helpers who were there all the time and were always glad to tell me what had been going on, what that guy had been doing, and so on. In the study of drug crisis intervention we found several people like that at the national institutes of health. These people had been involved in things like heroin policy, ambulances and emergency medicine for many years, always close to the throne but never quite in power. In the study of drug dealers Peter and Patti Adler uncovered a brilliantly articulate insider who went to great trouble for months to get contacts for them and report on deals. These were inside-dopesters who were tremendously helpful.

The everyday life philosophers are harder still to detect because most people don't care to listen. But these are people who have thought about the setting from every angle and may or may not have a systematic theory about it. The one thing they do have is lots of ideas and thoughts about it. If the researcher shows he's interested, they're more than glad to talk about it, up, down, over and across. In the drug study we found quite a few of them. The observer of emergency medicine was helpful with his ideas and insights.

Field researchers have traditionally used marginal people as informants, always with cautions about getting stigmatized by associations with them and the dangers of biased views.

A lot of literature exists on marginal man theory in field research. The basic idea is that, because they are ambivalent in their feelings and identities in the group, they are better able to see what others take for granted and more willing to talk with outsiders about it. The ideas seem sound enough. The only disagreement I have with it is that I have found most people are marginal in varying ways, to varying degrees, and in varying situations within any setting. It's mainly a matter of finding a way to get them to talk about their ambivalent feelings, to stand back and evaluate the whole setting. Sometimes the most marginal people of all are the leaders who seem so supercommitted. The commitment is a front to hide the fact that they don't believe in what they are asking others to die for, pay for, or simply believe in. They may even be selling out the organization to the competitors. Investigative reporters have relied far more on internal enemies to reveal the inner secrets of organizations. I think the internal enemies can be the most important in research precisely because they are so anxious to talk to someone who can "get the bastards."

Unfortunately, sociologists have little direct help to offer and their commitment to anonymity makes them immensely less useful than journalists. Still, people like Altheide have found the enemies of the leaders very useful in getting the "dirt" on the leaders. Such information merely has to be carefully checked out. It is mainly used as an insight and data for trying to draw other people out, especially to do phased-assertive work on them.

Providing Support, Cross-Checking and Balancing Each Other

Team field researchers are rarely called upon to play the lone ranger type. Even when there are just two people on the team, they provide a great source of support and stimulation to each other. Unlike taking a trip to the mailbox to deposit one's questionnaires, in almost any field research project there are many times when the researcher faces situations that are embarrassing, scary or unpleasant in other ways. Sometimes fellow researchers do nothing more than go along to hold each other's hands, but this is sometimes the most important thing. Having someone to give emotional support may make all the difference between getting it done right away or putting it off for months and maybe never getting to it. Support can be especially important if the research becomes frightening. I have spent many hours reassuring shell-shocked field researchers, especially those studying drug dealers. But in most instances team members provide not only support but stimulation as well. They keep one's thoughts about the setting moving, give different perspectives on a meeting, and so on.

Support and stimulation are especially important in the early stages of research. It is at this stage that we have found it useful for a small group of people to be involved in attempts at entree. This way they all learn the basic things at the same time, meet key people from the beginning, and pool their many ideas. This also makes it easy to use specialization. The setting may not warm up to the team as a whole, but if they like just one person, it's easy to instantaneously switch that team member onto them.

A common thing I've noted in these initial group meetings is that the quarterback (seen as the director by the people to be studied) has to start the discussions because it is expected of him. In many settings, predominately the closed settings of organizations, he must provide the aegis of authority and show that he knows what he's doing, that the project is worth the people's time. But the talk then shifts, with his support, to the team members most likely to be inserted in the setting. If it develops that someone else is more likable to the people, the talk can be shifted to them and the switch made right there. In any event, the director and other team members progressively provide support for the team member who is going to be immediately involved in studying them. He takes the stage, does the main performance, and they support his act. This is an important part of boosting him into the setting. It is also of real value just to let the members see how many people are involved in the project, that they already know so many things about what they're studying, that they are bright and effective people. (If they are not, hide them.) They get the immediate sense that they're involved in an important project, that it's worth helping. It's at this point also that the researcher can casually refer to all the other settings he is already involved in studying, to show them that they aren't the only victims, that it probably doesn't hurt as much as they fear, and that they'd better get on the research bandwagon before he withdraws his offer to study them. Well, it's rarely quite that effective a group demonstration, but it's a fine ideal to keep in mind—bringing the members to their knees, begging to be studied on any terms the researcher is willing to offer!

But team members do not merely provide support. They also provide a vital check on each other. Field researchers have always bemoaned the almost total lack of internal checks and of retesting their studies. The few instances of retesting that have been done, such as the famous retest of Redfield's study of Tepotzlan by Lewis, have shown that they need it badly. Retests tend to show that each participant observer has gotten at different parts or given different interpretations to things. And yet retests continue to be rare. Team field research provides built-in retests, especially if handled the right way. And these retests are only part of the more general checks on each other and balancing of each other that goes on.

With a team it is relatively easy to get retest checks on research, both on one setting and between comparative settings. For example, when Altheide and Rasmussen did their two studies of the different network-affiliated TV newsrooms in one city, they were doing a comparative study in which the external factors that might be important, of being in this particular city, were controlled pretty well. They were able to easily do the first field research on TV news that was really comparative. But we also had other team members involved, especially an insider at Altheide's station, who could provide evidence about the possible effects upon their findings of their individual characteristics and situations of observation. We thus had retest between comparable settings and some important retest within one setting. Both the between and the within independent observations are what we call cross-checks on each other. As we know from Chapter 1, they give us greater reliability of our findings—independent retest observations, or objectivity.

In the drug crisis intervention study we were able to do far more of this cross-checking of comparable settings and of one setting. We had massive cross-checks on the comparable settings because we had many different, partly independent studies of emergency rooms going on. That part was no problem at all and proved tremendously valuable. We found that what we found in one emergency room was important in finding out what was going on in the others. The reader will remember, for example, the vital importance of simply knowing what is likely to be going on in opening up a setting by fishing, drawing out, phased assertion and confrontation. It is often easy for many comparable settings to hide things, but it is likely that at least one setting will reveal things—someone will talk or one may accidentally find something.

We all understood that different individuals might see different things or think differently about them, or be shown or told different things, and so on. So we would make independent or partially independent observations of the same setting to check this out. Probably even more important, since we had researchers working partly independently on different parts of the settings, such as in the emergency rooms and in the ambulances, we sometimes had researchers coming at the same setting from different angles, providing pincers or multiperspectival checks on what we were getting in each part of the setting. In the nude beach study we used a special form of this which we called insider-outsider cross-checks. As one part of our checking out of people in the scene, we would deliberately keep one of us as an outsider to observe from the outside people who had been observed already from the inside by insiders. Since we could see a lot of what people were up to by just watching them in such an open setting, the outsider would be able to see how what the people did when the insiders were not with them, compared to what they did and said when the insiders were there. For example, Rasmussen and Carol Ann were insiders with the Doc group and the beach politicos described earlier, and I was the outsider. They knew I existed somewhere, but we kept my identity secret for months. They finally spotted me talking with Rasmussen one day, but until then I was just another creep creeping around the beach, casually watching them and making mental notes on what they were doing. (They didn't blow my cover. I simply felt it didn't matter much anymore. We had all the goods on them.)

The insider-outsider strategy, even in the form of a two-member team, can be of tremendous value in other ways as well. Remembering our long discussion of the pros and cons of in-depth involvement, it should be evident that an insider-outsider team combines the values of both, especially when the outsider then moves in to become enough of an insider to better know how to communicate with the insider. We've done this in many different ways. Though it was done for more personal reasons, this proved to be of real value at times in the massage parlor study. I was the outsider, though one who was in direct contact with some of the members through in-depth interviews, and the others (Rasmussen, Kuhn, Carol Ann) the insiders. The balance between the cool detachment of the outsider and the more committed view of the insiders proved important at certain points.

Another crucial aspect of the insider-outsider strategy can be checking the uncertainty effects of the insider researcher. In this case the outsider may in fact be an insider who is part of the team, but not known to be working with them. Either as an insider to the setting or someone from outside not known to be working with the team, he draws out the members on their views and feelings about the researcher. He especially invites negative views, maybe by phased assertions. For example, by being an outsider in the beach scene, I was able to get some independent evidence on Rasmussen and Flanagan. In the TV news study Altheide's insider, while known to be associated with him, picked up a lot of evidence about his observational problems in the setting. In a big open setting the researcher can sometimes even play his own outsider, because people will tell him that they've heard about someone doing research on the setting and he can pretend he doesn't know anything about it. (Even more sinister, he can send in a *researcher provocateur* to attack the researcher in a confrontational tactic. He might tell the members he's heard about the researcher and assert things such as, "Hey, man, don't you think all them sociologists are a bunch of dumbasses? They never ask the important questions and spend all their time watching themselves in the mirror.") I've never tried that one, but I think it would be interesting to try it.

It is easy to build such cross-checks into one's team design. For example, with the understanding of the other team members, the quarterback can arrange to have one researcher study a setting, then send in another blind, or totally independently, to retest his findings. The second would not be told what the first had found until he had finished, then they can all put it together and see what they have. This kind of independent cross-checking works against the equally important integration of a team effort and is time-consuming. It can generally be done only in a basic science team design, but it can at least be done partially in policy-oriented research to provide crucial checks on the most important aspects of the settings.

In addition to cross-checking each other, team members tend to balance each other in the collective grasps, understandings and reports that emerge from the work. The various self-deceptions, political commitments, and so on, of each member tend to be balanced by those of other members– unless, of course, someone has conspired to produce a monolithic team. We have always promoted this balancing from early in the work, at least by the stage of grasping it all, by getting together to talk about our thoughts on the work, taping these talks, and considering how and why we might have different senses and ideas about it. These become more crystallized as our understanding grows. It is then possible to cross-check on differences, to see if it's something about the individuals, something about different settings or what. The quarterback needs above all to be open to these. He is, presumably, the person most responsible for writing it all up (though this can vary) and he must come up with a true statement, which is much more likely if the balancing has been promoted. I've always found this team balancing to be important.

The Problems of Team Field Research and Attempted Solutions

That flippant reminder of the possibilities of covering up serves to introduce us to the problems of team field research. All methods have their problems and, considering the pains we've gone to in this book to penetrate others' cover ups, it would be unfitting to end with a cover up of these problems. Our experience has shown that the major problems are those of trust, timidity at being independent (or problems of authority), and the usual organizational problems.

Trust is no doubt the crucial problem in team field research, as in most human enterprises. This became apparent in our first big team effort, the study of the political convention. It will be remembered that this study involved the multiperspectival study of groups in conflict, especially the potential demonstrators and the police. We realized after a while that we were not getting much information from the person studying the demonstrators. We mainly got surface stuff that told us little more than we could get in the newspapers. Just as in espionage work, when one gets "filler," one has to suspect, if there are potential trust problems because of great conflict, that the person producing filler doesn't trust him. Not having enough experience at that stage, I didn't. This person was one of the weak points in the web of commitments, simply because I had few direct ties to him and did not know him well. But I discounted that too much. Fortunately, in this instance I learned from two other team members that this person was highly committed to the cause he was studying, which I more or less knew, and that his political commitments made him suspicious of me and the whole effort. He simply was not wiling to tell us much of the internal workings we needed to know. About that time the convention disappeared, so it did not matter much. But it is easy to see how one could be fed a whole line by an errant team member. How is it dealt with?

Three crucial things must be done. Naturally, one would like to avoid catastrophes and to minimize the need for any internal security measures. This is done by taking the first step, that of being careful to choose people with whom one is on friendly and trusting terms, then building their commitments him (the researcher) and the others in the project, and by maintaining open lines of communication at all times. It is also done by making sure everyone realizes that internal cross-checking will most likely reveal traitors and slaggards.

Second, while the team members, especially the quarterback, must have some trust in people, they must also be realists—that is, suspicious. They must be open to something going wrong. When they are getting filler or nothing or things that don't test out in terms of their grasps of the setting, they should look into the matter of possible betrayal. By the time we got to the drug crisis intervention study I had this attitude. When I was being continually put off and fed previously known information by two hired-hand researchers, I looked into it. How? Check 'em out, of course.

Checking out, as part of cross-checking more generally, is the third thing to do. The researcher goes to the team members he can trust most by all considerations (see Chapter 7) and have them check these people out. Or he can make direct observations and so on. We did. They were simply not doing the job, so we fired them.

Unfortunately, one of the factors leading to trustworthiness in our team efforts also tends to decrease the expression of independent points of view and initiative. To build trust, we build feudal relations to tie people to us. As an academic, this is easily done by using graduate students, who have career commitments in addition to everything else. This can be a very tight bond, especially because graduate students tend to overemphasize their dependence on faculty members. But it can by that very fact be stifling of independence. The more equality, the more independent action on both sides; but the less trust. One obviously has to balance these factors and try to find ways of diminishing their negative effects. I try to use many different bonds of friendly commitments, play down the professorial ones at all points, be egalitarian, and emphasize the importance of independent contributions. The benefits of the professorial relation are probably outweighed by the disadvantages, and they are hard to overcome on any front, whether dealing with members or students, but they can generally be kept in bounds.

The organizational problems of team field research do not differ much from those of any entrepreneurial activity. Some are obvious and easy to take into account; some are much less so. The bigger the team, for example, the greater the problems of communication and integration of effort; and the greater the tendency for the quarterback to become a manager, then a director. By the time there are a dozen members delegation of authority and tasks is critical. I suspect that, like sociability gatherings, the ideal team project is six members for a pure science project. For policy-oriented research it is impossible to say how many are needed to get the necessary in-depth understanding and the representative findings. Some may demand dozens, but my suspicion is that the larger the organization the blunter the cutting edge. After some point, which I cannot yet specify, I expect one necessarily gives up truth for representativeness. But that point is certainly not one lone ranger, nor six team members, nor a dozen. The team is a powerful technique in social research, both in getting the truth and in getting practical results. It has problems, but these are far more easily managed than those of the lone ranger model. Field research will no doubt continue to be a haven for rugged individualists who do not fear to single-handedly attack the citadels of secrecy in our society. But there are now more powerful methods for most purposes. They should be used whenever possible and appropriate. In the same way, cooperative methods will continue to be important, but they must be seen as being merely part of the more general, far more powerful investigative team field research methods.

NOTES

1. For example, while Suttles (1968) has provided a creative and, I suspect, insightful understanding of the construction of a moral order in a slum inhabited by three different ethnic and racial groups, I do not believe it possible for one person to get the in-depth involvement needed to get that kind of information in the three different groups. All of my experience, some of which we shall deal with below, indicates that is almost impossible and Suttles has not provided the evidence that he was able to do it.

2. I might point out that even the Lone Ranger had Tonto to help him. This not only provided him support and inspiration, but was often the only thing that saved him from early extinction. Using a multiperspectival approach, Tonto often appeared at the rear of the bad guys when they had the drop on the Lone Ranger.

3. The research director, often the principal investigator as well, has certainly served in many cases as an inspiration and support. Generally, however, this was all done in the office. An experienced researcher certainly develops the *feel,* a generalized grasp, of research settings and problems and possible solutions. Graduate students generally talk with them in detail about what is going on and I do not dispute its importance. But I myself have always found that, regardless of how much of a generalized feel I have for such things, it's difficult to help much with the big problems, such as getting a grasp and a creative understanding of the setting unless one has some direct involvement in the setting. Even brief direct involvements can be of crucial value.

4. This demand for the universal individual and insistence on rugged individualism in field research is well-embedded in the traditional form of scholarship. I have always found great resistance among sociology faculty to the idea that a team of students should do a study together and receive collective credit for it. They always want one individual to be responsible. Otherwise, they insist, "How will we know how to grade them? How will we know who really did the work?" While I myself am pretty much of a rugged individualist by deep feeling, it seems obvious that most of the worthwhile forms of research can be better done by teamwork. The old forms must be changed so that it is even possible to have team doctoral dissertations, the way it is possible to have multi-authored books. Bush pilots were fine in the days of the single-seated biplane, but it's better to have a crew with a pilot in the days of intercontinental flights. The same holds even more for research. It is a common belief that truly creative work always springs from an individual, not a group. But that's nonsense, based, presumably, on lack of experience with creative work. People commonly believe that because of the great man theory of genius in the Western World and because those making use of others commonly pretend to be doing it all alone. I think we need a flexible strategy— individuality when it works, especially when it's necessary, but team efforts when they work better, which is the case most of the time.

5. After a talk I had given on team field research methods, a member of the audience began the questioning with one of life's ultimate questions, "Well, okay, so maybe team field research is a good idea, but how do you choose the team? How do you tell whether a person is going to do good field work and work well in a team?" My immediate reaction to such a question is, "How the hell do you choose a good anything

in people—a good wife, a good friend, a good graduate student, a good business advisor, a good president, a good survey researcher, a good any kind of person?" In my more restrained moments I have a few hints that might be helpful in this matter, but I make no pretense of being able to give a thorough understanding of it. I think I have a pretty good grasp of the problems and a good idea of the possible way of choosing people. I even like to think I have great abilities to sense who is and who is not hard-working, creative and productive. I base this on my experience in editing a dozen books and working with large numbers of young sociologists in which I was concerned with getting at just those things as the basis for my choices. But I also know from my experience that I have made any number of mistakes about who is going to get the work done well. I believe I have rarely misestimated, up or down, anyone's intellectual ability. That tends to be more stable. But productivity, getting the work done, is dependent on one's life situation and it's easy to be wrong. It is also problematic to tell who will be able to get along with people and who will get bounced quickly. Certainly the crucial thing for me in choosing field researchers is the ability of people to get along with other people of any kind—people who have a feeling and concern for other people, even when it's just to manipulate them. The second thing is someone's ability to get a job done. Are they reliable and do they have initiative? Some people can give a dozen reasons why they can't try to get into an emergency room, while someone else is blowing it open. Closely related to this is commitment to the project and to me. Researchers, like business associates, have to be tied to one by the iron bonds of feudalism, not by the impersonal and tenuous bonds of hired labor. And, of course, experience with me in a previous research setting is vital. When someone has proven himself, only drastically changed personal circumstances lead me to doubt his ability in a new setting.

6. This team field research design probably has more in common with analytic induction methods than any other method. But it is different in important ways.

7. To give a few hints of the complexities involved in what might appear to be a simple decision, let me mention that we had to decide on our universe from among the city, the metropolitan area of city and county, and the standard metropolitan statistical area used by the Census Bureau and other government agencies. Traditional methodologists make their decisions on an abstract basis, which is generally really an ad hoc basis butressed by abstract rhetoric. Given our primary commitment to the concrete realities of the social world, our universe would have to correspond to the natural structure of the social world. We had to determine much of this for our universe, since it was by no means apparent. Something that is commonly decided before the study begins thereby becomes one of the important products of the study. In both cities we had to determine the general nature of emergency room, hot line and free clinic services before we could decide on the general boundaries of our study. In Western City we chose to study the metropolitan area because of the specific nature of the county contract system for emergency medicine. This also corresponded well enough to the National Commission's desire to have as broad an area as possible. They really wanted us to choose the standard metropolitan statistical area because this would be more acceptable to government agents used to thinking in those terms, but that would have forced us to study a number of different subuniverses because of the different governmental service systems. This was too much, given our time and manpower constraints. We compromised and they got four fifths of their whole pie.

8. Given the intense time pressures in this study, and the fact that we were able to determine some parts of the core sample quickly, we already had most field researchers working on the core sample before we knew the dimensions of the universe.

9. We had an excellent example of role specialization in this natural experiment. Steven Siegel was the ringleader. Siegel had grown up with an interest in acting. I think

he must have spent many of his teen years making prank phone calls, because he really took to this natural experiment. We casted well for this study.

10. The organizer of this demonstration was also a bitter enemy of the managers of one of the TV stations. It was important to hide all relations with him. This is just one more example of the double-agentry of field research, which isn't too different in this way from other aspects of life.

11. Americans are on a secret taping binge. It's shocking to find how many people are taping all kinds of secret, really intimate things, all unknown to the other people involved. In the study of massage parlors we even found one of our good contacts had made secret recordings of some visits to the parlor. And some of the girls had recorded their work to prove "the vice" had entrapped them. I even found a student who secretly recorded his argument with a professor. *That* really shocked me.

12. Cloyd's thesis, like almost everything we touch, provides another excellent example of how vital contacts are. Cloyd had already decided to do a study of plea bargaining. When I learned of it I remembered that one of the team members in another city who had worked on drug crisis intervention, Stouffer, had mentioned that he had a lifelong friend who had become an assistant city attorney in the city Cloyd was studying. We got hold of Stouffer, he put in the word with his friend, the friend was contacted, responded warmly, and Cloyd was able to get excellent access to his work, including tapes of his plea bargaining.

13. Whenever I think of this, I remember my first day in graduate school. I had taken a Greyhound bus from Miami, Florida. I had to spend the early morning hours wandering around the downtown section of Philadelphia, observing the remnants of nightlife, wandering down Market Street, feeling the quickening pulse of urban America in the grey dawn. I finally got a local bus to Trenton, where I had to wait in a teeming black slum for the even more local bus to Princeton. When I got off at Princeton, suitcase in hand, I discovered that the Graduate College (which I later learned was known as "Goon Castle") was a mile away from the seamy downtown area. I wound up a hill along a path rimmed with flowering shrubbery (rhododendron, no less). And suddenly there before me on top of the hill was a Medieval English castle, set in the midst of a beautiful golf course and looking exactly like something out of a fairy book. I soon discovered that it was indeed a fairy castle. It had a wood-paneled commons room, complete with sherry with the master before dinner. It even had a miniature Gothic cathedral, complete with an organ, where the young scholars ate dinner each night, draped in long black robes, and watched over by a high table from which grace was said before dinner each evening—intoned in Hebrew: "Adenoy aluhenu, adenoy echod!" (Which was my common-sense transliteration.) And about my first day there I met an older aspiring graduate student in sociology, who talked exactly as if he came as part of the castle. He needed some band-aids, so I accompanied him down the hill to the drugstore in the seamier part of Princeton. He ordered his band-aids and paid for them in such a manner that in two minutes he had made the cashier one of his mortal enemies. I discovered that I could escape some of the castle's influence by eating dinner in the breakfast room with some other vulgar American types. (We dubbed it "The Outhouse" and took pride in our exile.) But the castle's almost total isolation from American society complemented my booky isolation. After two years I almost wound up feeling like I belonged in the Castle. (One more year and I would have joined the Carthusian monks for dinner.) Looking out the little window in the turret where I lived, I came to think of American society in terms of beautiful mathematical abstractions. It took me years to rediscover the vulgar realities of American society.

14. It is important not to allow one's general social evaluations of such roles and activities to affect one's evaluations of them in field research. Most people would

probably think of a front man or sociability gadfly as somehow a shady character, or of lower prestige than the others. I never do. In research they are vital and highly prized, especially because there are so few of them. At the risk of looking like a shady character myself, I would point out that I have come through experience to have much the same attitude in these matters as people in sales work or con games. While I have almost always learned about team research from direct experience of it, I find that we obviously make use of many of the same devices as people in these other activities that deal with people. Con men and salesmen, for example, make tremendous use of sociability types who serve as outsiders to hook the marks and pass them on to the inside man who tries to make the deal. They support each other's stories, complement each other's characteristics, etc. It is easy to see the relations between some of our forms of specialization and those in these activities and many others, especially politics—advance men, detail men, idea men, P.R. men, bag men, and so on. It may be that we can profit from a more explicit consideration of their activities, but we have almost always created our ideas as we went, often dragging them after us, but sometimes letting them lead us.

15. Most sociologists and graduate students today are careerists, so it is inevitably hard to get much done in these ways. I feel most appreciative of the efforts of the people who have worked with me under these circumstances.

BIBLIOGRAPHY

Adams, R.N. and J.J. Preiss (eds.), *Human Organization Research*. Homewood, IL: Dorsey Press, 1960.

Adler, Peter and Patti, Jack D. Douglas with Paul K. Rasmussen, "Drug Dealing for Pleasure and Profit," in Douglas, *Observations of Deviance,* 1977c.

Altheide, David, *Creating Reality*. Beverly Hills: Sage, 1976.

———, John Johnson and Robert Snow, "Counting Souls," in Altheide and Johnson, *Modern Propaganda*. Boston: Allyn and Bacon, 1977.

Becker, Howard S., *Outsiders*. New York: Free Press, 1963.

———, "Whose Side Are We on?" *Social Problems,* 14, 1967.

———, *Sociological Work*. Chicago: Aldine, 1970.

———, "Participant Observation: The Analysis of Qualitative Field Data," in R.N. Adams and J.J. Preiss (eds.), *Human Organization Research*. 1960, pp. 267-289.

Becker, Howard S. and Blanche Geer, "Participant Observation and Interviewing: A Comparison," reprinted in McCall. Chicago: Aldine, 1969, pp. 322-331.

Bernstein, Carl and Bob Woodward, *All the President's Men*. New York: Simon and Schuster, 1974.

Bogdan, Robert and Stephen J. Taylor, *Introduction to Qualitative Research Methods*. New York: John Wiley, 1973.

Bruyn, S.T., *The Human Perspective in Sociology: The Methodology of Participant Observation*. Englewood Cliffs, NJ: Prentice-Hall, 1969.

Cicourel, Aaron V., *Methods and Measurement*. New York: The Free Press, 1964.

———. *The Social Organization of Juvenile Justice*. New York: Wiley, 1968.

Dalton, Melville, *Men Who Manage*. New York: Wiley, 1959.

Davis, Fred, "The Martian and the Convert: Ontological Polarities in Social Research," Urban Life, 3, October, 1973, pp. 333-343.

Deutscher, Irwin, *What We Say/What We Do*. Glenview, IL: Scott, Foresman, 1973.

Douglas, Jack D., *The Social Meanings of Suicide*. Princeton: Princeton University Press, 1967.

———, *Deviance and Respectability*. New York: Basic Books, 1970a.

———, *Youth In Turmoil*. Washington, D.C.: U.S. Government Printing Office, 1970b.

———, *The Relevance of Sociology*. New York: Appleton Century-Crofts, 1970c.

———, *Understanding Everyday Life*. Chicago: Aldine, 1970d.

———, *American Social Order*. New York: Free Press, 1971.

———, *Perspectives on Deviance*. coedited with Robert Scott, New York: Basic Books, 1972a.

———, *Research on Deviance.* New York: Random House, 1972b.

———, *Introduction to Sociology.* New York: Free Press, 1973.

———, *Defining America's Social Problems.* Englewood Cliffs, NJ: Prentice-Hall, 1974a.

———, *Drug Crisis Intervention, Research Appendix.* National Commission on Marijuana and Drug Abuse, Washington, D.C.: U.S. Government Printing Office, vol. 4, 1974b.

———, *Newspower: The Growing Power of The News.* Forthcoming, 1977a.

———, with Paul K. Rasmussen and Carol Ann Flanagan, *The Nude Beach.* Forthcoming, 1977b.

———, *Observations of Deviance.* New York: Random House, 1977c.

———, and John M. Johnson (eds.), *Existential Sociology.* New York: Cambridge University Press, 1977.

Easthope, Gary, *A History of Social Research Methods.* London: Longmon, 1974.

Erikson, Kai, "A Comment on Disguised Observation in Sociology," *Social Problems,* 14, Spring 1967, pp. 366-373.

Faris, Robert E.L., *Chicago Sociology.* San Francisco: Chandler, 1967.

Garfinkel, Harold, *Studies in Ethnomethodology.* Englewood Cliffs, NJ: Prentice-Hall, 1967.

Goffman, Erving, *Behavior in Public Places.* New York: The Free Press, 1963.

———, *The Presentation of Self in Everyday Life.* Garden City: Doubleday, 1959.

Gold, Raymond, "Roles in sociology field observations," *Social Forces,* XXXVI, March, 1958, pp. 217-23.

Gouldner, Alvin, "The sociologist as partisan," *American Sociologist,* 3 (1968), pp. 103-16.

Habenstein, Robert, *Pathways to Data.* Chicago: Aldine, 1970.

Hammond, P.E. (ed.), *Sociologists at Work.* New York: Basic Books, 1964.

Hughes, Everett C., *The Sociological Eye.* Chicago: Aldine, 1970.

Humphreys, Laud, *The Tea-Room Trade.* Chicago: Aldine, 1970.

Johnson, John, *Doing Field Research.* New York: Free Press, 1976.

Jules-Rosette, B., *African Apostles: Ritual and Conversion in the Church of John Maranke.* Ithaca, NY: Cornell University Press, 1976.

Junker, B.H., *Field Work.* Chicago: University of Chicago Press, 1960.

Lazarsfeld, Paul S., *Qualitative Analysis.* Boston: Allyn & Bacon, 1972.

Lewis, Oscar, *Life in a Mexican Village; Tepotzland Restudied.* Urbana, IL: University of Illinois Press, 1951.

Liebow, Elliot, *Tally's Corner.* Boston: Little, Brown, 1967.

Lofland, John, *Analyzing Social Settings.* Englewood Cliffs, NJ: Prentice-Hall, 1971.

McCall, George J., "The Problem of Indicators in Participant Observation Research," in McCall and Simmons, 1969, pp. 230-238.

McCall, George J. and J.L. Simmons, *Issues in Participant Observation.* Reading, Mass.: Addison-Wesley, 1969.

Madge, John, *The Origins of Scientific Sociology.* New York: The Free Press, 1962.

Manning, Peter K., "Police lying," *Journal of Urban Studies,* 3, Oct., 1974, pp. 283-306.

Mauksch, Hans O., "Studying the Hospital," in Habenstein, 1970.

Maurer, David, *The Big Con.* New York: Signet, 1962.

Mehan, Hugh and Houston Wood, *The Reality of Ethnomethodology.* New York: Wiley, 1976.

Miller, S.M., "The participant-observer and 'over-rapport,' " *American Sociological Review,* 17, February 1952, pp. 97-99.

Miller, Walter, "Lower class culture as a generating milieu of gang delinquency," *Journal of Social Issues,* 14, 1958, pp. 5-19.

Minor, Dole, *The Information War.* Tulsa: University of Oklahoma Press, 1970.

Naroll, Raoul, *Data Quality Control*. New York: The Free Press, 1962.

Palmer, V.M., *Field Studies in Sociology: A Student's Manual*. Chicago: University of Chicago Press, 1928.

Park, Robert, *Human Communities*. Glencoe, IL: The Free Press, 1952.

Rasmussen, Paul and Lauren Kuhn, "Massage Parlors," in Douglas, 1977c.

Redfield, Robert, *Tepotzlan*. Chicago: University of Chicago Press, 1930.

———, *Chan Kon*. Washington, D.C.: Carnegie Institute of Washington, 1934.

———, *The Folk Culture of Yucatan*. Chicago: University of Chicago Press, 1941.

———, *The Little Community*. Chicago: University of Chicago Press, 1960.

Riesman, David, "Tocqueville as Ethnographer," in *Abundance for What?* Garden City, N.Y.: Doubleday, 1965.

Roy, Donald, "The Study of Southern Labor Union Organizing Campaigns," in Habenstein, 1970.

Schatzman, L. and A. Strauss, *Field Research: Strategies for a Natural Sociology*. Englewood Cliffs, NJ: Prentice-Hall, 1973.

Scott, Marvin, *The Racing Game*. Chicago: Aldine, 1969.

Sudman, S. and N.M. Bradburn, *Response Effects in Surveys*. Chicago: Aldine, 1974.

Suttles, Gerald, *The Social Order of the Slum*. Chicago: University of Chicago Press, 1967.

Talese, Gay, *Honor Thy Father*. Greenwich, CT: Fawcett Crest, 1971.

Thompson, Hunter, *Hell's Angels*. New York: Random House, 1966.

Thrasher, F., The Gang. Chicago: University of Chicago Press, 1927.

Trow, Martin, "Comment," in McCall and Simmons, 1969.

Vidich, A.J. and M.R. Stein (eds.), *Reflections on Community Studies*. New York: Wiley, 1964.

Warren, Carol A.B., "Fieldwork in the gay world," *Journal of Social Issues*, January, 1977.

———, "Field Research in A Courtroom Setting." Unpublished manuscript.

———, *Identity and Community in the Gay World*. New York: Wiley, 1975.

Wax, Murray, "Tenting with Malinowski," *American Sociological Review*, 37, February 1972, pp. 1-13.

Wax, Rosalie, *Doing Field Work*. Chicago: University of Chicago Press, 1971.

Webb, Beatrice Potter, *My Apprenticeship*. New York: Longmans, Green and Co., 1926.

Webb, E.J. et al. *Unobtrusive Measures*. Chicago: Rand-McNally, 1972.

Webb, Sidney and Beatrice, *Methods of Social Study*. (Originally published 1932), New York: Kelley, 1968.

Weinberg, Martin, "Sexual modesty, social meanings, and the nudist camp." *Social Problems*, vol. 12, pp. 311-318, 1969.

Whyte, William F., *Street Corner Society*. Chicago: University of Chicago Press, 1955.

Wolfe, Tom, *The Pump House Gang*. New York: Bantam Books, 1969.

Wolff, Kurt H., "Surrender and Community Study," in A.J. Vidich et al. (eds.), *Reflections on Community Studies*. New York: Wiley, 1964.

SAGE LIBRARY OF SOCIAL RESEARCH

1. **DAVID CAPLOVITZ:** The Merchants of Harlem: A Study of Small Business in a Black Community
2. **JAMES N. ROSENAU:** International Studies and the Social Sciences: Problems, Priorities and Prospects in the United States
3. **DOUGLAS E. ASHFORD:** Ideology and Participation
4. **PATRICK J. McGOWAN and HOWARD B. SHAPIRO:** The Comparative Study of Foreign Policy: A Survey of Scientific Findings
5. **GEORGE A. MALE:** The Struggle for Power: Who Controls the Schools in England and the United States
6. **RAYMOND TANTER:** Modelling and Managing International Conflicts: The Berlin Crises
7. **ANTHONY JAMES CATANESE:** Planners and Local Politics: Impossible Dreams
8. **JAMES RUSSELL PRESCOTT:** Economic Aspects of Public Housing
9. **F. PARKINSON:** Latin America, the Cold War, and the World Powers, 1945-1973: A Study in Diplomatic History
10. **ROBERT G. SMITH:** Ad Hoc Governments: Special Purpose Transportation Authorities in Britain and the United States
11. **RONALD GALLIMORE, JOAN WHITEHORN BOGGS, and CATHIE JORDAN:** Culture, Behavior and Education: A Study of Hawaiian-Americans
12. **HOWARD W. HALLMAN:** Neighborhood Government in a Metropolitan Setting
13. **RICHARD J. GELLES:** The Violent Home: A Study of Physical Aggression Between Husbands and Wives
14. **JERRY L. WEAVER:** Conflict and Control in Health Care Administration
15. **GEBHARD LUDWIG SCHWEIGLER:** National Consciousness in Divided Germany
16. **JAMES T. CAREY:** Sociology and Public Affairs: The Chicago School
17. **EDWARD W. LEHMAN:** Coordinating Health Care: Explorations in Interorganizational Relations
18. **CHARLES G. BELL and CHARLES M. PRICE:** The First Term: A Study of Legislative Socialization
19. **CLAYTON P. ALDERFER and L. DAVE BROWN:** Learning from Changing: Organizational Diagnosis and Development
20. **L. EDWARD WELLS and GERALD MARWELL:** Self-Esteem: Its Conceptualization and Measurement
21. **ROBERT S. ROBINS:** Political Institutionalization and the Integration of Elites
22. **WILLIAM R. SCHONFELD:** Obedience and Revolt: French Behavior Toward Authority
23. **WILLIAM C. McCREADY and ANDREW M. GREELEY:** The Ultimate Values of the American Population
24. **F. IVAN NYE:** Role Structure and Analysis of the Family
25. **PAUL WEHR and MICHAEL WASHBURN:** Peace and World Order Systems: Teaching and Research
26. **PATRICIA R. STEWART:** Children in Distress: American and English Perspectives
27. **JUERGEN DEDRING:** Recent Advances in Peace and Conflict Research: A Critical Study
28. **MOSHE M. CZUDNOWSKI:** Comparing Political Behavior
29. **JACK D. DOUGLAS:** Investigative Social Research